RESULTS OF THE 2001 KERAK PLATEAU EARLY BRONZE AGE SURVEY

TWO EARLY ALPHABETIC INSCRIPTIONS FROM THE WADI EL-ḤÔL

NEW EVIDENCE FOR THE ORIGIN OF THE ALPHABET FROM THE WESTERN DESERT OF EGYPT

THE ANNUAL OF
THE AMERICAN SCHOOLS OF ORIENTAL RESEARCH

Volume 59

Series Editor
Nancy Serwint

Billie Jean Collins
ASOR Director of Publications

RESULTS OF THE 2001 KERAK PLATEAU EARLY BRONZE AGE SURVEY

By
Meredith S. Chesson, Cheryl Makarewicz,
Ian Kuijt and Charlotte Whiting

TWO EARLY ALPHABETIC INSCRIPTIONS FROM THE WADI EL-ḤÔL

NEW EVIDENCE FOR THE ORIGIN OF THE ALPHABET FROM THE WESTERN DESERT OF EGYPT

By
John Coleman Darnell, F. W. Dobbs-Allsopp,
Marilyn J. Lundberg, P. Kyle McCarter, Bruce Zuckerman
with the assistance of Colleen Manassa

American Schools of Oriental Research • Boston, MA

ANNUAL OF THE AMERICAN SCHOOLS OF ORIENTAL RESEARCH
VOLUME 59

ISBN: 0-89757-071-5

Library of Congress Cataloging-in-Publication Data

Results of the 2001 Kerak Plateau Early Bronze Age survey / by Meredith S. Chesson ... [et al.]. Two early alphabetic inscriptions from the Wadi el-Hol : new evidence for the origin of the alphabet from the western desert of Egypt / by John Coleman Darnell ... [et al.]. -- 1st ed.
p. cm. -- (The annual of the American Schools of Oriental Research ; v. 59)
Includes bibliographical references.
ISBN 0-89757-071-5 (alk. paper)
1. Kerak Plateau (Jordan)--Antiquities. 2. Excavations (Archaeology) --Jordan--Kerak Plateau. 3. Bronze age--Jordan--Kerak Plateau. 4. Inscriptions--Egypt--Hol, Wadi el- 5. Alphabet--History. I. Chesson, Meredith S. II. Darnell, John Coleman. III. Two early alphabetic inscriptions from the Wadi el-Hol. IV. Series.
DS101.A45 vol. 59
[DS154.9.K47]
930 s--dc22
[933]

2005032533

Printed in the United States of America on acid-free paper

Contents

Results of the 2001 Kerak Plateau Early Bronze Age Survey

MEREDITH S. CHESSON
University of Notre Dame

CHERYL MAKAREWICZ
Harvard University

IAN KUIJT
University of Notre Dame

CHARLOTTE WHITING
University of Durham

Contents

Acknowledgments

This research has been supported financially and logistically by several institutions and granting agencies, including the Institute for Scholarship in the Liberal Arts at the University of Notre Dame, the National Science Foundation (grant BCS01-04422), the Council for British Research in the Levant and the Graduate School of Arts and Letters at Harvard University. The authors especially wish to thank the Department of Antiquities of Jordan, especially Dr. Fawwaz al-Kraysheh, Director; Dr. Mohammed Najjar, Director of Excavations; and Khalid Tarawneh, Kerak Representative. This field research benefited greatly from the support of Dr. Marwan Khoury, Isabelle Ruben, Nadja Qaisi, Alison McQuitty and Dr. Bill Finlayson; the report has benefited from the support and comments of Tom Schaub and two anonymous reviewers. While benefiting from the insights and critiques of several generous individuals, the authors accept responsibility for all ideas and errors within this article.

List of Figures

Results of the 2001 Kerak Plateau Early Bronze Age Survey

by Meredith S. Chesson, Cheryl Makarewicz, Ian Kuijt and Charlotte Whiting

From late May until the final week of June a team from the University of Notre Dame, Indiana, USA, conducted a series of surface assessments and test excavations at eight Early Bronze Age settlement sites previously identified in a project directed by J. Maxwell Miller (Mattingly 1983, 1984; Miller 1991). Of the hundreds of sites identified by Miller's team, these eight were chosen from their published descriptions as settlement sites with substantial Early Bronze Age occupations (fig. 1). At each site the team conducted a walkover survey, noting architectural features and the nature of preservation of the site (Appendix A). In most of the cases, the sites are in very poor condition of preservation, Umm el-Habaj and Lejjun being the only exceptions (Appendix B). Most sites had been terraced and plowed extensively or were damaged by later construction. The project's main aims were to conduct impact assessments of these eight Early Bronze Age urban settlements on the Kerak Plateau, record the environmental and developmental impact on each site to aid the Department of Antiquity's management of these resources, and investigate the suitability of these sites for future research projects. The 2001 season combined macroscale (regional) and microscale (site by site) approaches to preliminarily examine the chronological development of urbanism and ruralization, and the relationship between environmental and ecological zones and the scale of settlement in the region.

METHODOLOGY

Site Surveys

In the first stage of the project, the team visited the eight Early Bronze Age settlements. At all of these sites, the team attempted to discern the boundaries of the site by identifying potential Early Bronze Age fortification walls, where possible, and taking into account the distribution of Early Bronze Age sherds on the surface. Additionally, the team noted and judgmentally mapped architectural remains visible on the surface with a GPS unit (Garmin Etrex Vista, with an error of 4 m). The team collected the following data by surface reconnaissance at each site: (a) estimated size of site; (b) nature of exposed architecture, if any; (c) periods of occupation of site, based on collected surface materials; and (d) preservation of site and nature of modern disturbances. When suitable, a portion of each site was selected to conduct a systematic collection of artifacts lying on the surface in at least one circular ("dog-leash") 8-m radius unit (approximately 200 square m).

Limited Soundings at two Sites: Lejjun and Khirbet el-Minsahlat

After the initial survey and data collection was completed at the eight sites, the team selected Lejjun and Khirbet el-Minsahlat for limited test

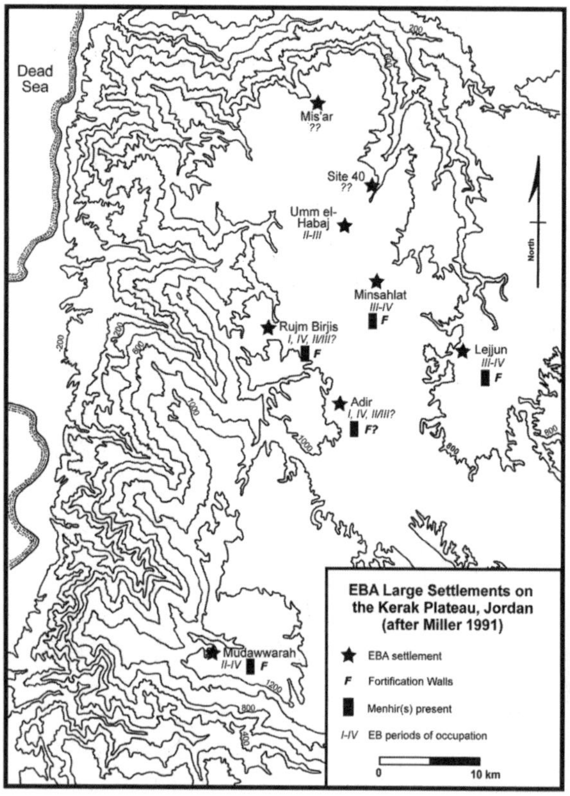

Fig. 1. Early Bronze Age large settlements on the Kerak Plateau surveyed in 2001.

excavations. These tests were conducted in controlled 2 × 1 m units, which were expanded when deemed necessary. The units were placed in order to assess the nature of architectural and artifactual preservation, and to recover a sufficient sample of chipped stone, ceramic, groundstone, faunal and paleobotanical remains, radiocarbon samples, and architectural remains. All sediments were screened with 2.5 mm mesh, unless the deposits had been badly disturbed and therefore held little contextual information for analysis. Radiocarbon samples were collected from both sites to provide absolute chronological dates and to offer an absolute framework in which to relate the other six surveyed sites on the Plateau. All soundings were backfilled at the completion of excavation to preserve the site for future research opportunities. Results of the test excavations follow the discussion of the results from the surface surveys.

RESULTS OF SURFACE SURVEYS

The following description provides a short summary of the survey findings for each of the sites visited by the team. For each site, the name of the site and Miller's site number (Miller 1991) is provided.

Mis'ar (Miller site #25)

This site is situated on a south-facing slope rising from a tributary of the Wadi Dafali. The site is currently occupied by the modern, small village of Mis'ar, which has expanded to cover the entire original site. Areas of the site where no houses have been constructed have been plowed. Due to the modern disturbances, it was not possible to discern the original boundaries of the site from any period. Clear architectural remains can be found in the northern section of the site in the modern village. In one particular case, two buildings have been built over the foundations of a large ancient building, whose walls can be easily traced (and which unfortunately was not associated with any diagnostic pottery). Miller (1991: 39) mentions that he found occupational remains on both sides of the tributary, but the southern banks have been terraced and planted extensively and no remains were recovered. Two rock-cut cisterns were noted to the west of the village. The overall state of preservation of this site is extremely poor due to the modern village, terracing, plowing, and erosion.

Few pottery and groundstone artifacts were noted on the surface. Of the thirty diagnostic ceramic sherds collected across the site, the chronological periods spanned from the Early Bronze Age through the modern periods, with Iron Age II pottery dominating the collection (fig. 2:d–l). Of the fifteen sherds dated to a period later than the Early Bronze Age, ten were dated to the Iron Age II, three to the Late Byzantine period, and one to the Middle Islamic period. The ten Iron Age II rim sherds fit in well with the common repertoire of late Iron Age forms from the Kerak Plateau, such as holemouth jars, necked jugs/jars, jars with folded rims, and bowls (Brown 1991: 198–202). Especially characteristic were the holemouth jar (fig. 2:j), the jars with folded rims (figs. 2:g and 2:i), and the bowl with ridged rim (fig. 2:d). The fabric

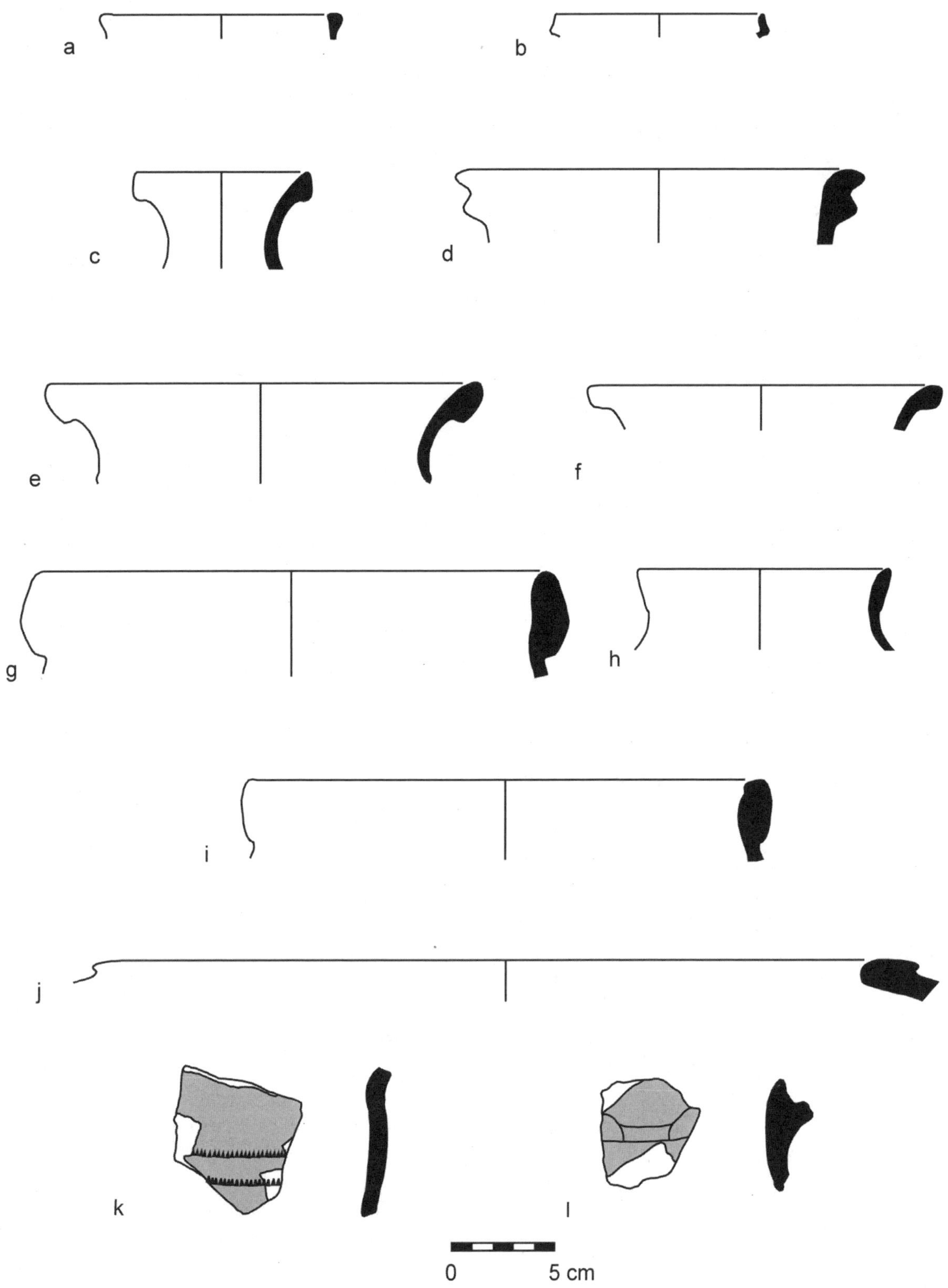

Fig. 2. *Historic periods pottery from surface collections at Mis'ar, Adir and Rujm Birjis.*

of these sherds ranged in color from pink to pale yellow to pale brown, with light grey cores and they were heavily tempered with shale fragments, limestone, and quartz (for detailed descriptions of all sherds illustrated, see Appendix D). The Late Byzantine body sherds were characterized by their distinctive "pie-crust" and incised decoration (figs. 2:k–l; Brown 1991: 221). In addition, the sherds were characterized by their distinctive fabric of a red (2.5 YR 5/6) core and pale yellow (5 Y 8/3) interior and exterior surfaces, heavily tempered with well-sorted, sub-angular quartz. Although heavily abraded, a handle of Hand Made Geometrically Painted Ware (HMGPW), dated to between the twelfth and up to at least the fifteenth century (Johns 1993: 65–67), was also identified, based on its distinctive fabric and surface decoration, characterized by a thick grey core, pale brown surface slip, and poorly sorted abundant chaff, shale, and limestone inclusions.

Site 40 (Miller site #40)

Site 40 is located to the south of the Iron Age site of Khirbet el-Balu', on the same track traveling southeast from the modern village of Jad'a. The site has been extensively plowed and terraced, and a house has been built on its northwest portion (Miller's main landmark of the house, an adjacent eucalyptus tree, still stands). Site 40 is located on two hills (separated by a small tributary) rising gently from the Wadi Balu'. Very few architectural remains were evident on the surface, with the exception of a few putative wall lines. In the eastern portion of the site, there is a large boulder field, and we were unable to discern a clear edge to the site in any direction. The overall state of preservation is very poor, owing to modern building, plowing and terracing.

Of the thirty-two diagnostic sherds collected in a general surface collection, most were Early Bronze Age, including diagnostic body sherds of combed storage jars, red slip and burnishing on bowl rims and body sherds, holemouth jar rims, platterbowls and ledge handles. Four sherds of later dates were collected. One undecorated body sherd of Hand Made Ware (HMW), usually dated to between the twelfth and at least the fifteenth century (Johns 1993: 65–67), was identified on the basis of its distinctive fabric. In addition, a ribbed body sherd, a body sherd possibly from the neck of a vessel, and a very abraded handle were dated to the Roman/Byzantine period on the basis of their fabric and morphology.

Rujm Birjis (Miller site #73)

Rujm Birjis is located on a low rise near the western edge of the Kerak Plateau and has been heavily disturbed by later occupations, especially by terracing and plowing. The construction of a modern road and several modern houses has cut through the eastern portion of the site. In the bulldozer cuts associated with these structures, one can see several large stone walls exposed in the section, particularly in the cut behind the house by the main section of the site. Rujm Birjis is roughly 4 ha today; however, the eastern edge is not well defined, and the northeastern edge has been destroyed by modern building (fig. 3). Terrace wall systems across the site may have been be built over older (EB) fortification walls, since some of these walls can be seen to be several meters in height and width in the bulldozer cuts. In addition to more modern terrace walls and rubble heaps from field clearing and building, three cisterns were recorded, as well as a fallen menhir next to its socket in the southeastern portion of the site. Schaub (personal communication, 2003) notes that in previous visits east of the road, he found significant amounts of pottery similar to the EB IB pottery at Bab edh-Dhra', including some examples of the C cemetery ware. The jar illustrated in fig. 5:d is an example of the C cemetery ware, and this piece had been collected and given to the team by the inhabitants of the house on the site. In 2001, this area was heavily disturbed from plowing and planting, and the team found few materials. Overall, the state of preservation of Rujm Birjis is very poor.

Pottery, chipped stone and groundstone artifacts were noted on the surface. Of the 661 sherds collected, 278 were diagnostic in form and/or decoration. The majority of pottery collected can be assigned to the Early Bronze Age I and IV periods by form, technique of manufacture or fabric. The most common diagnostic forms included body sherds of combed storage jars, red-slipped

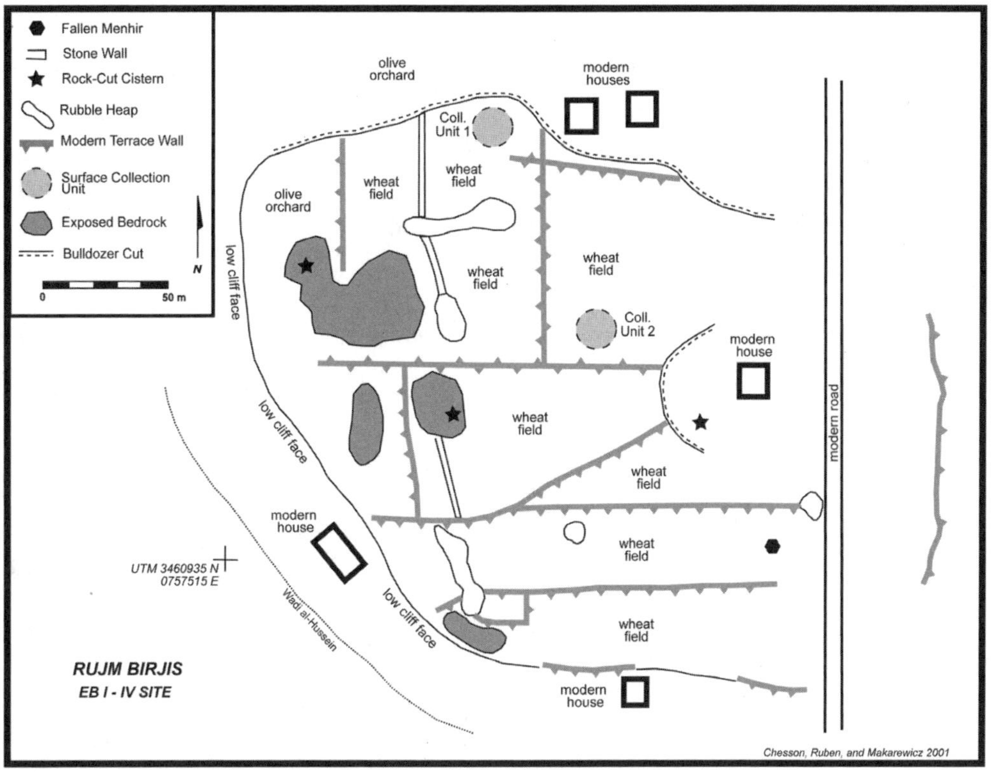

Fig. 3. Schematic plan of Rujm Birjis.

and burnished decoration on bowl rims and body sherds, holemouth jar rim sherds, and sherds from platterbowls and ledge handles. Nabataean and Roman pottery was also noted (see below, figs. 2:c, 4, and 5). One reused Canaanean blade with slight sickle sheen was collected along with one groundstone weight.

Several sherds from later periods were recovered in the surface collections. Twenty-two of these were collected in Collection Unit 1, which comprised seventeen Roman/Byzantine body sherds and a Late Roman handle (Parker 1987a: 534; Brown 1991: 216). The remaining four sherds were classed as Nabataean on the basis of fabric and form, and included an undecorated Nabataean fine ware body sherd, a base (Brown 1991: 211), a decorated body sherd dating approximately to the first and second centuries C.E. (Stucky et al. 1994: 283; Schmid 1995: 645), and a body sherd with rouletted decoration (Khairy 1982). Collection Unit 2 yielded fifty-nine non-Early Bronze Age sherds, and apart from one sherd of HMGPW, all of them were Classical in date. Twelve of these were classed as Nabataean on the basis of form and fabric, characterized by its fine texture, light red (2.5 YR 6/8) color and no visible inclusions. The Nabataean sherds included three typical Nabataean bases (Brown 1991: 211), three painted sherds of Nabataean fine ware dating to approximately the second century C.E. (Stucky et al. 1994: 283; Schmid 1995: 645), two Nabataean fine ware bowl rims (fig. 2:b; Stucky et al. 1994: 282; Schmid 1995: 645; 1996: 187), and four Nabataean/Early Roman body sherds. In addition, forty-six Roman/Byzantine body sherds were identified.

Umm el-Habaj (Miller site #88)

The site is located on a low rocky hill located approximately 2 km ENE from Qasr off the road to Smekkiyeh. Umm el-Habaj is surrounded by wheat fields, and the old fields (which the team judges to be based at least partly on earlier Roman field systems) immediately around the site are under cultivation. The site is covered with wall lines, although there are no obvious remains of Early

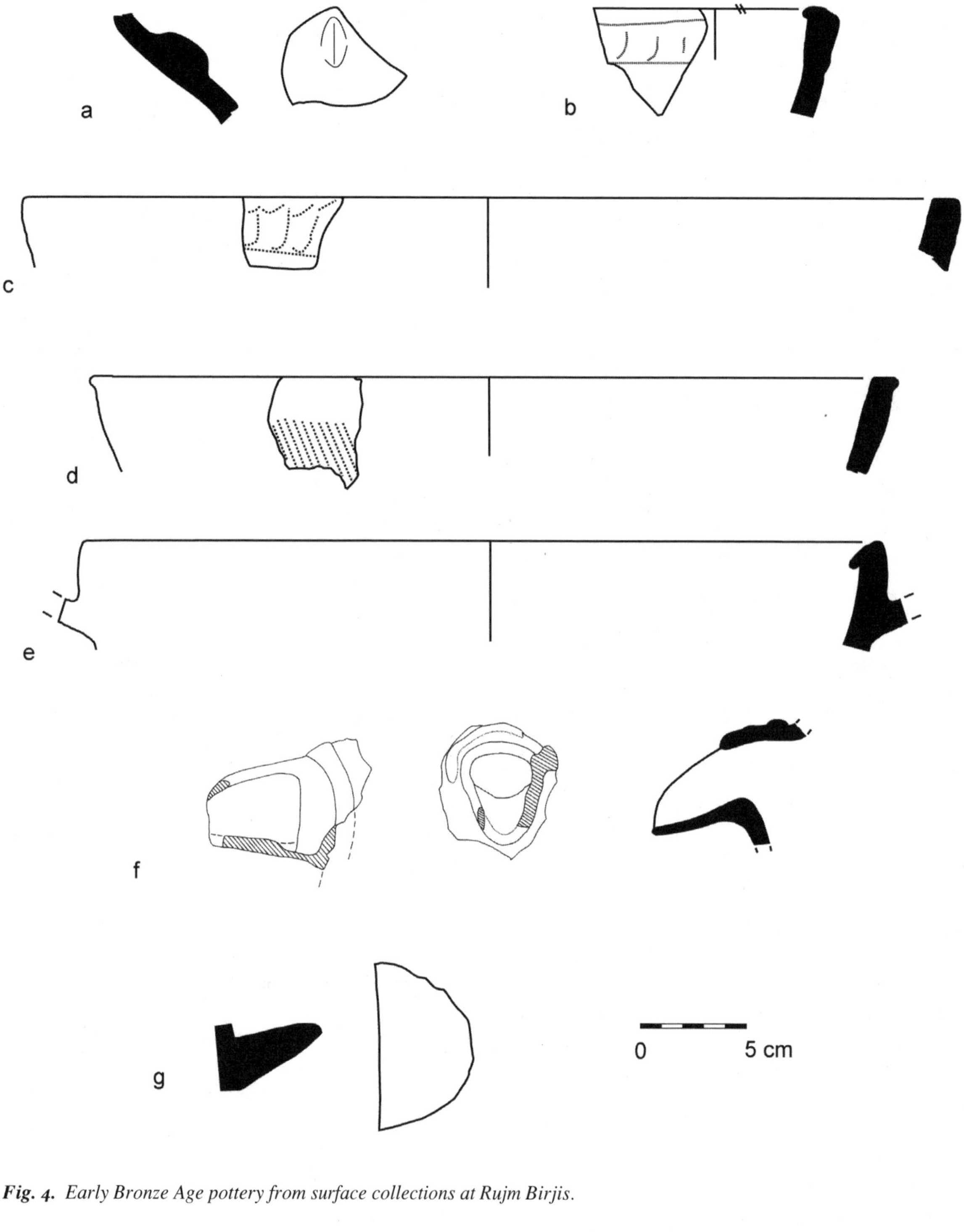

Fig. 4. *Early Bronze Age pottery from surface collections at Rujm Birjis.*

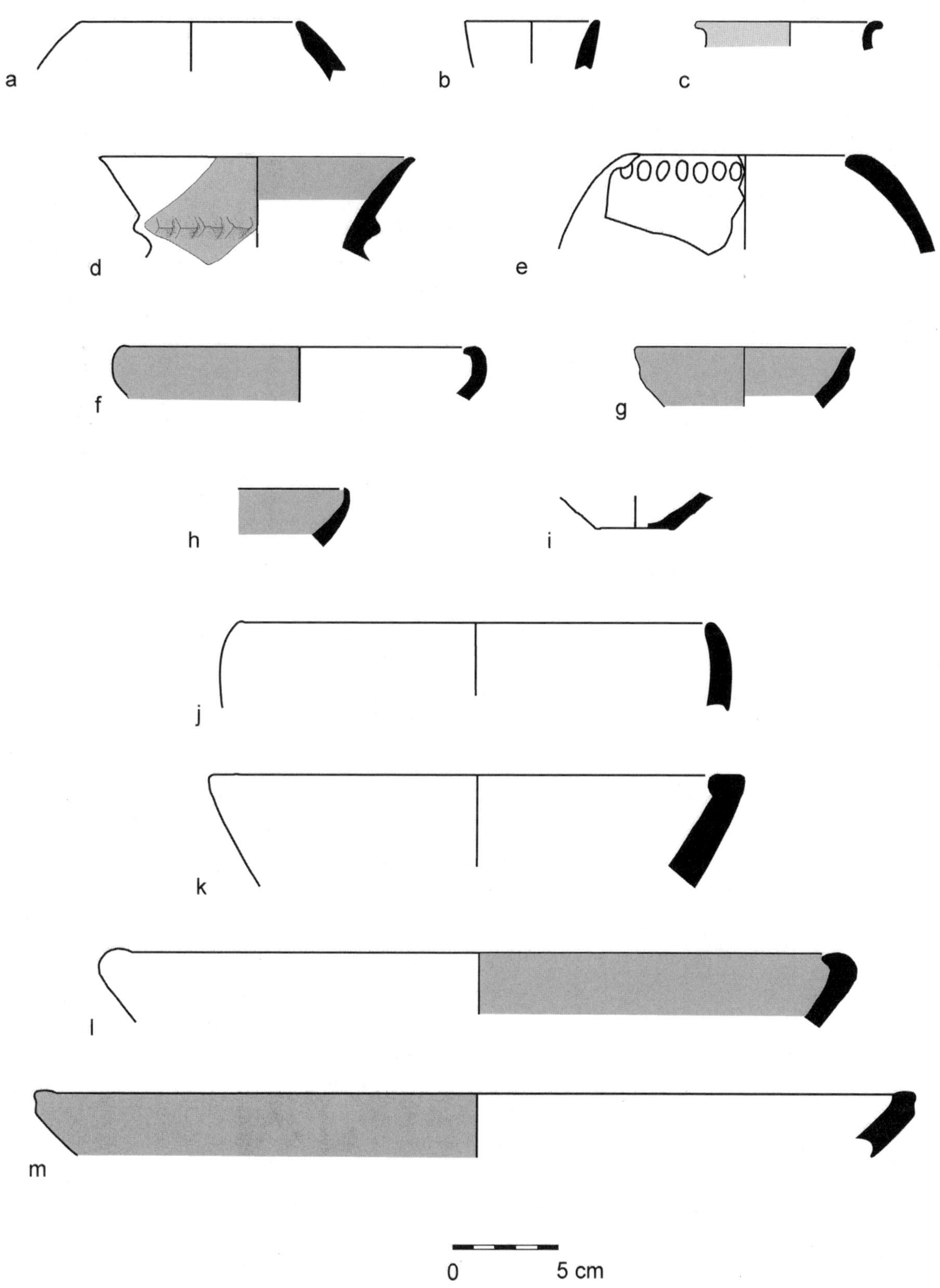

Fig. 5. *Early Bronze Age pottery from surface collections at Rujm Birjis.*

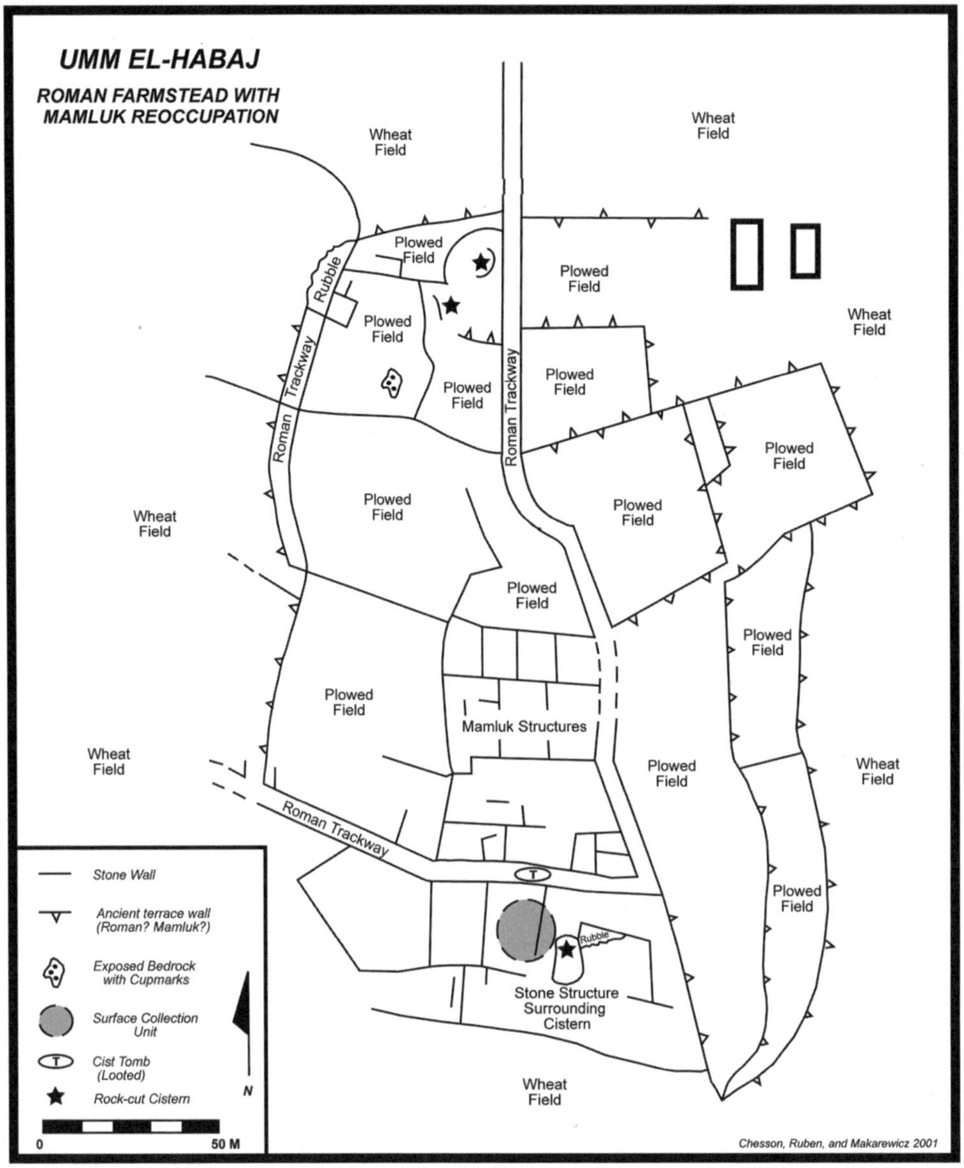

Fig. 6. *Schematic plan of Umm el-Habaj.*

Bronze Age fortification walls or structures (fig. 6). Several cisterns were noted, many of which have been reused over several occupations and show evidence of modification. Later occupations, especially the construction of trackways and a large building complex in the south–central portion of the site (probably Mamluk, given the pottery collected and the construction methods), have heavily disturbed any Early Bronze Age deposits. The trackways are well-built with faced walls in the main portion of the site and appear to be the remains of a reoccupied Roman farmstead, based on pottery collected. One of the trackways travels at least a few hundred meters to the north of the site, and the fieldwalls also appear to be very ancient and associated with the Roman farmstead. The Mamluk occupation was built on earlier foundations in the south–central part of the site. Adjacent to the Mamluk remains there is a cistern, which itself is associated with the remains of a structure. The location of all of these remains suggests that they may represent some form of water

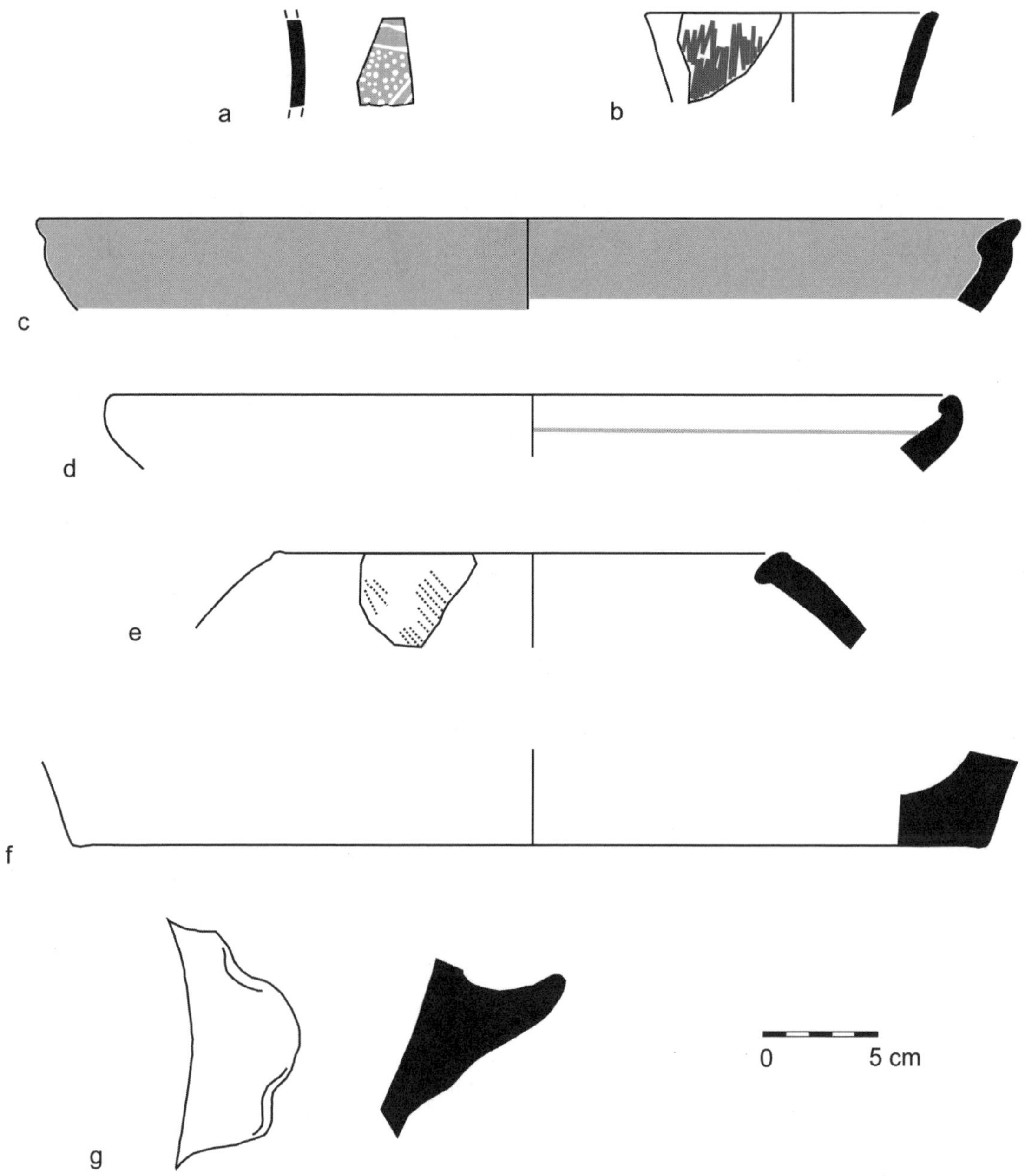

Fig. 7. Early Bronze Age pottery from surface collections at Umm el-Habaj, Lejjun and Khirbet Mudawwarah.

management and administrative structures. One stone-lined cist burial of a young adult female had been built in the middle of one of the trackways in the southern part of the site, and this grave had been disturbed in antiquity. From the paucity of Early Bronze Age ceramics and architecture visible on the surface, later occupations have made serious inroads towards destroying the earlier occupational remains. However, the overall state of preservation for the later periods is very good. The site has suffered little from erosion or later building, and the plowed fields seem to be very ancient ones. Bedouin tents are set up on the northeast edge of the site, but their presence and the use of the ancient field systems are the extent of modern occupation and alteration of the site.

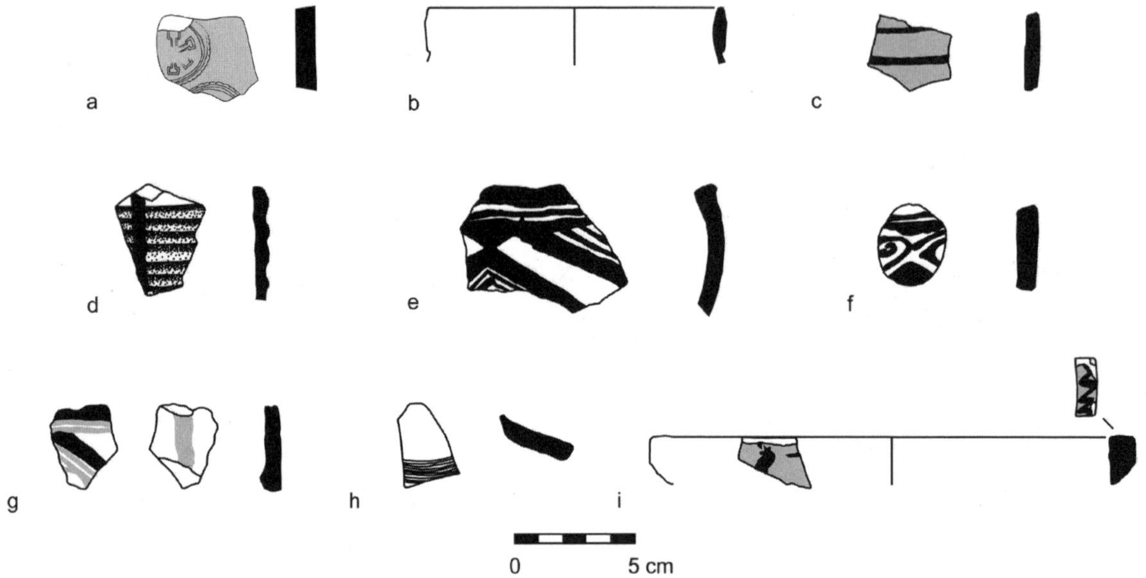

Fig. 8. *Historic periods pottery from surface collections at Umm el-Habaj.*

Of the 426 sherds collected in a general surface collection and from one collection unit, few Early Bronze Age sherds were identified among the 201 diagnostic pieces. While most of Early Bronze Age sherds dated to the EB II–III and IV and were unremarkable (fig. 7:a–e), one sherd of white-on-red ware (Genz 1993) was collected (fig. 7:a). The vast majority of the sherds (169) were late in date, with Nabataean, Roman, Early and Late Islamic being the most common (fig. 8). In Collection Unit 1, seventy non-Early Bronze Age sherds were collected, notably a Late Roman jar rim (fig. 8:b; Fellmann Brogli 1996: 253), four Roman handles, two of which are "casserole" handles (Parker 1987a: 534; Brown 1991: 216), and eight Roman/Byzantine body sherds. Sherds dated to the Byzantine period included twenty-five handles and twenty-one body sherds in dark grey metallic ware and orange ware with cream slip (Brown 1991: 221–23). One African Red Slip (ARS) ware body sherd was also identified, usually dated to between the fourth and sixth centuries (Hayes 1972: 217). In addition, seven handles and one body sherd of HMGPW were identified, along with an Early Islamic bowl rim decorated with a motif in red paint on a cream slip (fig. 8:i), and characterized by a fine textured, pink (7.5 YR 7/4) fabric with frequent, well-sorted quartz inclusions. A very fragmentary jar rim in heavy dark grey ware was also identified as of probable Early Islamic date (Kareem 2001: 85, figs. 16–17).

In the general surface collection across the site, ninety-nine non-Early Bronze Age sherds were identified. Seventy-seven of these sherds were identified as Roman/Byzantine body sherds, along with one Byzantine lid (Parker 1987a: 538) and seven Roman/Byzantine bases (Parker 1987a: 532–46; Brown 1991: 217, 277). Particularly characteristic were two body sherds in dark grey ware decorated with wavy band combing (fig. 8:b) and a body sherd with painted black bands (fig. 8:d), dating to the Late Byzantine period and probably extending into the Early Islamic period (Parker 1987a: 544; Brown 1991: 221; Walmsley 1995: 665–66). A decorated ARS body sherd was also identified, dating to between the fourth and sixth centuries C.E. (fig. 8:a; Hayes 1972: 217). In addition, two body sherds of Nabataean fine ware, both decorated and undecorated, were identified. Due to the small size of these sherds, however, a closer dating was not possible. Sherds dating to the Islamic periods included seven sherds of HMGPW (fig. 8:e–g; Johns 1993) and an Early Islamic sherd decorated with red painted bands on white slip (see fig. 8:c; Sauer 1982: 331; Dornemann 1990: 174).

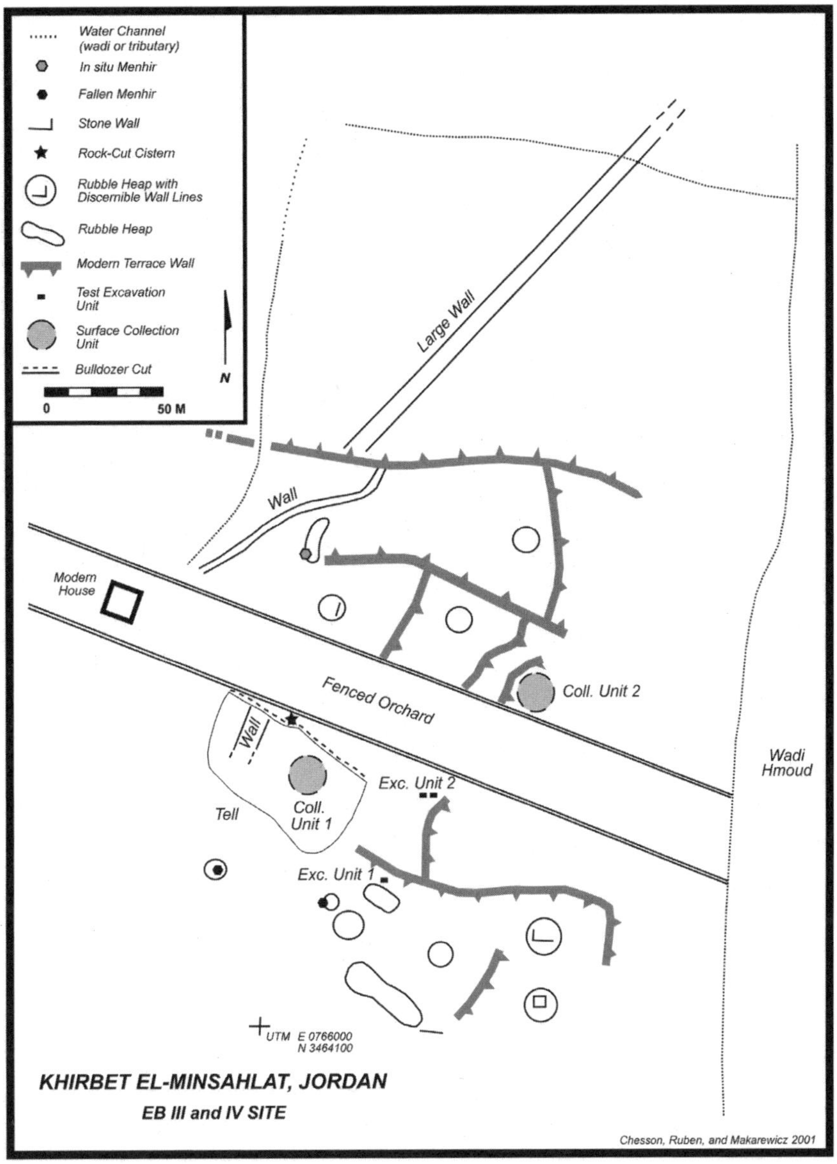

Fig. 9. *Schematic plan of Khirbet el-Minsahlat.*

Khirbet el-Minsahlat (Miller site #101)

Khirbet el-Minsahlat is situated on a hill rising from Wadi Hmoud southwest of the village of Hmoud. The site is approximately 5.5 ha in size; however, a large portion of the site has been destroyed by the construction of an orchard that cuts a transect through the center of the settlement (fig. 9). The landowner has used a bulldozer to destroy approximately one half of a large mound to clear space for the orchard. In this bulldozer cut, several large walls are visible (one is approximately 10 m wide) and the deposits range from 2 to 3 m in depth. Pottery collected from the bulldozer cut spoil was predominantly late EB III/EB IV. At the base of the bulldozer cut, there is a cistern that would have been covered by the tell, suggesting that what is considered to be a typical rock-cut Byzantine cistern may in fact be much older in origin.

Several heaps of stones across the site have discernible lines within them and may represent the remains of towers or other large structures. There is one clear, large, well-built stone wall extending from the northern part of the site and running into the wadi in a roughly northeastern heading. This wall seems to be outside of the main site, and we do not clearly understand its relationship to the other parts of the site, where the main evidence for habitation occurs. On the southern half of the site, two fallen menhirs associated with what seem to be the remains of their sockets were found, and on the north side of the site one menhir is still standing *in situ* (although the top half has fallen off and is lying beside the base). Each of these menhirs measures approximately 1.5 to 2 m in height. The major occupation of this site is clearly late EB III/IV, based on the pottery and the presence of the menhirs. The construction of the orchard has heavily impacted the preservation of Minsahlat, since it cuts through the middle of the site. However, the orchard and some plowed terraces in the north are the only evidence of modern occupation, and the overall preservation of the site is fair, especially in the southern half of the site.

Of the 202 sherds collected in two collection units—from a bulldozer cut, and generally across the site—108 were diagnostic. The vast majority of sherds were EB III and IV (body sherds of combed storage jars, red slip and burnishing on bowl rims and body sherds, holemouth jar rims, platterbowls and ledge handles being the most diagnostic forms), with only a handful of Roman/Byzantine body sherds, rims, and bases (figs. 10–11; see also excavated pottery in figs. 25–26). One Canaanean blade was collected while walking across the site, and four fragments of basalt grinding stones were also noted. Nine of the diagnostic sherds were of non-Early Bronze Age date. Six of these sherds were collected in the general surface collection across the site, and included five Roman/Byzantine ribbed body sherds and one Nabataean handle (Brown 1991: 276). The remaining three sherds were recovered in Collection Unit 1 and consisted of one body sherd of painted Nabataean fine ware, probably dating to the first century C.E. (Stucky et al. 1994: 283; Schmid 1995: 645), and two Nabataean/Early Roman body sherds.

Adir (Miller site #227)

The Early Bronze Age site of Adir is situated below the modern settlement of Adir, one of the largest towns on the Kerak Plateau. The main tell has been extensively altered by modern and ancient occupation, and modern bulldozing and building have destroyed most of the site. Owing to the density of settlement and building, it was impossible to discern any clear boundaries of the site beyond the rough outline of the main tell on which several old (early twentieth-century) buildings sit. Along a long bulldozer cut (ca. 100 m long and at least 3–4 m high) on the main tell, ceramics were collected that suggested an occupation from the EB IV through modern periods (fig. 12; fig. 2: a–b). In the northeastern reaches of the town, one standing and two fallen menhirs are located in a bedrock field along with two cisterns. One of the cisterns had been altered in antiquity to be used as a tomb, and the tomb has been emptied out at some point in time. To the southeast of the modern town, located by the modern cemetery and between two extensions of the town, lies a cistern field with the foundations of water catchment walls. The field also shows evidence of quarrying and is now being bulldozed for modern building materials. Among the cisterns, there are the foundations of a very large building, possibly associated with water management. Overall, the state of preservation of Adir is extremely poor, owing to modern occupation and building.

The forty sherds collected from the general surface and the bulldozer cut, represent a wide range of periods, mostly Classical and EB IV. Seven of the twenty-six diagnostic sherds collected from the bulldozer cut were identified as non-Early Bronze Age in date. A base, a spout in orange ware with cream slip, a jar handle, and a possible jug rim in dark grey ware were dated to the Byzantine period (Brown 1991: 277). In addition, a lid and a ribbed body sherd were dated to the Roman/Byzantine period. The remaining jar rim was identified as Iron Age II in date (fig. 2:a).

Lejjun (Miller site #239)

Lejjun is located on a hill rising from the Lejjun spring, across from the Roman fort, and approximately 4.5 km southeast of Jdeidah on the road leading to the Kerak–Qatrana road. Lejjun is not currently occupied and exhibits little evidence for occupation following the Early Bronze Age.

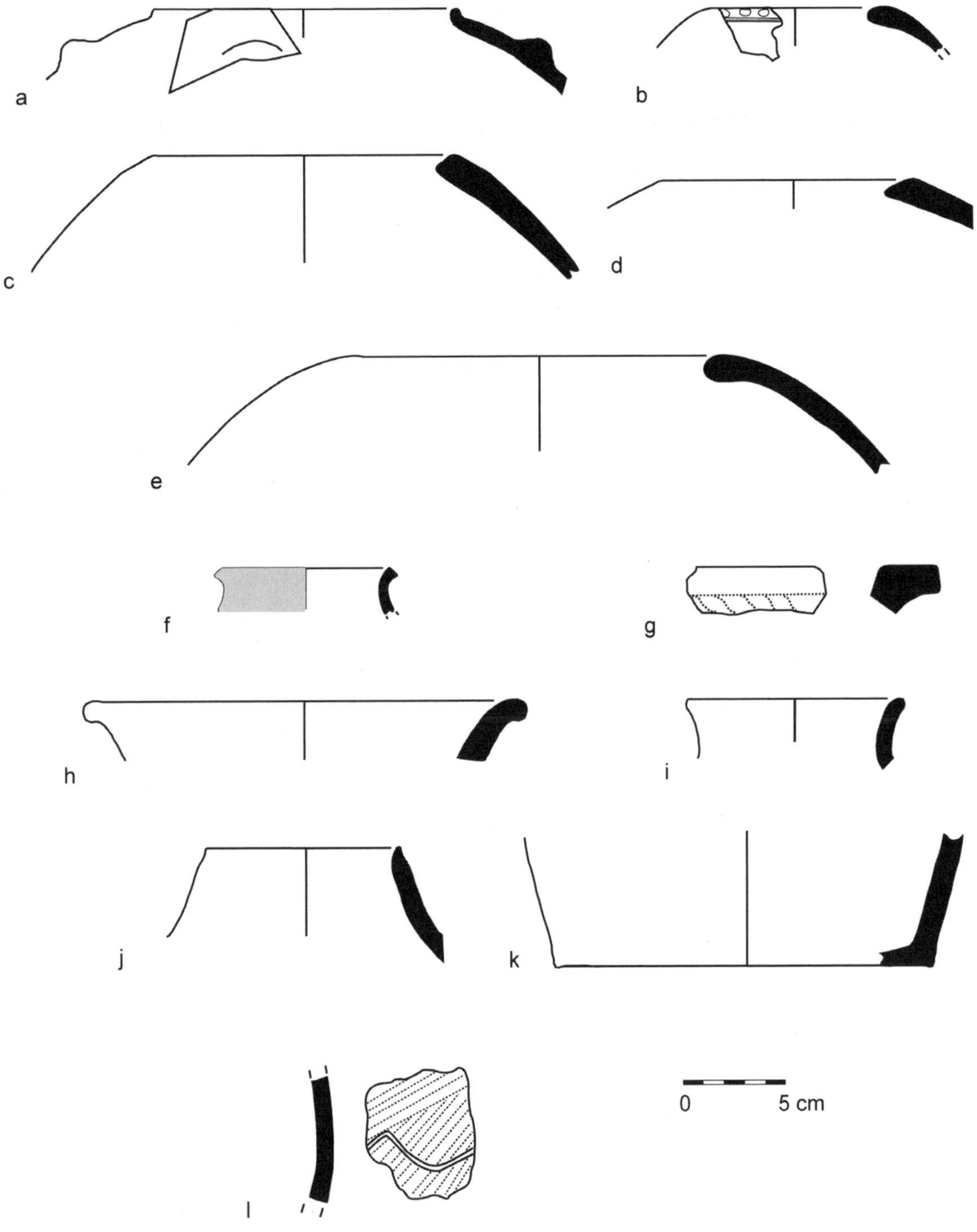

Fig. 10. *Early Bronze Age pottery from surface collections at Khirbet el-Minsahlat.*

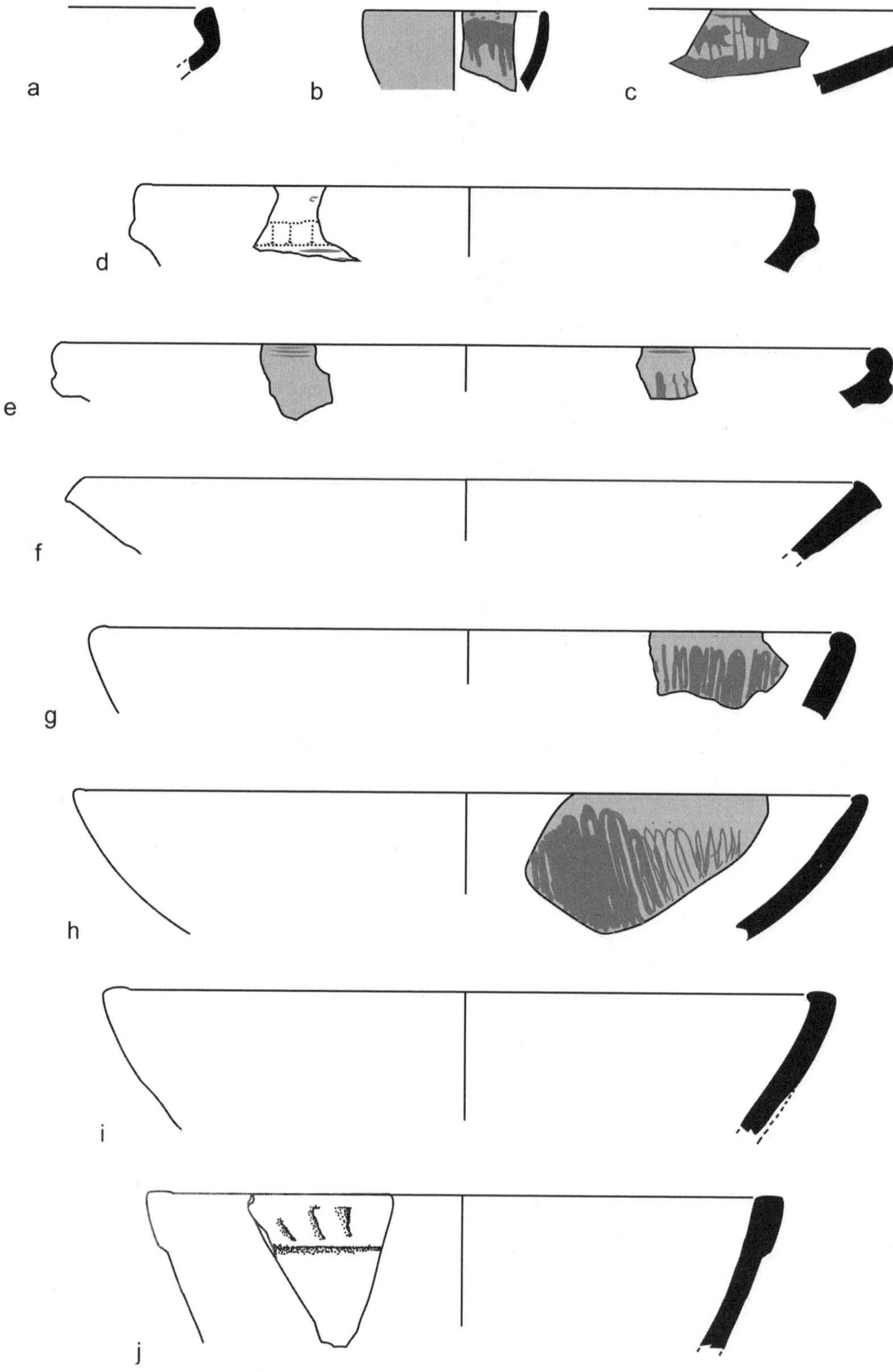

Fig. 11. *Early Bronze Age pottery from surface collections at Khirbet el-Minsahlat.*

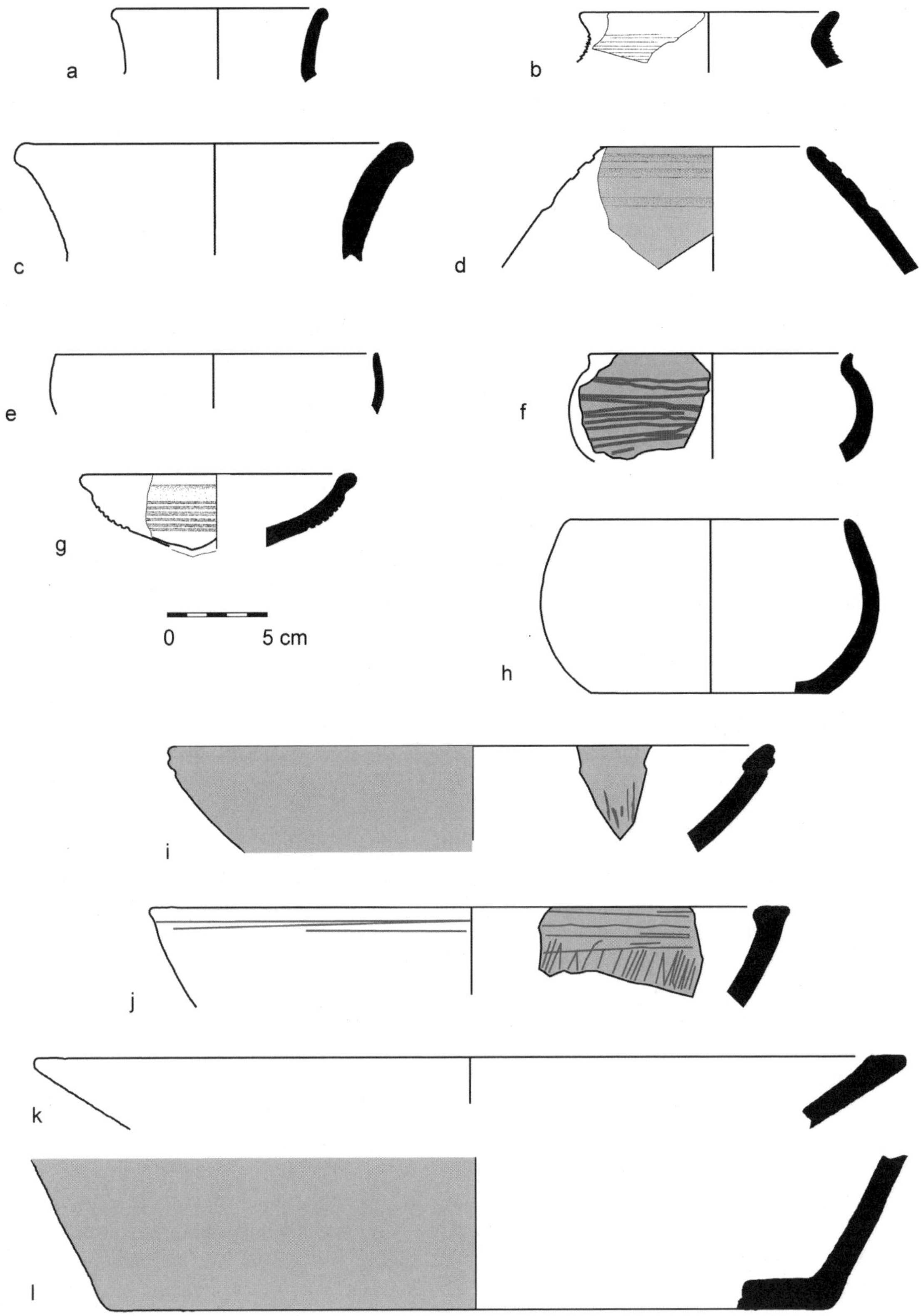

Fig. 12. Early Bronze Age pottery from surface collections at Adir.

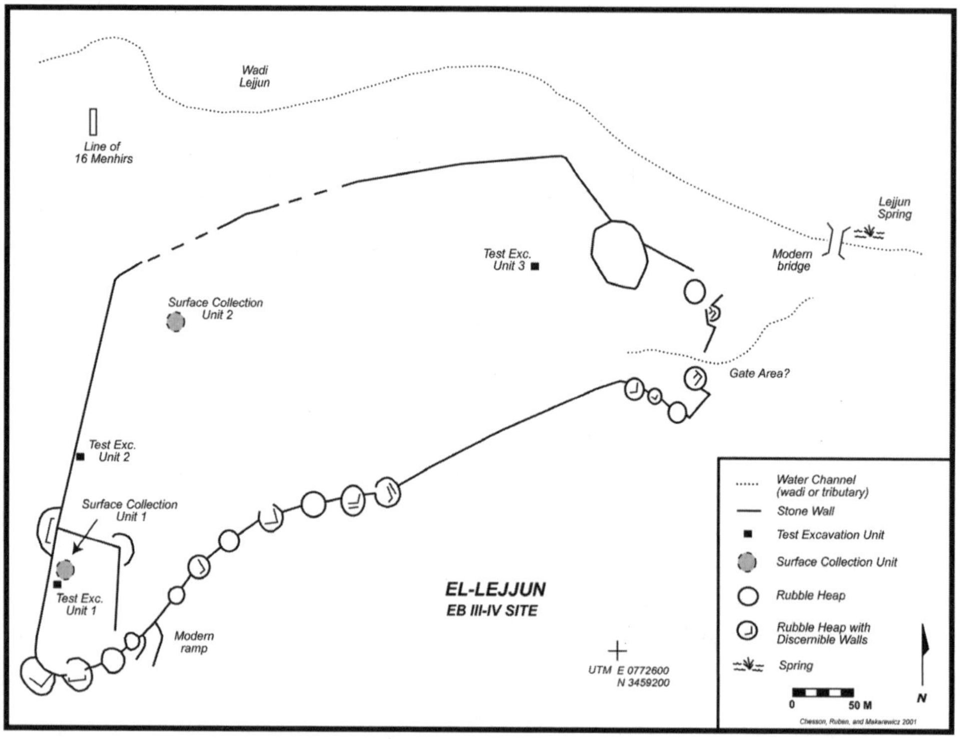

Fig. 13. *Schematic plan of Lejjun.*

The site is approximately 10–11 ha in size, enclosed by large stone fortification walls that can be traced around the entire site (fig. 13). Several structures inside the walls can be discerned through aerial photographs (see Parker 1987b: pl. 20) and in walking on the surface. There may be a gate system in the eastern reaches of the settlement overlooking the spring, based on the large rectangular structures and the general topography of the area. There also is a large, roughly oval-shaped structure along the eastern fortification wall, which is approximately 37 × 42 m in size. In the southwest portion of the fortification wall, there are eleven large stone mounds spaced at approximately 20-m intervals. Two of these mounds seem to form "dog-legs" in the fortification wall. The final large mound of rubble forms the southwestern corner of a large, rectangular structure inside the main fortification wall. This structure measures approximately 60 × 110 m, and the two southernmost rubble mounds along the edge of this building show signs of being reused for at least two burials. In the northwest, downslope from the fortification walls, there are sixteen menhirs (eleven of which are still standing *in situ*) aligned on a north–south axis. The state of preservation of Lejjun is good, although the site has suffered from erosion and the occasional pot hunting. Overall, the site has changed very little from Miller's descriptions of his visit twenty-five years ago, although it is used by the local Bedouin for grazing.

Of the 119 ceramic sherds recovered in one collection unit and in a general collection across the site, almost all date to EB II–III (fig. 7:f; also see excavated pottery in fig. 20). Interestingly, the fabric of the pottery is very different from that of ceramics from all the other surveyed sites. The Lejjun fabric seems to be finer in general, with smaller-sized inclusions, and it contains a substantial amount of shiny (micaceous?) grit temper. This difference in temper may be significant and will be followed up later with petrographic surveys and analyses of pottery samples from various sites on the Kerak Plateau. Only four collected sherds were non-Early Bronze Age in date. From the sample collected in the general collection across

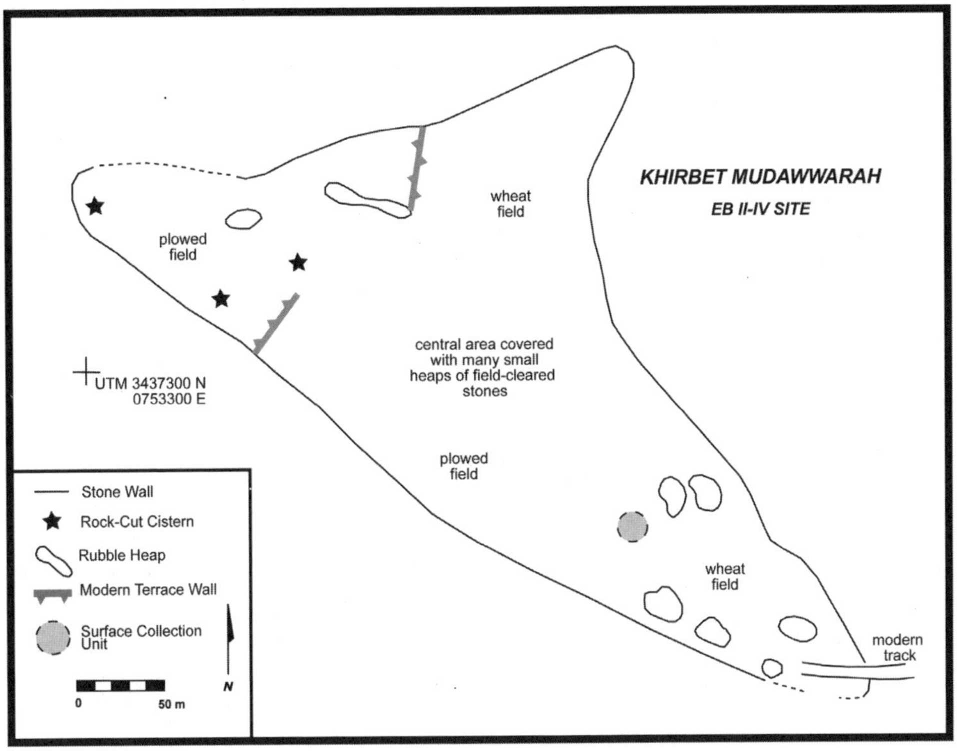

Fig. 14. Schematic plan of Khirbet Mudawwarah.

the site, two rim sherds of bowl forms dating to the Iron Age II were identified (Brown 1991: 274). One Late Byzantine bowl rim was identified in the sample from surface Collection Unit 1 (Brown 1991: 277), and one ribbed body sherd in dark grey ware, probably dating to the Byzantine period, was identified in the sample from surface Collection Unit 2.

Khirbet el-Mudawwarah (Miller site #390)

Khirbet el-Mudawwarah is located on a spur overlooking the Wadi Juhra. The site has been heavily disturbed by plowing and terracing. Many of the terrace walls may actually have been built upon the Early Bronze Age fortification walls. The size of the site is approximately 5.5 ha, based on the outlines of the fortification walls that are visible around the entirety of the site (fig. 14). There are several heaps of stones across the site, possibly from field-clearing or from structures within the fortification walls. Three cisterns were recorded within the bounds of the site. One of the cisterns is being currently used and has been capped with a cement installation. Another cistern has been partially cleared recently. This cistern's spoil heap was filled with diagnostic EB II–III pottery, including red-slipped and patterned burnished sherds. Overall, the state of preservation of Khirbet el-Mudawwarah is very poor, and the site has been extensively modified through terracing, field-clearing and plowing.

In the surface collection unit, 193 sherds were collected, of which seventy were diagnostic in form and/or decoration. The vast majority of the sherds were EB II–III and EB IV forms (fig. 7:g). While a few later, wheel-turned forms from Roman and Byzantine periods were collected, there is no architectural or artifactual evidence to suggest any major occupation of the site after the Early Bronze Age. Only five non-Early Bronze Age sherds were identified. Three Roman/Byzantine body sherds were present in the sample from the general surface collection. The sample from Collection Unit 1 included two very abraded Roman/Byzantine body sherds.

Discussion of Early Bronze Age Pottery from Surface Collections

The majority of Early Bronze Age pottery collected at the eight sites demonstrates the presence of EB I–IV occupation on the Kerak Plateau, although the sample is heavily weighted toward the EB II onward. As Brown notes (1991: 173–84, especially 176–84), the Early Bronze Age pottery from the Kerak Plateau presents an interesting combination of continuity with the earlier Chalcolithic forms and an impressive diversity of forms and improved manufacturing techniques. For example, holemouth jars, flat bases, and raised band decorations find clear antecedents in the Chalcolithic period (Brown 1991: 176). Brown (1991: 176–77) also notes that by the EB II–III period, the manufacturing techniques were producing better-fired and -finished vessels, in some cases formed on slow wheels. Furthermore, fabrics were harder and thicker than in previous periods, and different and finer tempers were used from the earlier EB I and Chalcolithic periods. In the Miller survey pottery, Brown described that certain vessel forms were associated with particular tempers (e.g., holemouth jars contained large-sized white, calcite inclusions) and that these differences in tempers might have reflected differences in use (cooking in holemouth jars vs. storage and serving in platterbowls, storage jars, and bowls). Red slips, self slips, combing, and burnishing were common decorative elements on closed and open forms, with slipping and burnishing found primarily on bowls and platters, and self-slipping and combing associated with jars. Holemouth jars were rarely slipped or decorated in any way.

In analyzing the EB IV pottery from Miller's survey, Brown (1991: 180–81) states that there was no major development in either fabric composition or manufacturing techniques to differentiate this corpus from the EB II–III assemblage. Red slips and burnishing continued to be widely used. Grooving or "rilling" around the exterior rim of bowls and holemouth jars appeared more frequently on EB IV vessels, and envelope ledge handles predominated the handles assemblage. The EB IV vessels exhibited more examples of plastic decoration (scalloping, "pie crust," and finger impressions) on rims or appliqué bands close to rims of large bowls and basins. The 2001 Kerak Plateau Survey provided ample data to confirm Brown's characterizations of the Early Bronze Age pottery corpus on the Kerak Plateau (for detailed descriptions of all sherds illustrated, see Appendix C). Based on her typology, the majority of the 2001 survey assemblage contains EB I–IV pottery.

Discussion of Non-Early Bronze Age Pottery from Surface Collections

Non-Early Bronze Age sherds were collected from all eight sites targeted by the survey. The vast majority of the pottery dated to the Nabataean, Roman, and Byzantine periods, although some Iron Age II pottery was identified at three sites (Lejjun, Adir, Mis'ar). In addition, pottery dated to the Early and Middle Islamic periods was identified at four sites (Umm el-Habaj, Mis'ar, Rujm Birjis, Khirbet el-Mudawwarah). No examples of Neolithic, Middle or Late Bronze Age, or Iron Age I material were noted (Table 1). Distinctive fabric types, in addition to morphology and decoration, were used as the primary indicators of date. Most samples were not large enough to make general comments on fabric types. Overall, the fabrics, forms and decoration of the collected sherds fit in well with Brown's characterization of the Iron Age II through Islamic periods pottery of the Kerak Plateau (Brown 1991: 197–241). Detailed descriptions of the form, fabric, and decoration of a representative selection of diagnostic sherds are provided along with their illustration for comparative purposes (Appendix D). The following discussion provides a summary of the findings of the ceramic analysis of the non-Early Bronze Age pottery collected from each of the sites surveyed by the project.

To facilitate an overview of the ceramic periods represented at each of the sites, Table 1 presents the results of the pottery analysis according to collection unit (see also Appendix D, figs. 2 and 8). Most of the samples of non-Early Bronze Age pottery were not large enough to make general comments on the settlement or other activities at the sites in question. In general, ceramics from

Table 1. Historic ceramic periods present at each site by collection unit.

Site	Sample	Periods Represented
Mis'ar	General surface collection	10 Iron Age II, 3 Late Byzantine, 1 Middle Islamic
Site 40	General surface collection	3 Roman/Byzantine, 1 Middle Islamic
Rujm Birjis	Collection Unit 1	4 Nabataean, 1 Late Roman, 17 Roman/Byzantine
	Collection Unit 2	12 Nabataean, 46 Roman/Byzantine, 1 Middle Islamic
Umm el-Habaj	General surface collection	2 Nabataean, 84 Roman/Byzantine, 5 Byzantine, 1 Early Islamic, 7 Middle Islamic
	Collection Unit 1	4 Roman, 1 Late Roman, 8 Roman/Byzantine, 47 Byzantine, 1 Early Islamic, 9 Middle Islamic
Khirbet el-Minsahlat	Collection Unit 1	1 Nabataean, 2 Nabataean/Early Roman
	General surface collection	1 Nabataean, 5 Roman/Byzantine
Adir	Bulldozer cut	1 Iron Age II, 2 Roman/Byzantine, 4 Byzantine
Lejjun	General surface collection	2 Iron Age II
	Collection Unit 1	1 Late Byzantine
	Collection Unit 2	1 Byzantine
Khirbet el-Mudawwarah	General surface collection	3 Roman/Byzantine
	Collection Unit 1	2 Roman/Byzantine

the Roman/Byzantine period made up the greatest proportion of the samples collected from all eight sites. In comparison, Iron Age II, Nabataean and Islamic pottery only made up a small proportion of the samples. Iron Age pottery, for example, occurred only in small quantities at Lejjun, Adir, and Mis'ar. Similarly, Nabataean pottery was only found in small quantities at Rujm Birjis, Khirbet el-Minsahlat, and Umm el-Habaj. Early Islamic ceramics were found in small quantities only at Umm el-Habaj. Middle Islamic pottery was found in greater quantities at Mis'ar, Umm el-Habaj, Rujm Birjis and Khirbet el-Minsahlat. The majority of the pottery of this date fell into the category of distinctive handmade wares with geometrically painted decoration. Because most samples were not large enough to make general comments on fabric types, fabrics were only recorded in detail for the diagnostic sherds from each sample. Overall, the fabrics, forms and decoration of the examined pottery fit well with Brown's characterization of the Iron Age II through Islamic period pottery of the Kerak Plateau (Brown 1991: 197–241).

RESULTS OF TEST EXCAVATIONS

Test excavations conducted at Lejjun and Khirbet el-Minsahlat offer several interesting avenues for exploring the Early Bronze Age on the Kerak Plateau, which will be discussed briefly at the end of this section. All excavated sediments were screened with 2.5 mm mesh and soil samples were collected for flotation from priority contexts, such as floors, pits and hearths. This section briefly outlines the preliminary results from the excavations at both sites.

Lejjun

Three test trenches were opened at Lejjun to determine the depth of deposits and the nature of preservation of architecture and material culture (fig. 13).

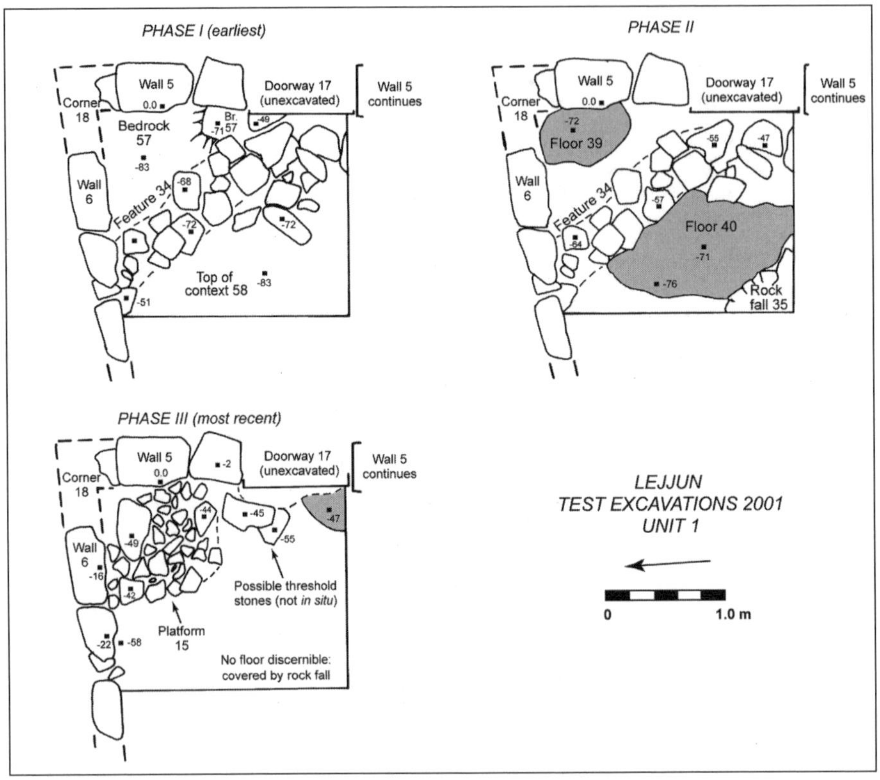

Fig. 15. *Plan of architectural phases in Unit 1, Lejjun.*

Unit 1 (fig. 15)

A 2 × 1.5 m unit was placed inside the large, rectangular structure in the southwestern portion of the site. This large structure can be easily seen in the aerial photograph of the site (Parker 1987: pl. 20) and has been mapped into the team's plan of the site (fig. 13).

Three phases of occupation were noted in Unit 1, all associated with walls 5 and 6. Walls 5 and 6 were constructed from a single line of very large stones, in some places situated on a single layer of small stones on bedrock or with the large stones lying directly on the bedrock. The walls were not bonded, and corner 18 seems to have collapsed or been robbed out from a very early stage. Blocked doorway 17 does not seem to be an intentional blockage, as there is no clear face to the block and the stones seem to be very haphazardly arranged, as if they are the product of fall rather than human placement. Overall, the construction method of walls 5 and 6, and especially corner 18, did not emphasize the importance of building clear interior faces to the walls, and none of the stones exhibit any signs of modification.

In the most recent phase, platform 15 was associated with walls 5 and 6, built into the northeast corner (18) of the building. Unfortunately, no surface was associated with this platform. This may be due to the destruction of the surface by stones fallen from the building's walls, blocking doorway 17 and covering the unit and platform 15.

The middle occupation is represented by a floor (39 and 40), which abuts and partially covers a line of stones (34) that runs through the middle of the unit on a southeast–northwest axis. Interestingly, 34 runs from the lower levels of doorway 18 across the unit and under wall 6.

The oldest occupational layer is associated with the construction of walls 5 and 6 on bedrock (57; approximately 65 cm below the modern ground surface of the site) and the placement of stone line 34 across the edge of bedrock before it descends to an unknown depth. We were unable to reach bedrock to the south of stone line 34, but it is interesting to note that 34 travels under wall

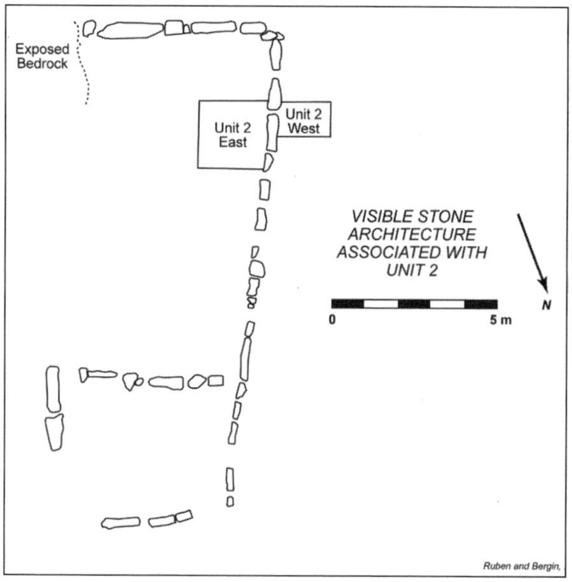

Fig. 16. Plan of structure associated with Excavation Units 2 East and 2 West, Lejjun.

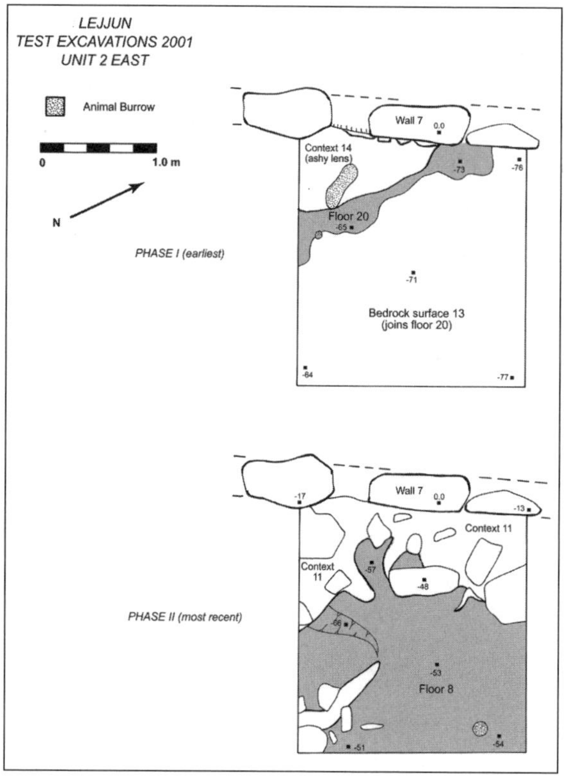

Fig. 17. Plan of architectural phases in Unit 2 East, Lejjun.

6. While 34 seems to be designed in some way to provide a footing for floors 39 and 40, it is clearly the product of an earlier occupational phase. It may have been an internal dividing wall in this earlier phase, but we were unable to ascertain its original function as we did not reach bedrock on its southern "face," stopping on the top of another layer of sediment (58). From the small excavation unit it is difficult to determine whether the excavated area was inside a roofed structure or situated in an unroofed courtyard space.

The amount of collected materials—before and after screening began—was very small, especially in comparison to the amount of materials collected at similar sites in the region. For example, while the screening increased the appearance of juvenile animals in the sample, overall very few bones were collected, and of these few could be identified to the species level. The vast majority of ceramic sherds collected were body sherds of what seem to be cooking holemouth jars, based on the fabric and blackening of the sherds' surfaces. Very few diagnostic pieces were found, and no reconstructible (or portions of reconstructible) vessels were found, even on solid floors. Very few chipped stone artifacts and no groundstone objects were recovered.

Unit 2 (figs. 16–18)

Unit 2 was placed approximately 100 m to the northeast of Unit 1, on both sides of a wall running parallel to the western fortification wall (fig. 16). Unit 2 East was opened first to the east of wall 7 (fig. 17). This 2 × 2 m trench contained two phases of occupation, each associated with a clearly defined floor surface and both associated with wall 7. Like the walls of the structure in Unit 1, the single line of stones of wall 7 was laid directly on bedrock or on top of a single, thin layer of small stones. The most recent occupational phase in Unit 2 East was associated with a floor (context 10) approximately 40 cm below the modern ground surface and sloping westward toward wall 7. The floor was constructed of crushed limestone and soil. No artifacts were found on floor 8, and the floor partially covered several large stones. The oldest occupational phase in Unit 2 East was a floor (13) composed of bedrock and a small section of crushed limestone flooring material where the bedrock dipped down near wall 7. On this floor, the

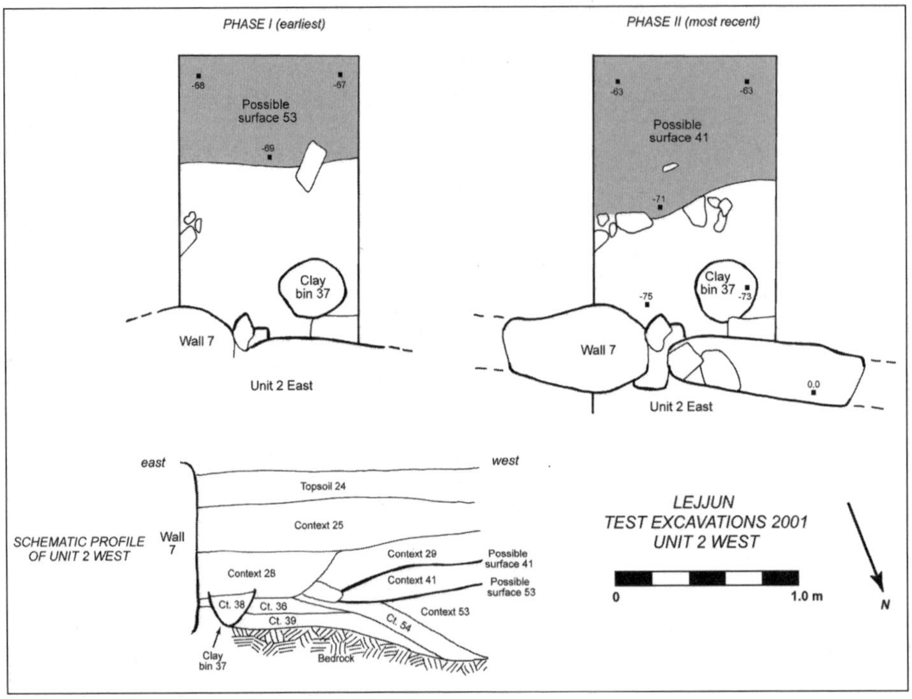

Fig. 18. *Plan of architectural phases in Unit 2 West, Lejjun.*

excavators recovered a single, small groundstone object of unknown function and no other materials. Below the sediment portion of floor 13, the excavators uncovered fill and the single line of small stones used as a foundation for portions of wall 7.

Two radiocarbon samples were collected from the removal of floor 10, the later of the two floors. Both samples were wood charcoal and were processed by accelerator dating:

Sample	Context	Age	$\delta^{13}C$	Cal Date 1-Σ (Calib 4.3)
ISGS-A0242	Floor removal	4314 ± 52	-22.4	2923–2884 CAL B.C.E
ISGS-A0243	Floor removal	4393 ± 42	-25.5	3088–22919 CAL B.C.E

These dates place occupation of Lejjun at EB II, and the fortifications at Lejjun suggest an extensive EB II occupation. While the test excavation units provide a very small sample of data on occupation at the site, the radiocarbon dates indicate that it was settled as early as the EB II, and we suggest that the extensive fortification system may have been in place at least in the EB II.

Unit 2 West was a 1.5 × 1 m trench adjacent to Unit 2 East across wall 7 (fig. 18). Below topsoil, the excavators found a series of what seemed to be layers of dump. At approximately 60 cm below ground surface, they found a circular clay bin set into the ground (context 36) adjacent to wall 7. The sediments to the west of this bin, and above the context 36, continued to be layers of dump or fill. Two potential surfaces were found in these layers of sediments, although the surfaces were less clearly defined (i.e. showing signs of definite construction or creation) than those in Unit 2 East. With these potential surfaces, it can be suggested that there are also at least two occupational phases on the west side of wall 7, although it cannot be determined if each of these phases corresponds to one or both of the floor surfaces in Unit 2 East. Even with excavation trenches on both sides of wall 7, the size of the units prevents any way of clearly determining the "inside" or "outside" (or roofed or unroofed) nature of the spaces on both sides of wall 7.

Like in Unit 1, very few artifacts or materials were recovered. The vast majority of ceramic sherds collected were body sherds of what seem to be cooking holemouth jars, based on the fabric and blackening of the sherds' surfaces. Very few diagnostic pieces were found, and no reconstructible (or portions of reconstructible) vessels were recovered, even on solid floors. Very few chipped stone artifacts and only one groundstone object were retrieved in Units 2 East and West.

Unit 3 (fig. 19)

A 2 × 1 m unit was opened along a line of stones (wall 46) in the southeastern portion of the site, near the largest heap of rubble along the southeastern portion of the fortification wall. Though the depth of deposits in this area was very shallow (approximately 40 cm of sediments from ground surface to bedrock), the excavators uncovered two phases of occupation, each associated with a floor surface and separated by a layer of fill. The later occupational phase was represented by a floor (context 45) approximately 20 cm below the ground surface. This surface ran up to wall 46 and was associated with a potential installation (context 51; stone work surface?). The earlier phase was associated with the construction of wall 46, either directly on bedrock or on a few centimeters of sediments lying on top of bedrock. Adjacent to the wall (almost covered by a stone in the wall) excavations uncovered a cupmark in the bedrock surface (context 48). It is impossible to clearly associate this cupmark with the wall. The placement of the cupmark under one of the wall's stones suggests that it is an older feature that may or may not have been associated with the living surface of the earlier phase of occupation. Similar to the other two units, very few finds were recovered in fills or on floors.

Discussion of Lejjun Test Excavations

Test excavations at Lejjun have produced information on the architectural and artifactual remains at the site, and the radiocarbon samples from the later of the two floors in Unit 2 place this structure and its floors to the EB II. Overall, the architectural remains are in fairly good shape, although the depths of deposits are very shallow (ca. 40–60 cm in the units tested). The shallow nature of deposits may reflect post-depositional processes (erosion, for instance) of later occupational phases, the continuous reuse and modification of structures over a long occupational history, differential use across space and through time, or a rather short occupational period. Obviously, the small sample size of three test trenches in an 11 ha site provides limited clarification with regards to our understanding of Lejjun's occupational history. The fortification structures and remains of large buildings suggest a long, or at least intense, occupation of the site. If this is the case, the question of the relationship between shallow deposits and the length and intensity of settlement begs examination.

Interestingly, the pottery collected in the surface survey showed a marked difference in temper and fabric from other sites on the plateau and from that collected in the test excavations. At this time, it is not possible to explain this difference within the region or even within the same site.

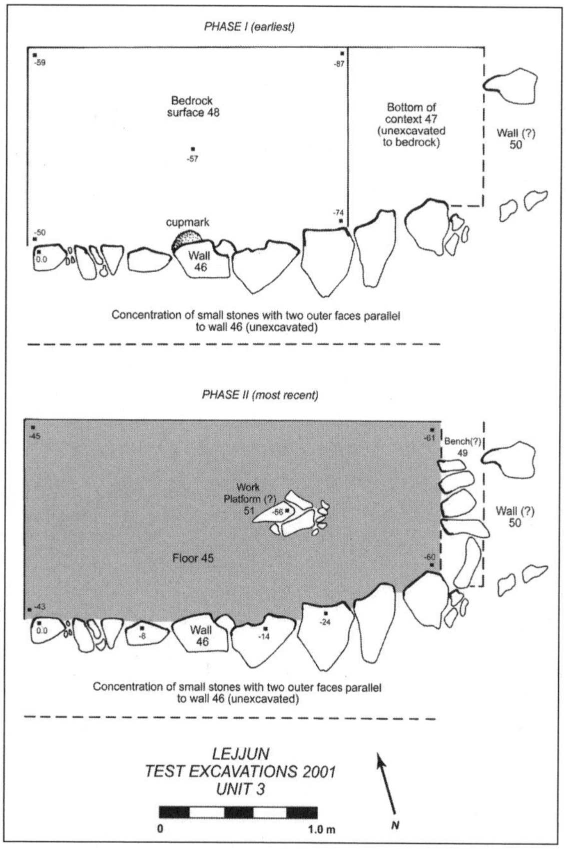

Fig. 19. *Plan of architectural phases in Unit 3, Lejjun.*

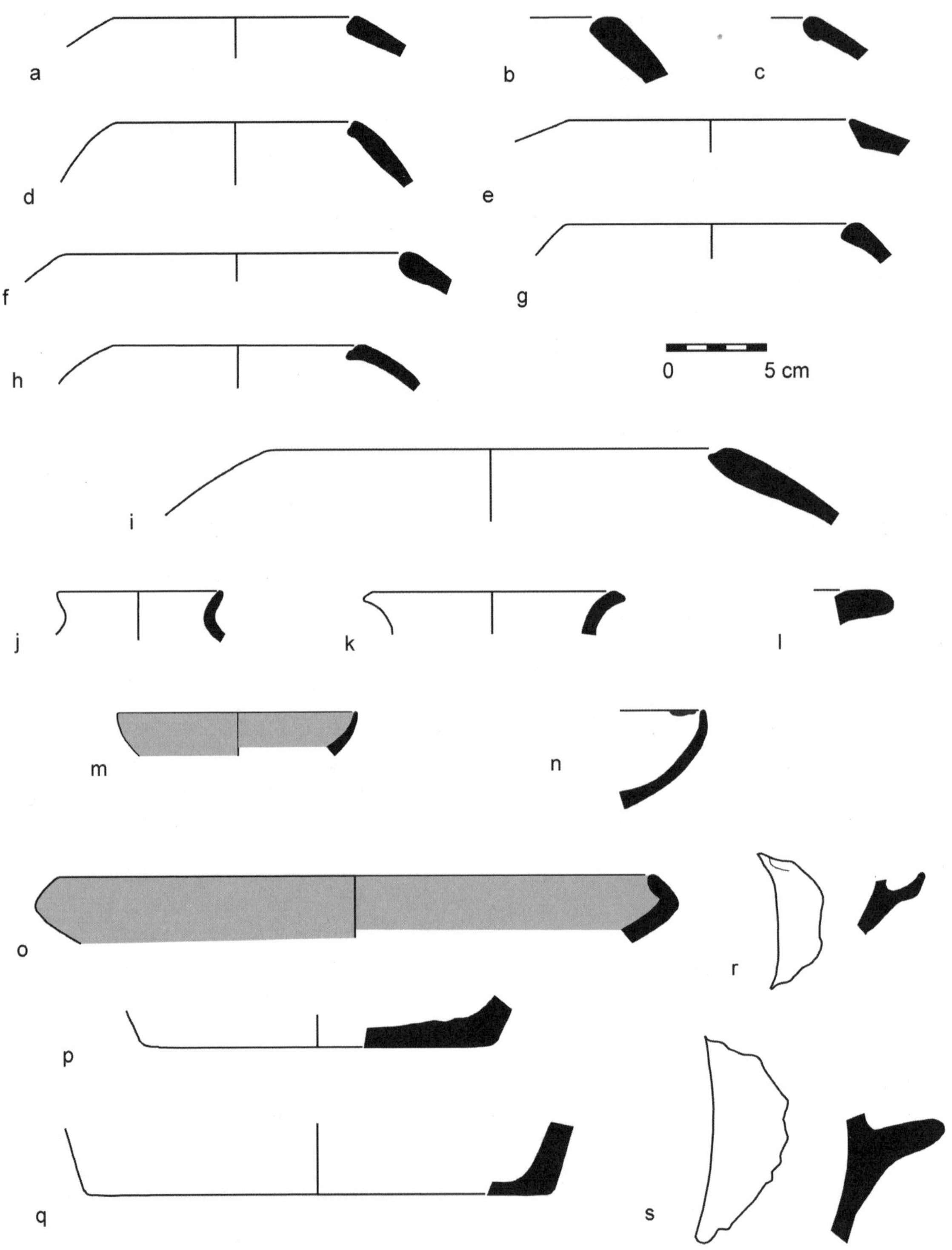

Fig. 20. *Early Bronze Age pottery excavated at Lejjun.*

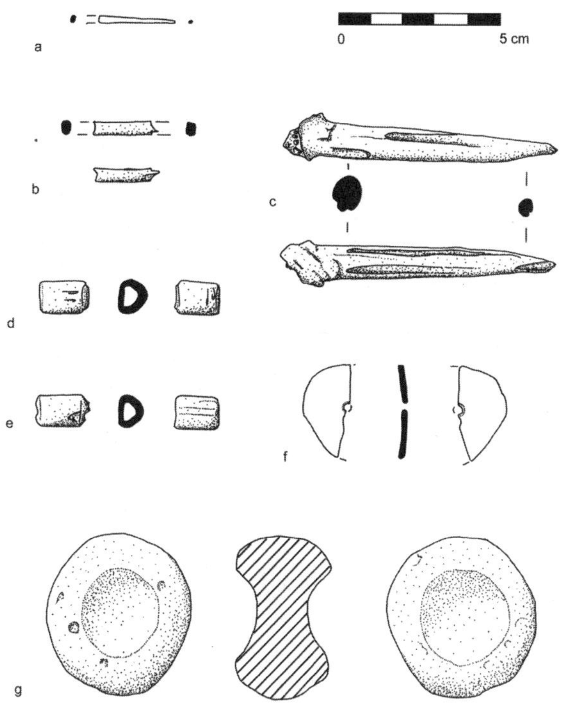

Fig. 21. Small finds excavated at Lejjun and Kh. el-Minsahlat.

A systematic petrographic study of the region's sites and clay sources will need to be undertaken to begin to understand this discrepancy. The relative absence of pottery (or other artifact types) in relation to Early Bronze Age sites in other areas is interesting. In most excavations, all non-diagnostic sherds are returned to a sherd dump on the site; if this practice had been followed at Lejjun, the sample would have contained less than thirty sherds. Thus, all sherds were kept and logged in terms of fabric, surface treatments and probable form. The dominance of cooking holemouth jar body sherds, with their coarse fabric and burning on exterior and interior surfaces, in the assemblage is noteworthy (fig. 20). Why people on the plateau (because this trend is not limited to Lejjun) did not discard their pottery even when broken may reflect the paucity of clay sources in the region. Again, only a systematic petrographic study of the Kerak Plateau's sites and clay sources can begin to address this issue.

In addition to ceramic and chipped stone artifacts, the excavations recovered several small finds (fig. 21:c–g). These objects include a worked gazelle horn core, two polished bone beads, a shaped and pierced piece of shell, and a small groundstone object. While the overall ceramic, faunal, and lithic assemblages may be "impoverished" in terms of quantity and quality, the remains of Lejjun's impressive fortification system and interior architecture offer an exciting avenue for exploring issues of social and economic organization from a city-planning perspective. A worthwhile project would be the mapping of the surface architecture of the site with a total station to create a city plan. Overall, Lejjun offers very interesting possibilities for investigating sociopolitical and socioeconomic structures of Early Bronze Age life in a more marginal environment.

Khirbet el-Minsahlat

Two test trenches were opened, and one portion of a bulldozer section was cleaned and drawn at Khirbet el-Minsahlat.

Section Cleaning (fig. 22)

The construction of an olive orchard involved the bulldozing of the main tell of the settlement, located in the western portion of the site. The bulldozer cut exposed at least 3 m of deposits and measures approximately 70 m in length. Several walls were easily identified in this section, one of which is 10 m wide (fig. 9) and may be part of a fortification wall or gate on the western edge of the settlement. Nine meters of the bulldozer section were drawn, illustrating the remains of at least four walls and two occupational phases, represented by separate floors. At the western end of the drawn section lies a cistern cut into the bedrock. Previous to the bulldozer cut this cistern would have been covered. As mentioned earlier in the results of the survey at Minsahlat, this "typical" Byzantine cistern must be more ancient and can clearly be attributed to the Early Bronze Age whose deposits surround it.

Within the section, walls were placed directly on sediments and there is no sign of any special preparation of foundations for these stone walls. Wall B is an excellent example of this practice. It is actually the outer face of a wall (based on tracing walls on the surface of the mound behind the bull-

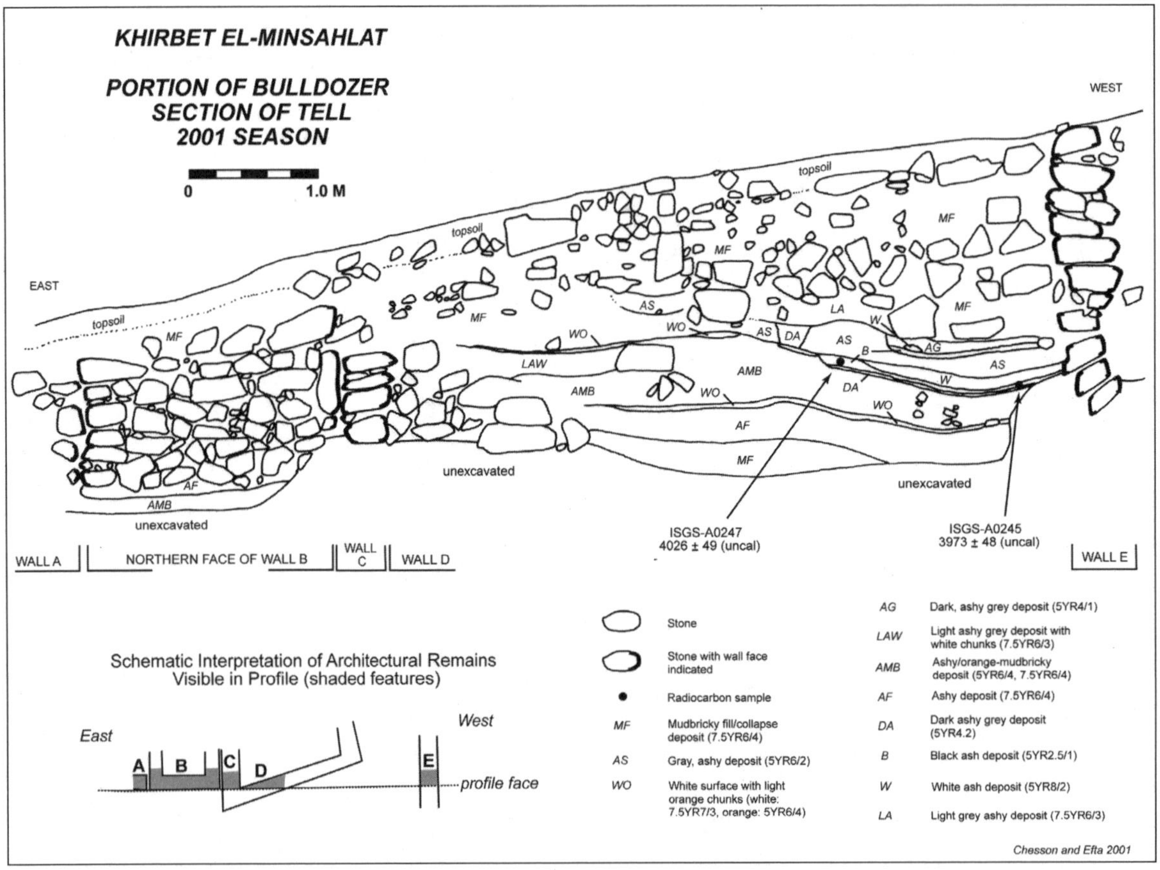

Fig. 22. *Stratigraphic profile of a portion of the bulldozer cut, Khirbet el-Minsahlat.*

dozer cut), placed on ashy sediment that overlays mudbrick fill mixed with ashy sediment.

Between Walls D and E there are two clear floors visible in the section. The earlier floor seems to be a hard, crushed limestone surface similar to those found in the other units at the site. The later floor is associated with intense burning, and it seems that these burning episodes can be divided into earlier and later phases. Above this second surface the section shows approximately one meter of wall fall, with stones mixed with pockets of ash and mudbricky material.

From the section, it is clear that the depths of deposits in this portion of the site are extensive, ranging from 2 to 4 m at least. Moreover, the preservation of architecture in this section of the site is excellent, with at least two occupational phases present.

Unit 1 (fig. 23)

A 2 × 3 m trench was opened in line with a wall visible on the surface, in which at least four phases of renovation of the structure were noted. After clearing the topsoil across the entire unit, a perpendicular crosswall (wall 3) was found. Wall 3 is abutted by wall 34, which is a short wall ending in a possible entranceway (further excavation is necessary to clarify the nature of wall 34). On the northern side of wall 3, the excavators found the stone foundation of a work platform (14), but no floor associated with this feature. This stone platform is the most recent phase of architecture. No corresponding floor was found to the south of wall 3, and we surmise that any surface that may have existed has eroded away. Below feature 14, the team encountered a level of fall composed of large stones. Due to the depth of deposits on the southern side of wall 3, it was decided to stop

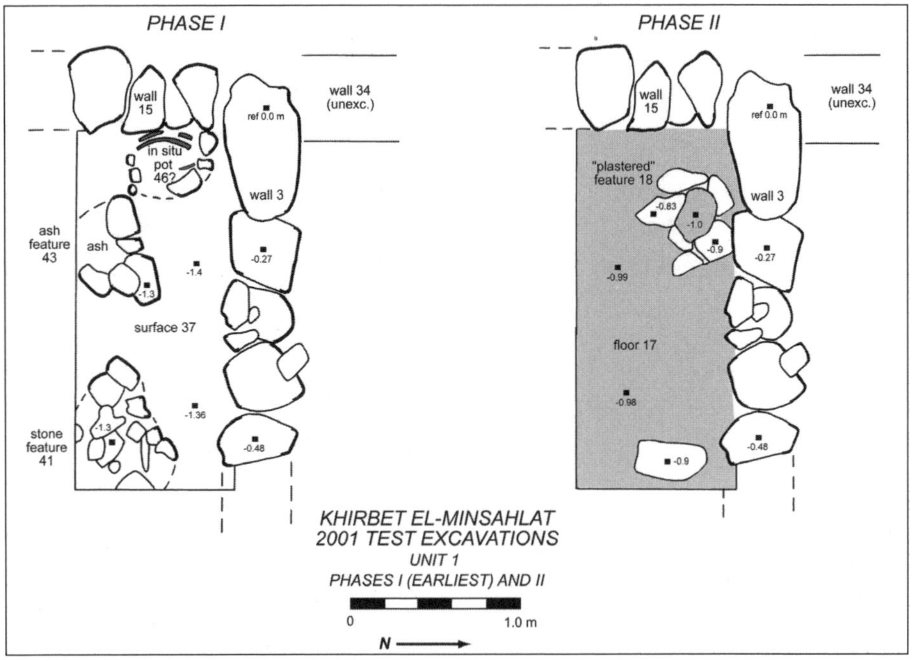

Fig. 23. Plan of architectural phases in Unit 1, Khirbet el-Minsahlat.

excavations on the northern side because of time constraints.

On the southern side of wall 3, excavations reached the bottom of the wall (approximately 1.4 m below the ground surface), which was bonded with wall 15. Interestingly, these stone walls were placed on loose sediment and their builders did not prepare any type of foundation trench or solid surface for them (this was also the case with wall B in the section). There were three renovation episodes found in this structure (not including the phase that may have been associated with feature 14 to the north of wall 3). The most recent phase was represented by a floor (10) that continued up to walls 3 and 15. The floor was constructed of a mixture of hard-packed mud, ash and soil, and was associated with no features or *in situ* artifacts.

In the middle phase, another mud/ash surface (17) was found, associated with a small depression (18) built into the surface and surrounded by stones over which the surface lapped. Another stone feature (a platform or work surface) was encountered in this phase, but its location in the southwest corner meant that only a small portion of it could be excavated.

In the earliest phase, walls 3 and 15 were constructed on loose, silty soils. The earliest floor or surface associated with these walls is not very clear, but there are a number of installations found at locus 37, which suggests that a floor did not survive. Nevertheless, the combination of a stone platform (41), a small stone storage feature (43) and the remains of part of a holemouth jar (46) set into the earth and surrounded by small stones strongly suggests that a floor existed in this area at one time. It is likely that the floor did not survive within the small space excavated in the corner of the building (since the section also did not show any signs of flooring or a surface), but may have survived in other areas of the room. All of these installations and the probable floor surface were encountered at the same level as the bottom of walls 3 and 15, further supporting the interpretation of a floor at this level to coincide with the construction of both walls.

It is estimated that at least one to two more meters of deposits remain in this area, since the sediments below walls 3 and 15 are anthropogenic in nature. In addition, Unit 1 is situated approximately 2 m higher on the slope than Unit 2, which also did not reach bedrock after excavating for well over a meter.

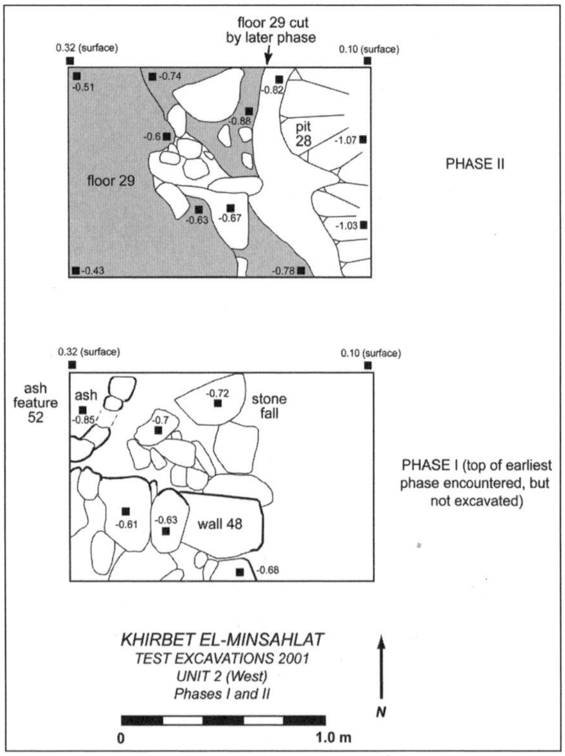

Fig. 24. Plan of architectural phases in Unit 2 West, Khirbet el-Minsahlat.

Unit 2 (fig. 24)

A 2 × 1 m trench was opened to the east of the main tell on the site, to the west of what seemed to be a wall. The stones of this "wall" turned out to be positioned by erosion and slopewash, but the unit (Unit 2 East) was placed serendipitously in a dump of considerable depth. A second 1.5 × 1 m unit (Unit 2 West) was opened to the west of the original unit to increase the area covered by the testing and to provide a series of soil samples, since the preservation of paleobotanical materials was good.

In these two units, three general phases of occupation were noted. The latest occupation of this area of the site focused on the dumping of garbage and ashy sediments. In both the eastern and western units one meter of loose, ashy deposits were encountered below topsoil. The preservation of bone and paleobotanical remains was particularly good in these units, where 100 percent of all sediments were screened through a 2.5 mm mesh.

Corresponding to the middle phase of activity in this area, the team encountered more compact layers of sediment associated with the abandonment of a stone structure below the later layers of dump in Unit 2 West. A hard layer (29 and 38) of whitish material directly covered the stones, which may represent the collapse of wall and roof material of the structure that over time hardened into a layer of mudbrick, limestone and sediments. It seems that a later pit was cut into this layer, although in such small units it was difficult to ascertain whether this pit encompassed the eastern end of the west unit as well as the western end of the east unit.

The earliest phase of activity in this area corresponds to the construction and use of the building associated with wall 48. So little of wall 48 was uncovered in this test unit that it is difficult to say more about it. However, there is an ash pit (52) associated with wall 48, although it was impossible to say whether the ash pit was contemporaneous with 48 or existed after its abandonment. With the good preservation of stone architecture in Unit 1, and judging by the slope of the site, it seems that there is at least one more meter of deposits in this area associated with this earlier phase of occupation.

Radiometric Dates at Minsahlat

Three radiocarbon samples were collected and processed from the test excavations: two samples from the bulldozer cut and one sample from Unit 1. The two samples from the bulldozer cut were taken from dark ash features, probably hearths, associated with floors. The third sample, from Unit 1, was collected from the removal of a poorly-preserved surface associated with a broken pottery vessel and a stone installation.

Sample	Context	Age	$\delta^{13}C$	Cal Date 1-Σ (Calib 4.3)
ISGS-A0244	Floor removal in Unit 1	4081 ± 48	-24.4	2840–2500 CAL BCE
ISGS-A0245	Hearth/ash feature in section	3973 ± 48	-24.5	2565–2460 CAL BCE
ISGS-A0247	Hearth/ash feature in section	4026 ± 49	-23.2	2618–2471 CAL BCE

In recent synthesis articles, Phillip (2001) and Palumbo (2001) both accept the traditional span of the EB IV as ca. 2350–2000 B.C.E.; however, neither author uses calibrated radiocarbon dates to confirm this chronological designation. Instead, they rely on published calibrated dates from EB III sites to provide an ending date to the EB III and a potential beginning date for the EB IV. At this time, with so few calibrated EB IV dates published, we believe that the pottery and the calibrated dates together suggest a terminal EB III/very early EB IV occupation. The pottery at Minsahlat, particularly the envelope ledge handles, the red-slipped and burnished bowls with exterior grooves below the rim, and the incised decorations encircling the rims of holemouth jars support a late EB III/early EB IV date to the excavated contexts. Further research, based on a combination of ceramic chronologies and absolute dates, will be necessary to confirm the date of the site before any resolution can be offered.

Discussion of the Test Excavations at Khirbet el-Minsahlat

Despite the destruction of a portion of the site by the orchard, the site of Minsahlat nevertheless offers a substantial amount of information on the architectural and artifactual characteristics of the settlement. Similar to Lejjun, the architectural preservation is very good, and in the case of Minsahlat the depth of deposits is considerable. Bedrock was only encountered in the cistern next to the bulldozer section, at least four meters below the mound's surface. Furthermore, in Units 2 East and West bedrock was never reached, and the discovery of wall 48 approximately 1.3 m below ground surface suggests that there may be at least one more meter of deposits on the lower elevations of the site. In Unit 2, excavations encountered at least two occupational phases, an earlier stone wall covered by more than a meter of ashy dump deposits from the later phase.

Though the test excavations in the dump encountered a high quantity of ashy sediments, no charcoal samples were encountered. Soil samples were collected and perhaps with their flotation there may be some small samples of charcoal gathered for radiocarbon analysis. On the other hand, preservation of paleobotanical and faunal remains were very good in Unit 2 (see below). All the pottery and chipped stone tools collected in excavation were diagnostic Early Bronze Age forms, particularly late EB III pottery forms (figs. 25–26). As at Lejjun, a few small finds were collected, namely, two polished bone tools (fig. 21:a–b). In terms of pottery, flint, and other artifactual remains, the quantities of materials at Minsahlat were slightly higher than at Lejjun and the paleobotanical and faunal remains were much better preserved.

Preliminary Paleobotanical Analysis from Minsahlat and Lejjun (based on Bending 2002)

Preservation of paleobotanical remains at both sites was good, with burnt seeds found during sieving as well as in soil samples floated at the end of the field season. The species identified were hulled barley grains, einkorn and emmer wheat grains, chickpea, lentil, grass pea, olive and grape. The only wild species identified was a grass. Table 2 outlines the species present in each unit at each site. Both Lejjun and Minsahlat, located only a few kilometers from each other, are on the borders of the dry-farming region of the Kerak Plateau. All species identified at Lejjun and Minsahlat are well documented at other EB II–III sites in the greater region, and demonstrate that the people at these sites combined agricultural and pastoral elements in their daily economic practices (Genz 2003; Grigson 1995; Horwitz and Tchernov 1989; Philip 2001). Continued research at Minsahlat in the future will augment this record of human–plant relations during the Early Bronze Age on the Kerak Plateau.

Preliminary Faunal Results (Table 3)

The 2001 excavations at Minsahlat and Lejjun offer well-preserved faunal remains, an archaeological data set that had been largely neglected in Bronze Age studies until the last decade (Bartosiewicz 1998; Dechert 1995; Greenfield 2002; von den Driesch 1993; Levy 1992: 74). While early analyses of Early Bronze Age faunal assemblages generally suffered from poor collection procedures and

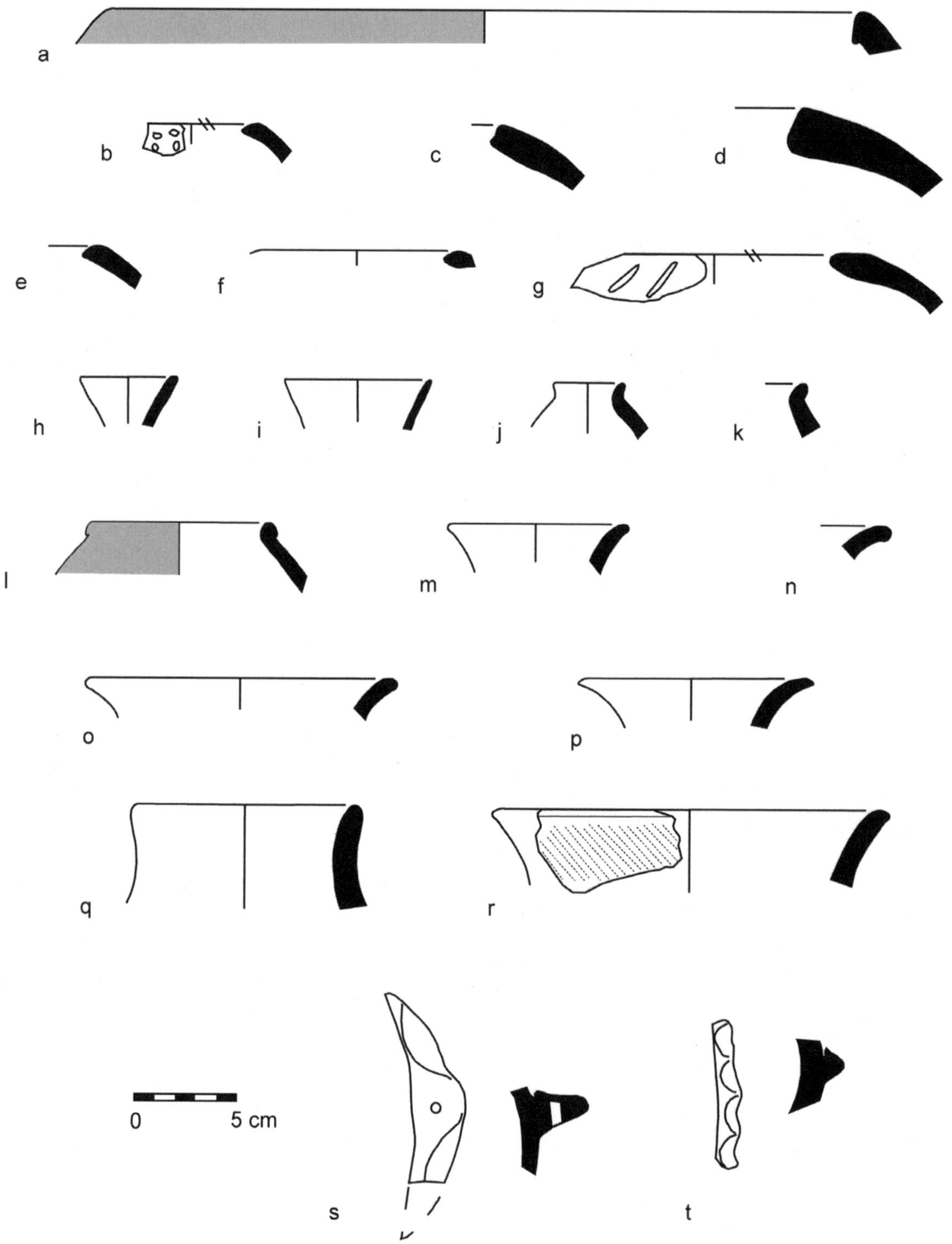

***Fig. 25.** Early Bronze Age pottery excavated at Khirbet el-Minsahlat.*

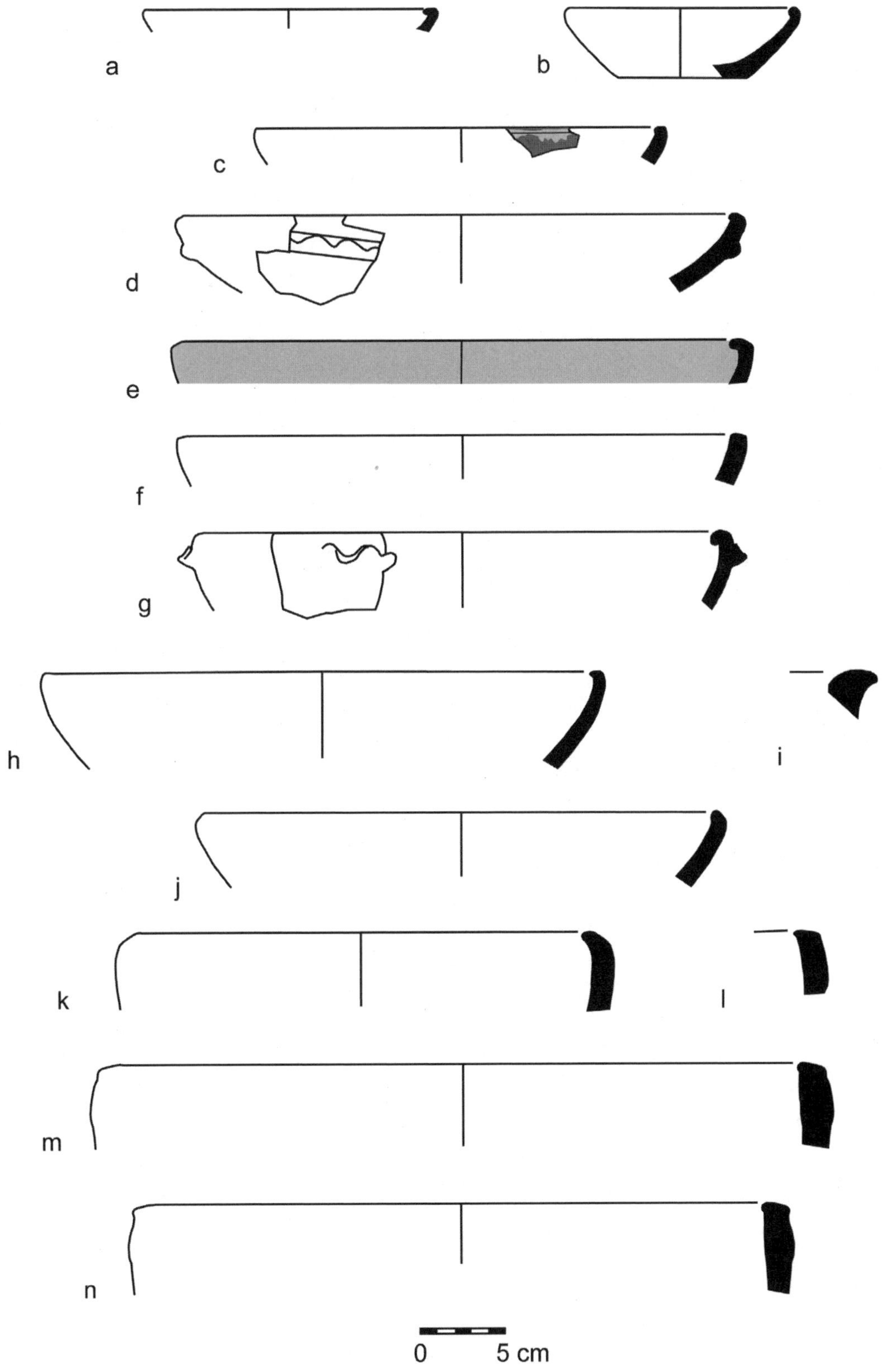

Fig. 26. *Early Bronze Age pottery excavated at Khirbet el-Minsahlat.*

Table 2. Plant species collected in excavations at Lejjun and Khirbet el-Minsahlat (Bending 2002).

Excavation Unit	Species present
Lejjun Unit 1 (inside structure)	Grass pea, common pea, large legume (indet.), olive, grape
Lejjun Unit 2 (inside and outside of structure)	Barley wheat (indet.), einkorn grain, emmer grain, olive
Minsahlat Unit 1 (inside structure)	Chick pea, lentil, grass pea, barley grain (indet.), hulled barley grain, emmer grain, olive
Minsahlat Unit 2 (ash dump)	Chick pea, lentil. grass pea, hulled barley grain, barley grain (indet.), emmer grain, einkorn grain, glume what (indet.), olive, grape

conflation of data from different levels (Horwitz and Tchernov 1989), recent zooarchaeological analyses focusing on these periods are grounded in more rigorous excavation techniques, with attention paid to fine-screen sediment sifting, careful contextual control and reporting of faunal material beyond broad stratigraphic level.

All sediments at Minsahlat and Lejjun were sieved using a 3-mm mesh screen, since small screen size greatly increases the quality of bone recovery and subsequent faunal analyses (Payne 1972). While small-screen sifting potentially reduces excavator-induced bias, various taphonomic processes may impact the character of a faunal assemblage, especially in terms of skeletal element and demographic representation and potentially biasing conclusions regarding human use of animals (Bar-Oz and Dayan 2002, 2003; Lyman 1994). The extent to which taphonomic processes impacted the Minsahlat and Lejjun faunal assemblages has not yet been assessed in this preliminary report.

Faunal assemblages from Southern Levantine Early Bronze Age occupations are dominated by domestic sheep and goat, with cattle third in relative importance. Pigs and equids are also found, as are wild species including roe deer (*Capreolus capreolus*), fallow deer (*Dama dama*), red deer (*Cervus elaphus*) and gazelle (*Gazella gazella*), although these wild taxa are minor contributors to overall subsistence. The distribution of taxa from both Lejjun and Minsahlat similarly follows this general pattern of Early Bronze Age faunal subsistence. Relative abundance of taxa was calculated

Table 3. NISP of Lejjun and Khirbet el-Minsahlat fauna, 2001 season.

Taxon	Lejjun	Minsahlat
Mammal	75	140
Medium mammal	103	94
Small mammal	4	3
Medium artiodactyl	231	569
Small bovid	5	17
Ovis/Capra	62	150
Ovis/Capra/Gazella	4	5
Capra sp.	17	45
Ovis sp.	8	18
Gazella sp.	3	3
Large mammal	13	8
Large artiodactyl	7	7
Large bovid	4	3
Bos/Equus	1	2
Bos sp.	11	7
Equus sp.	2	6
Canis sp.	1	–
Aves	2	–
Crustacean	–	1
Total NISP	553	1078

as an adjusted percentage, where skeletal elements assigned to broad categories such as medium artiodactyls and medium mammal were proportionally allocated to taxon (Table 3). It is likely that the unidentified portions of each assemblage will most likely reflect the proportions of identified taxa. Therefore, most of the shaft fragments, ribs, and skull fragments that are classified as medium mammal or medium artiodactyls are likely to have come from sheep or goat.

Goats were the most commonly identified taxon at both Minsahlat and Lejjun, comprising over fifty percent of proportionally allocated taxa in each assemblage. Sheep were the second most abundant taxa, followed by cattle. Equids and gazelle were also recovered from both sites. The presence of gazelle may indicate that an open parkland environment was in close proximity to Lejjun and Minsahlat. However, it is also possible that gazelles were traded in from a different environmental zone, or that site occupants were moving into different zones to catch their prey (Horwitz and Tchernov 1989: 289). Two bird shaft fragments and a single canid metapodial were recovered from Lejjun. Bird bone fragments have been recovered from Yarmouth, Tel Dalit, and Tel Aphek (Davis 1976, 1988; Hellwing and Gophna 1984; Lernau 1978). A single crustacean claw was found at Minsahlat; freshwater aquatic crabs inhabit running water in the Southern Levant and have been reported from Early Bronze Age Numeira (Finnegan 1984). However, it is unclear if crabs were a human food source or not. Pigs are absent from both Minsahlat and Lejjun. This is probably due to small assemblage size, although it is possible that the Kerak Plateau was too arid during the EBA to support habitats appropriate for pig populations. In the Southern Levant, faunal assemblages contain proportionally few pig remains in arid areas compared to wetter ones (Grigson 1987).

Capra sp. *and Ovis* sp.

At both Lejjun and Minsahlat, goats were relatively more abundant than sheep. The Lejjun assemblage contained ca. 51 % goats and ca. 38 % sheep, while the Minsahlat assemblage contained ca. 63 % goats and ca. 29 % sheep. As a point of comparison, EB III Khirbet ez-Zeraqon, also located in a steppic zone, has a similar goat:sheep ratio as Minsahlat and Lejjun at 55 goats:45 sheep (Dechert 1995). Early Bronze Age Jericho is also dominated by goats, which comprise 64 % of the total assemblage (Clutton-Brock 1979). At Tel Erani and Tel Yarmouth, however, there is a significantly higher relative frequency of sheep over goat with 80 sheep:20 goats at Tel Erani and 75 sheep:25 goats at Tel Yarmouth (Ducos 1968; Davis 1988). The decision to herd goats over sheep at Lejjun and Minsahlat may be an environmentally based one; goats are better adapted to drier environments and more marginal food sources. Unlike Tel Erani and Tel Yarmouth, which are located in the Mediterranean ecotone, Minsahlat and Lejjun are situated on the edge of a steppic region. Alternatively, the relatively large abundance of goats at Minsahlat and Lejjun may be due to economic factors; goats generally produce significantly larger quantities of milk than sheep (Palmer 2002).

Goat skeletal elements recovered from Minsahlat include an unfused distal femur, an unfused distal humerus, three fused and three unfused first phalanges, two fused and two unfused second phalanges, one fused distal radius, one fused distal tibia and three fused distal metacarpals. Sheep remains from Minsahlat include a fused distal humerus, a fused and an unfused first phalanx, two fused second phalanges and one unfused second phalanx. Both a left and right mandible from a juvenile sheep were also recovered. Each mandible displays a dp2 and dp3 in moderate wear, the left mandible a dp4 at wear stage 9 according to criteria established by Payne (1973), and the broken dp4 from the right mandible is exhibiting heavy wear. Although an attempt to refit right and left mandibles proved to be unsuccessful, the similar wear stages suggest that both mandibles may have originated from the same individual. It is most likely that extremely young caprines are underrepresented in the Minsahlat assemblage. Sixteen percent of specimens categorized as medium artiodactyl have been characterized as 'juvenile,' defined as bone fragments displaying either an unfused epiphysis or under-developed cortical bone.

Goat skeletal elements recovered from Lejjun include three fused first phalanges, two fused second phalanges, one fused scapula, a fused pelvis, and one fused and two unfused distal metacarpals. Wear stages of a goat P/4 and a M/3 were categorized at I and H, respectively. The fusion and tooth wear data indicate a predominance of older goat individuals over extremely young ones. Sheep skeletal elements from Lejjun include a fused proximal femur, a pelvis fused at the acetabulum, and an unfused second phalanx. One right sheep mandible displays a moderately worn dp2, dp3, and dp4 at wear stage F. While fusion and tooth wear sample sizes from both Lejjun and Minsahlat are too small to construct age-curves and make any firm statements on goat herding strategies and product exploitation by the inhabitants of either site, the 2001 Minsahlat goat fusion data indicates a predominance of older individuals, but there is likely a much greater presence of younger animals if juvenile specimens from the medium artiodactyl category are considered. The Minsahlat goats potentially cover the entire age spectrum from very young to very old individuals and may indicate a complex exploitation strategy that includes secondary products. Interestingly, a different trend may be emerging at Lejjun, where most caprine skeletal elements are fused and tooth wear patterns indicate the presence of older animals.

Bos sp. *and Equus* sp.

Cattle are relatively well represented at Lejjun, comprising ca. six percent of the total faunal assemblage. Skeletal element fusion data indicate the presence of older animals. Recovered cattle skeletal elements are primarily from older individuals and include a fused second phalanx, a fused distal metapodial, a P/4 worn to stage J (Grant 1982), an upper M1 and M2 displaying moderate wear, and an unfused distal metatarsal. The presence of adult cattle at Early Bronze Age sites is generally interpreted to indicate the use of the animals for traction, although this issue remains to be systematically investigated. Cattle remains at Minsahlat include an upper third molar and a distal metapodial. The molar exhibits no wear and an undeveloped root system, indicating that it came from a juvenile animal. The distal metapodial was heavily fragmented, making it impossible to determine whether fusion had occurred or not.

Some equid elements were recovered from both Lejjun and Minsahlat. Lejjun equid elements include a second phalanx from Unit 3 (Bp = 40.0, GL = 34.0, Bfp = 36.0, Dp = 25.0 and Bp = 34.0; measurements according to von den Driesch 1978) and a lower first incisor from Unit 2 at wear stage E (Silver 1969). Equid remains from Minsahlat include a proximal left third metatarsal (Bp = 41.0), a fused distal tibia, two fibulae and an unfused lumbar vertebrae. These skeletal elements are relatively small and are probably from donkeys. The remains were removed from a discrete grouping of small stones containing ashy sediments and a high density of animal bone in the Unit 1 structure. While none of the equid skeletal elements display cut marks or burning, the presence of equid bone in these loci may suggest processing of some sort. Boiling, for example, is a method of cooking meat or extracting grease from bone and leaves skeletal remains unaltered macroscopically, although the integrity of internal bone structure may decrease.

Conclusions

Analyses of faunal assemblages such as those from Lejjun and Minsahlat contribute much needed information on general subsistence economies, but also provide an opportunity to carefully reconsider the overall role and importance of pastoralism within Early Bronze Age economies. While new models of Transjordanian EBA political, social, and economic structures and transactions have recently emerged (Chesson and Phillip 2003; Greenberg 2003; Harrison and Savage 2003; Philip 2003), conceptions of how agricultural and pastoral activities contributed to EBA economies have generally remained the same. There is an implicit assumption that economies relying heavily on pastoral products such as milk and wool are strictly a small village, homestead, or nomadic lifestyle phenomenon and that a pastoralist element can make only marginal economic contributions to larger, more urban communities. Discarding this perspective in favor of a different view that considers the possibility that pastoralism is an integrated element of the EBA large-scale economy in both the subsistence and subsistence-plus economic arenas may be appropriate for evaluating EBA communities on the Kerak Plateau as dynamic corporate structures and investigating risk-reduction strategies utilized by these communities.

While the arid Kerak Plateau may have not been well suited for intensive agriculture (Palumbo 2001: 293; Phillip 2001: 193–94), its location on the border of the dry-farming ecological zone was likely appropriate for intensive subsistence and subsistence plus animal husbandry. By maintaining a large, diverse livestock herd of sheep, goats and cattle, EBA communities on the Kerak Plateau could have created an extremely pliable economic structure that was much more flexible than one based on grain agriculture. Unlike those who rely on agricultural produce, individuals and communities with mixed herds can rapidly respond to environmental and economic dynamics by manipulating herd demography to focus on one type of animal over another, which subsequently alters the volume and type of animal product produced.

Once assemblage size is increased, faunal analyses from Minsahlat and Lejjun will add much need information on EBA subsistence economies on the Kerak Plateau, including (1) animal taxa chosen for exploitation, (2) use of secondary products and intensity of product production, and (3) the role of these products as part of a diversified economic strategy in an arid ecological zone. Through analysis of faunal remains, it may be possible to identify if the inhabitants of the Kerak Plateau utilized comparatively flexible resource exploitation systems in response to constraints imposed by local dry-farming and steppic ecological zones (Palumbo 2001; Phillip 2001) and to determine if this kind of environmental stress may have motivated individuals and groups to engage in highly regular reciprocation activities as a risk-reduction strategy that potentially result in archaeologically visible interactions between community institutions (Chesson 2003). It is possible that one way of identifying these social and economic relationships is through analysis and comparison of faunal remains derived from domestic and non-domestic contexts. With additional excavation at both Lejjun and Minsahlat, these concepts can be further developed.

Early Bronze Age Lithics from Minsahlat and Lejjun (Table 4; fig. 27)

Excavations at Minsahlat and Lejjun led to the recovery of a limited number of chipped stone tools representative of the Early Bronze Age occupations of these settlements. In contrast to the excavation of Early Bronze Age settlements located in more northern areas of Jordan, it appears that the occupants of Minsahlat and Lejjun used and produced only a limited number of chipped or ground stone tools (see Rosen 1997 and Philip 2001 for more detailed discussion of Early Bronze Age tool use). Despite the excavation of considerable cultural sediments and the employment of screening, remarkably few chipped stone debitage and tools were found during excavation, with a total of only twenty-two tools recovered (Table 4). In light of the limited sampling in each of these contemporary settlements, as well as the small sample size, the description and analysis of the tools from these sites will be combined.

Typology and Technology

Of the twenty-two tools that were recovered in excavation, five were tabular scrapers. Tabular scrapers are large retouched flakes characterized by intact cortex on the dorsal surface and abrupt retouch along the edges (see Rosen 1997: 71–80 for description and discussion). Tabular scrapers were recovered at both Minsahlat and Lejjun, and all of them appear to have been extensively used and retouched along the margins (fig. 27:b–d). According to Rosen (1997: 75) these tools were common in the Chalcolithic and Early Bronze Ages and disappeared with the end of the Early Bronze Age III. The use of these tools remains unresolved. Microwear analysis conducted by McConaughy (1979: 304) indicates that these tools may have been used as butchering knives. Alternatively, Henry (1995) suggests that they may have been used as wool shears. It has also been noted that tabular scrapers may have served a ritual function in Early

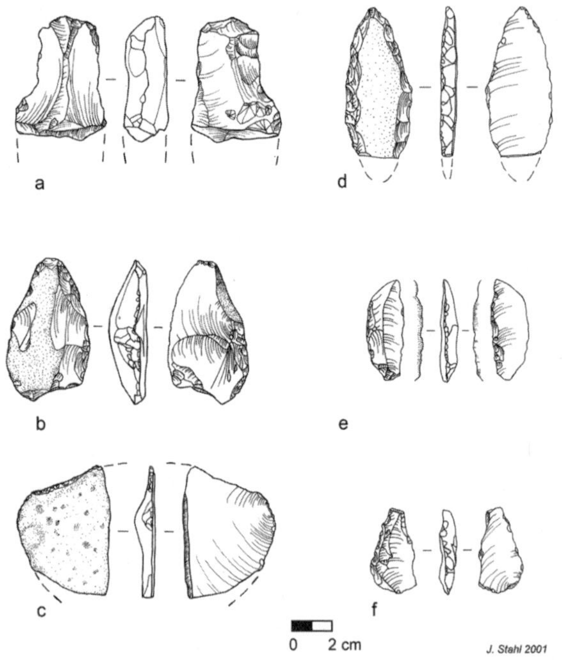

Fig. 27. *Chipped stone artifacts excavated at Lejjun and Khirbet el-Minsahlat.*

Table 4. Chipped stone tools from excavations at Lejjun and Khirbet el-Minsahlat.

Typology	Minsahlat Number	Minsahlat %	Lejjun No.	Lejjun %
Blade	–	–	2	25
Retouched blade	2	14.3	1	12.5
Retouched flake	3	21.4	2	25
Sickle Blade	1	7.1	–	–
Tabular Scraper	3	21.4	2	25
Bifacial Chisel	–	–	1	12.5
Bifacial Fragment	1	7.1	–	–
Borer/awl	1	7.1	–	–
End Scraper	1	7.1	–	–
Flake Core	2	14.3	–	–
Totals	14	100	8	100

Bronze Age communities (McConaughy 1979), although this remains to be demonstrated.

Interestingly, remarkably little evidence was found for the production or widespread use of Canaanean blade cores and sickle blades, a tool/technology that is widely held to be temporally and culturally diagnostic of the Early Bronze Age in select areas of the Near East. As outlined by Rosen (1997: 44), four basic technologies were employed for the manufacture of sickles; this includes Canaanean production of specialized prismatic blade technology, non-Canaanean prismatic blade production, simple blade production, and flake/blade production. Rosen (1997: 59) notes that the spatial distribution of Canaanean sickles is limited to more northern areas of the southern Levant, while areas south of Wadi Mujib in Jordan are more likely to be associated with simple and unbacked sickles, if they are present at all. A single, simple sickle blade with sickle sheen on two sides was recovered from the excavations at Minsahlat (fig. 27:e). This sickle blade was based on a relatively small blade that was retouched on one side. No prismatic cores or blades were recovered in excavation at either Minsahlat or Lejjun, a pattern that fits with our current understanding of the spatial distribution of different lithic technologies.

Other recovered tools include retouched flakes/blades (fig. 27:a). These are simple tools, apparently constructed by selecting a blade or flake with limited concern for shape or size. The function of these tools remains unclear. Perhaps they were used for ad-hoc tasks, possibly including scraping of wood or for modifying tools on a situational basis. Other tools include several fragments of bifacial tools. These include a borer/awl, a bifacial fragment, and part of what is probably a bifacial chisel tool. Finally, two unmodified blades were also recovered in excavations. All of these tools reflect a relatively simple technology that appears to be focused on a limited number of tasks requiring chipped stone tools.

Typical of the stone tool technology of the Early Bronze Age, the recovered tools were produced by hard-hammer core reduction of cores for flakes. In general, this appears to have been accomplished by the use of locally available raw materials. Most of the tools are manufactured on poor to medium quality flint materials, many of which were probably flintknapped in local areas.

The single clear exception to this pattern is that seen in the tabular fan scrapers. These appear to have been produced in areas south and east of Azraq (Rosen 1983; Rollefson, personal communication). While the specific source remains unknown, it is clear that they were manufactured elsewhere and traded in for local use. Collectively, the chipped stone tools recovered in the excavations of Minsahlat and Lejjun reflect a pattern that is typical of the Early Bronze Age—the situational use of local lithic raw materials for the manufacture of general tools coupled with the importation of select preformed tools, such as tabular scrapers, from distant areas.

DISCUSSION AND CONCLUSIONS

The most striking result of this research project was the immense negative impact economic development has had on the continued preservation of sites on the Kerak Plateau. Of the eight Early Bronze Age sites, only two showed minor signs of human impact, four showed significant signs of destruction, and at two sites we could no longer identify any Early Bronze Age remains due to building and field clearing. The rate of destruction of archaeological sites since the late 1970s, when Miller conducted the survey of the Plateau, is dismaying.

Aside from issues of preservation and heritage management, the analyses of ceramic, faunal, architectural and chipped stone remains provide preliminary insights into the material culture and architectural practices of these Early Bronze Age communities, particularly at Lejjun and Minsahlat, where test excavations were conducted. Architectural remains of large fortification systems typical of the Early Bronze Age were noted at several of the sites, as well as the use of rock-cut cisterns and menhirs. The analysis of ceramic forms from surface collections and test excavations demonstrates a significant degree of regionalism in terms of form and decoration, which has been previously been discussed in length by many scholars (see Palumbo 2001 and Philip and Baird 2000 for reviews of ceramic chronology and typology of the Early Bronze Age; compare Brown 1991 for discussion of the Kerak Plateau specifically).

Drawing on survey data, Philip (2001: 193–94) and Palumbo (2001: 243) point to the Central Jordanian Plateau, including the Kerak Plateau on which Minsahlat and Lejjun are situated, as a primary example of a loosely integrated network of EB II–III and IV settlements that demonstrates remarkable continuity in settlement patterns from the EB III to EB IV. Both Palumbo (2001: 243) and Philip (2001: 193–94) postulate that the location of the Kerak Plateau on the border of the dry-farming ecological zone and the steppe prevented the development of the highly intensive agricultural strategies found in large EB II–III walled communities in other areas. Life on the Kerak Plateau, especially in a community of 4–5 ha or more, required both the EB II–III and EB IV inhabitants to pursue a combination of subsistence practices, drawing on multiple sets of resources. Philip argues that this flexibility of economic practices would have granted greater resilience to the economic institutions of these settlements during stressful periods, particularly in the face of climatic, political and economic changes at the end of the EB III. Drawing on data from Miller (1991), Mattingly (1983, 1984) and Steele (1990), Philip and Palumbo suggest that the survey data from the Kerak Plateau shows greater levels of continuity in settlement from the EB III to EB IV because these Early Bronze Age communities pursued diversified economic strategies in a dry-farming environment.

Survey data from the Kerak Plateau, in comparison to several other areas, does demonstrate a remarkable continuity in settlement occupation from the EB II to the EB IV. Generally throughout the Southern Levant, the number of sites drops from the EB II–III to EB IV, and the numbers of EB II–III sites reoccupied in the EB IV vary greatly. Importantly, sixty percent of EB II–III sites on the Kerak Plateau are reoccupied in the EB IV, the highest percentage of reoccupation for any area in the region (Table 5). As Philip (2001) and Palumbo (2001) have noted, the Kerak Plateau involved a very high rate of reoccupation, and they suggest that we might expect some elements of continuity in economic, political, and social structures through the EB II–III and IV, despite clear shifts in settlement patterns elsewhere within the region. Palumbo (2001: 240–43) has also noted

Table 5. Number of EB II–III sites reoccupied in EB IV or EB IV/MB IIA periods.

Area	Source	Number of EB II–IV Sites	Number of reooccupied sites in EB IV	Percentage of reoccupied sites
Upper & Lower Galilee	Palumbo 1991: figs. 7–9	51	15	29.41%
Northern Coastal Plain & Coastal Plain	Palumbo 1991: figs. 7–9	54	8	14.81%
Huleh Valley	Palumbo 1991: figs. 7–9	16	5	31.25%
Jezreel Valley	Palumbo 1991: figs. 7–9	28	13	46.43%
Jordan Valley	Palumbo 1991: figs. 7–9	59	27	45.76%
North & South Central Hills	Palumbo 1991: figs. 7–9	124	15	12.10%
Golan	Palumbo 1991: figs. 7–9	8	2	25.00%
Northern & North Central Transjordan	Palumbo 1991: figs. 7–9	101	40	39.60%
Kerak Plateau	Miller 1991: 307–8	20	12	60.00%
Totals		461	137	29.72%

Table 6. Size of Early Bronze Age settlements in selected regions.

Sites	Period of occupation	Site size	Median site size	Mean site size	Published Sources
Rujm Birjis	EB I–IV	ca. 4 ha	n/a	n/a	Miller 1991
Kh. Muddawarah, Kerak Plateau	EB II–III (IV?)	ca. 5.5 ha	n/a	n/a	Miller 1991
Lejjun, Kerak Plateau	EB II–IV	ca.11 ha	n/a	n/a	Miller 1991
Jericho	EB II–III	ca. 4 ha	n/a	n/a	Amiran and Gophna 1989: figs. 1–2
Bab edh-Dhra'	EB II–IV	ca. 4 ha	n/a	n/a	Schaub and Rast 1989: fig. 2
Tell el-Far'ah (N)	EB II	ca. 5 ha	n/a	n/a	Amiran and Gophna 1989: figs. 1–2
Megiddo	EB II–III	ca. 6 ha	n/a	n/a	Amiran and Gophna 1989: figs. 1–2
Madaba Plains sites	EB II–III	n/a	4.4 ha	5.3 ha	Harrison 1997: 17
Northern Palestine	EB II–III	n/a	3.2 ha	4.84 ha	Esse 1991: 151, table 6
Madaba Plains sites	EB IV	n/a	2.3 ha	2.7 ha	Harrison 1997: 17
Northern Palestine	EB IV	n/a	0.84 ha	3.54 ha	Esse 1991: 151, table 6
Kh. Minsahlat, KP	EB IV	ca. 5.5 ha	n/a	n/a	Miller 1991

that the size of sites drops significantly in those cases where survey data has provided reliable size estimates for Early Bronze Age sites. For instance, Harrison (1997: 17) has documented that EB III site size on the Madaba Plains averages 5.3 ha, while in the EB IV sites drop to an average of 2.7 ha (Table 6). A similar reduction in size is reported by Esse (1991: tbl. 6) for northern Palestine sites, where the difference in size is even greater.

Interestingly, when comparing the drop in site size of Kerak Plateau sites, where reliable size and chronological estimates are available, EB IV sites are still quite large in relative terms. In 2001, the Kerak Plateau Survey team investigated the eight Early Bronze Age sites for which Miller's descriptions suggested the presence of a large Early Bronze Age settlement. Many of these sites had been drastically impacted by ancient and modern subsequent occupations; however, size data was available for several sites. Lejjun was the largest EB II–III walled community on the Kerak Plateau at 11 ha, while EB I–IV Rujm Birjis, EB II–III Mudawwarah, and EB IV Minsahlat are 4, 5.5, and 5.5 ha in size, respectively. While the size of settlements on the Kerak Plateau may drop by at least fifty percent from the EB II–III to EB IV, 5.5 ha Minsahlat is still larger than many EB III walled sites, including Bab edh-Dhra' and Numeira on the neighboring southeast Dead Sea plain (Table 6). In test excavations at Lejjun and Minsahlat, radiocarbon samples were collected and analyzed to link ceramic typology to an absolute chronological scale. Two samples from Lejjun have been analyzed and date Lejjun to the EB II. Three radiocarbon dates from Minsahlat date the site to the transitional late EB III/early EB IV, confirming the results from ceramic typological analysis.

The combined data from survey, test excavations and radiocarbon analysis of samples from Lejjun and Minsahlat strongly support the idea of continuity on the Kerak Plateau through the EB II to EB IV. We argue that with the scale of EB III– IV settlements on the Kerak Plateau, particularly at Minsahlat, in future research we might expect to find similar economic, political, and social structures as we have seen in similarly-sized EB II–III, dynamic corporate villages throughout the region.

APPENDIX A: SUMMARY OF DESCRIPTIONS OF SITES SURVEYED IN 2001

Name	Miller 1991 Site #	Description of Site	Material Culture observed	Major period(s) of occupation	EBA Material Culture observed
Mis'ar	25	Settlement site occupying the northern hill rising from a wadi tributary; modern town of Mis'ar now occupies the site; terrace walls on the southern slope of the site may be remains of EB fortification wall, but very difficult to say with any certainty; boundaries of site in all directions impossible to discern.	Pottery, groundstone fragments of grinding stones, walls from stone structures, cisterns and terrace walls.	Multiple periods (EB to modern), pottery collection very poor with Iron Age II dominating.	• small collection of not overly diagnostic pottery: EBII–III pottery with red-slip and burnishing; undecorated holemouth jars with EB fabric • groundstone fragments of grinding stones noted on site (could be any period) • cisterns (reused later?)
Site 40	40	Small settlement site located in the gently rolling hills around Balua; terrace walls and pottery scatters are the only remains observed and the extent of the site on any side was not discernible.	Pottery and terrace walls.	EBA (pottery)	• very little pottery: EBA pottery with red-slip and burnishing; undecorated holemouth jars with EB fabric
Rujm Birjis	73	Settlement site (approx. 4 ha) with traces of fortification walls, three cisterns, and multiple wall lines traceable on surface (beyond the terrace walls across the site); in main part of site up to 2 m of deposits present (seen in the bulldozer cut); a fallen menhir, surrounded by a heap of stones (with the original socket?), lies in a wheat field in the southeast portion of the site.	Pottery, chipped stone, stone walls, cisterns, cupmarks in exposed bedrock, terrace walls, fallen menhir and socket.	EB I, EB IV (pottery)	• pottery: EB I (spout, basin rims, fabric) and EB IV pottery • stone walls • cisterns (reused later?) • cupmarks in exposed bedrock (any period) • terrace walls (some may be constructed over old, large walls—EB?) • fallen menhir and socket
Umm el-Habaj	88	Settlement site with multiple periods of occupation on a low hill surrounded by wheat fields; architecture (multiple wall lines) and pottery from several periods observed, including a Roman track on the east side of the site and cisterns.	Pottery, stone walls, cisterns, structure walls	EB II–III, Classical Periods (Roman, Nabataean, Byzantine), Islamic (Mamluk especially).	• pottery: EB II–III pottery: white-on-red ware sherd, red-slipped and burnished bowls • cisterns (reused in later periods?) • terrace walls which may overlay EB fortification walls—this is a very tentative possibility
Khirbet El-Minsahlat*	101	Settlement site (approx. 5.5 ha) with traces of fortifications walls, one cistern, three menhirs, and multiple lines traceable on surface (beyond the terrace walls on site); in main portion of the tell there is a bulldozer cut from the construction of the orchard—this cut sections the main fortification wall, and exposed a cistern (EB).	Pottery, chipped stone, stone walls (some from very large structures), cupmarks in exposed bedrock, terrace walls, two fallen and one standing (but broken) menhir and sockets, fragments of groundstone grinding stones.	EB III–IV	• pottery • fan scrapers and sickle blade • stone walls (some from very large structures) • terrace walls • two fallen and one standing (but broken) menhir and sockets • fragments of groundstone grinding stones

Name	Miller 1991 Site #	Description of Site	Material Culture observed	Major period(s) of occupation	EBA Material Culture observed
Adir	227	Settlement site occupied by the modern town of Adir with no traces of EB fortification walls; two menhirs were found in the northern portion of the site/town.	Pottery, walls from stone structures, cisterns and terrace walls, caves, one fallen and one standing menhir.	EB IV, but traces of later periods in pottery.	• EB IV pottery from the long road cut in town (red-slipped, burnished bowls with grooves, storage jar rims) • walls from stone structures in road cut (period unsure) • cisterns and catchment walls associated with EB (and later) pottery on surface • and terrace walls, one fallen and one standing menhir
Lejjun*	239	Large (ca. 8–9 ha) settlement site with extensive remains of fortification walls, potential towers and structural remains within the settlement; a line of 16 menhirs (11 still in situ) lies to the northwest on the slope down to the wadi (outside the main settlement walls); there are a few more recent structures on the site, where people have reused some structures (potential burial site within remains of a tower on the southwest tip of the site, for instance, and a modern blind for hunting [?] on the northern section of the main walls).	Pottery, walls from stone structures, fortification walls and towers, menhirs.	EBA (EB II–IV)	• pottery • extensive walls from stone structures • fortification walls and towers • line of 16 menhirs (11 still standing)
Khirbet El-Mudawwarah	390	Large settlement site (5.5 ha) with extensive remains of fortification walls (now used as terrace walls), which follow the shape of the hill; little architecture beyond the fortification walls is discernible.	Pottery, fortification walls, cistern (one cleaned out with high quantity of EB pottery in spoil heap).	EBA (EB II–IV primarily)	• pottery: envelope and wavy ledge handles; red-slipped and burnished open and closed vessels • fortification walls now acting as terrace walls on hill • cistern (one cleaned out with high quantity of EB II–III pottery in spoil heap)

* Test excavations carried out at these sites.

APPENDIX B: SUMMARY OF IMPACT ASSESSMENTS ON SURVEYED EARLY BRONZE AGE SITES ON THE KERAK PLATEAU

Name	Map Reference	Miller 1991 Site #	State of Preservation 2001	Impact Assessment
Mis'ar	PG: 2105/90.0 UTMG: 61.8/77.5	25	Site occupied by modern settlement and heavily disturbed by construction, terracing and plowing.	Heavily impacted today; site in poor condition due to plowing, construction, and erosion.
Site 40	PG: 25.7/84.3 UTMG:65.9/71.4	40	Site occupied by modern building, Bedouin tents and terraced fields.	Heavily impacted today; site in poor condition due to plowing, erosion and building.
Rujm Birjis	PG: 17.2/73.9 UTMG: 57.7/61.2	73	80% of site plowed or occupied by orchards; three houses have been constructed on site and a bulldozer was used to remove large sections of fortification walls and deposits.	Heavily impacted today; currently under severe risk from bulldozing, construction and plowing.
Umm el-Habaj	PG: 23.0/81.0 UTMG: 63.4/68.4	88	Fields around the site are plowed, but there is too much stone on site to be plowed; Bronze Age occupation has been heavily impacted by later periods (especially Mamluk).	Overall state of preservation is good for more recent periods (Mamluk especially); very poor preservation for EB periods.
Khirbet El-Minsahlat	PG: 25.8/77.3 UTMG: 66.0/64.6	101	Orchard and house constructed through middle of main portion of site; majority of remaining portion of site terraced and plowed heavily.	Heavily impacted today; site in poor condition due to construction of orchard through the main portion of site.
Adir	PG: 22.5/68.5 UTMG: 63.1/55.7	227	90% of site covered by modern settlements and virtually all open space has been plowed; cisterns and foundation walls (for catchment systems?) still visible in an unoccupied area of town.	Heavily impacted today; site in poor condition due to construction, plowing and erosion.
Lejjun	PG: 31.7/71.9 UTMG: 72.3/59.6	239	Bedouin family lives on neighboring ridge and site is used for grazing; site has very little material culture on surface, in part this may be due to collecting by Parker and Miller in previous surveys; an additional menhir has fallen since Miller surveyed the site and there is evidence of people using the area of the menhirs for picnics/barbequeing.	Impact today moderate over most of site; menhirs see heaviest human impact.
Khirbet El-Mudawwarah	PG: 12.7/50.2 UTMG: 53.6/37.4	390	95% of site under cultivation; most of the main fortification walls still visible (used as terrace walls today); many terrace walls constructed across the site (likely built with stone robbed from EBA architecture) and several heaps of stone are present across the site from field clearing.	Heavily impacted today; site in poor condition due to terracing, field clearing and plowing.

APPENDIX C: DESCRIPTION OF ILLUSTRATED EARLY BRONZE AGE CERAMICS COLLECTED IN SURFACE SURVEYS

Fig.	No.	Site	Form	Diam. (cm)	Interior Surface	Exterior Surface	Fabric (Munsell)
4	a	Rujm Birjis	Jar shoulder	–	Smoothed 10R5/8	Red slipped and burnished 2.5YR5/8; appliqué knob	10YR7/4
	b		Basin rim	42	Smoothed 7.5YR6/3	Smoothed 7.5YR8/3; appliqué band below rim; top of rim has irregular incised scoring on it	5YR5/1
	c		Basin rim	42	Smoothed 2.5YR6/6	Smoothed 2.5YR6/6; impressed decoration at rim (decoration resembles appliqué, but no appliqué band applied)	7.5YR4/1
	d		Basin rim	36	Smoothed 10R6/8	Smoothed and combed 10R6/8–10R5/8	5YR7/4
	e		Vat rim	36	Smoothed 2.5YR6/6	Smoothed 2.5YR6/6 with ledge handle scar	2.5YR6/6
	f		Spout	–	Smoothed 7.5YR8/2, 2.5YR7/2	Smoothed 7.5YR8/2, 2.5YR7/2	2.5YR7/3
	g		Ledge handle	–	–	Smoothed 10YR7/3	10YR6/3
5	a	Rujm Birjis	Holemouth jar rim	10	Smoothed 5YR7/6	Burnished 5YR5/6	5YR7/4
	b		Small bowl rim	6	Smoothed 5YR7/6–5YR6/6	Smoothed 5YR7/6–5YR6/6	10R6/8
	c		Jar rim	8	Smoothed 10R5/6	White slip 10YR8/4	10R6/6
	d		Jar rim	14	Red slipped and burnished below rim, smoothed 2.5YR5/8	Red slip and burnished with impressed appliqué band 2.5YR5/8	2.5YR6/6
	e		Holemouth jar rim	10	Smoothed 5YR7/4	Smoothed with incised circles below rim 5YR5/3	5YR6/4
	f		Bowl rim	16	Traces of red slip 5YR7/6	Red slipped, burnished 10R4/6	2.5YR6/8
	g		Bowl rim	10	Red slipped and burnished 2.5YR6/6	Red slipped and burnished 5YR6/6	5YR7/3
	h		Bowl rim	?	Red slipped and burnished 2.5YR5/6	Red slipped and burnished 2.5YR5/6	7.5YR6/6
	i		Small bowl base (slow-wheel finished)	4	Smoothed 7.5YR7/4	Smoothed 7.5YR7/4	7.5YR7/4
	j		Bowl rim	22	Smoothed 5YR6/6	Smoothed 5YR6/6	2.5YR7/6
	k		Bowl rim	23	Smoothed 5YR7/4	Smoothed 5YR 8/4	5YR7/4
	l		Bowl rim	35	Red slipped and burnished 2.5YR6/6-2.5YR6/8	Smoothed, traces of red slip/burnish 10R5/4	10R5/3
	m		Bowl rim	44+	Smoothed with traces of red slip/burnish 10R3/6	Red slip/burnish 2.5YR6/6	5YR7/4

Fig.	No.	Site	Form	Diam. (cm)	Interior Surface	Exterior Surface	Fabric (Munsell)
7	a	Umm el-Habaj	Body sherd	–	Smoothed	White on Red Ware (red slip: 10R4/6, white paint: 2.5YR7/2)	Not read
	b		Bowl rim	12	Red slipped and pattern burnished 7.5YR7/6	Smoothed with traces of burnish 7.5YR7/6-7.5YR6/6	5YR8/4
	c		Bowl rim	42	Red slipped and burnished 2.5YR6/8	Red slipped and burnished 2.5YR6/8	7.5YR2/4
	d		Bowl rim	36	Smoothed with line of burnish 10R4/6	Smoothed 10R6/8	10R5/8
	e		Holemouth jar rim	22	Smoothed 5YR6/6	Combed 5YR6/6	5YR7/6
	f	Lejjun	Base	40	Smoothed with lime-white covering 7 5YR8/1	Smoothed 2.5YR6/8	5YR6/6
	g	Mudawwarah	Ledge handle	–	–	Smoothed 7.5YR7/2	7.5YR4/1
10	a	Minsahlat	Holemouth jar rim	14	Smoothed 5YR7/4	Smoothed with appliqué knob 7.5YR7/4	5YR7/4
	b		Holemouth jar rim	8	Smoothed 5YR5/1	Smoothed with incised line and circles below rim 7.5YR6/4	5YR4/4
	c		Holemouth jar rim	14	Smoothed 7.5YR6/3	Smoothed 7.5YR7/3	7.5YR7/4
	d		Holemouth jar rim	12	Smoothed 5YR6/4	Smoothed 5YR6/4	5YR6/4
	e		Holemouth jar rim	17	Smoothed 5YR6/4	Smoothed 5YR6/4	10R4/2
	f		Jar rim	8	Smoothed 10YR7/3	White/Cream slip 2.5YR8/2	5YR7/3
	g		Jar rim	–	Smoothed 5YR7/4	Smoothed with "pie crust-like" impressions below rim 5YR8/4	5YR5/6
	h		Jar rim	20	Smoothed 5YR7/6	Smoothed 5YR7/4	5YR6/6
	i		Jar rim	10	Smoothed 7.5R6/1	Smoothed Gley N/6	5YR5/1
	j		Jar rim	9	Smoothed 2.5YR6/6	Smoothed 2.5YR6/6	2.5YR7/8
	k		Base	18	Smoothed 2.5YR7/6	Smoothed 2.5YR7/4	5YR6/3
	l		Body sherd	–	Smoothed 5YR6/6	Combed with potter's mark 7.5YR7/3	7.5YR7/4
11	a	Minsahlat	Platterbowl rim	–	Smoothed 2.5YR5/6	Smoothed 2.5YR4/6	5YR4/2
	b		Bowl rim	8	Red slipped and pattern burnished 2.5YR5/6	Red slipped 2.5YR5/6	5YR7/3
	c		Bowl rim	–	Red slip and (pattern?) burnish 10R4/6	Red slip and (pattern?) burnish 10R4/6	2.5YR6/6
	d		Bowl rim	28	Traces of red slip/burnish 2.5YR5/6	Traces of red slip/burnish 2.5YR5/6; appliqué band with diamond impressed decoration	2.5YR7/6
	e		Bowl rim	32	Red slipped and pattern burnished 10R5/8	Traces of slip/burnish 10R6/8 with ledge handle (closed completely—envelope-like)	5YR7/4
	f		Bowl rim	34	Smoothed 7.5YR7/4	Smoothed 7.5YR7/4	7.5YR7/4
	g		Bowl rim	32	Red slipped and pattern burnished 10R4/6	Smoothed 7.5YR4/4	5YR7/6

Fig.	No.	Site	Form	Diam. (cm)	Interior Surface	Exterior Surface	Fabric (Munsell)
11	h	Minsahlat	Bowl rim	34	Red slipped and pattern burnished 10R4/8, 2.5YR5/6	Smoothed with red slip below rim 10YR7/6	7.5YR7/4
	i		Bowl rim	30	Smoothed 7.5YR6/4	Smoothed 5YR5/6	5YR5/2
	j		Basin rim	26	Smoothed 2.5YR6/4	Smoothed with appliqué band below rim 2.5YR6/4, 5YR5/2	10R6/4
12	a	Adir	Jar rim	10	Smoothed 5YR8/4	Smoothed 5YR7/8	2.5YR7/4
	b		Jar rim	12	Smoothed 2.5YR6/6	Smoothed with deeply incised, narrow gaged combing on neck 2.5YR6/6	5YR6/6
	c		Jar rim	18	Smoothed 2.5YR7/8	Smoothed 5YR7/6	10R6/8
	d		Holemouth jar rim	10	Smoothed 7.5YR7/4	Red slipped and burnished 7.5YR5/8 with incised concentric grooves (rilling)	7.5YR6/4
	e		Bowl rim	16	Smoothed 2.5YR3/1	Smoothed 2.5YR8/1	7.5YR5/3
	f		Bowl rim	13	Smoothed 5YR7/8	Red slipped and burnished 10R5/8	7.5YR7/4
	g		Bowl rim	12	Smoothed with traces of red slip 5YR5/6	Incised concentric grooves with traces of red slip 5YR5/6	5YR5/1
	h		Bowl rim and base	13/12	Smoothed 5YR7/8	Smoothed 7.5YR6/6	7.5YR7/6
	i		Bowl rim	30	Red slipped and pattern burnished 10R4/6	Red slipped 10R4/8	5YR7/6–5YR6/6
	j		Bowl rim	30	Pattern burnished 2.5YR4/8	Pattern burnished 2.5YR4/8	2.5YR6/6
	k		Bowl rim	40	Smoothed 7.5YR7/4	Smoothed 7.5YR4/2	5YR5/6
	l		Base	36	Smoothed7.5YR7/6	Combed and slipped 5YR6/6	7.5YR6/6

APPENDIX D: DESCRIPTION OF ILLUSTRATED HISTORIC PERIOD CERAMICS COLLECTED IN SURFACE SURVEYS

Fig.	No.	Site	Form / Date	Characteristics	Dominant Temper	Color / Decoration	Diam. (cm)
2	a	Adir	Jar rim / Iron Age II	Ext. Feel: harsh Int. Feel: harsh Hardness: hard Texture: irregular	Frequent, poorly sorted, sub-angular shale, 1.0–2.9 mm in size, with frequent, well-sorted, rounded basalt, 0.5 mm in size, and frequent, poorly sorted, sub-angular limestone, 0.4–2.7 mm in size.	Int.: 2.5 YR 6/6 (light red) Ext.: 5 YR 7/4 (pink) Core: 5 YR 7/3 (pink)	26
	b	Rujm Birjis	Bowl rim / Nabataean	Ext. Feel: very smooth Int. Feel: very smooth Hardness: very hard Texture: very fine	No visible inclusions.	Int.: 2.5 YR 6/8 (light red) Ext.: 2.5 YR 6/8 (light red) Core: 2.5 YR N5 (gray)	10
	c	Mis'ar	Jug / Jar rim / Iron Age II	Ext. Feel: rough Int. Feel: rough Hardness: hard Texture: irregular	Abundant, well-sorted, sub-angular quartz, 0.4 mm in size, with abundant, poorly sorted, angular shale, 0.5–2.1 mm in size, and infrequent, poorly sorted, limestone fragments, 1.5–3.3 mm in size.	Int.: 5 YR 7/6 (reddish yellow) Ext.: 5 YR 6/1 (gray) and 5 YR 6/4 (light reddish brown) Core: 2.5 YR N6 (gray)	8
	d		Bowl rim / Iron Age II	Ext. Feel: rough Int. Feel: smooth Hardness: hard Texture: irregular	Frequent, poorly sorted, angular shale, 0.7–3.3 mm in size, with infrequent, poorly sorted, sub-rounded limestone, 0.5-1.4 mm in size.	Int.: 7.5 YR 7/6 (reddish yellow) Ext.: 7.5 YR 8/4 (pink) Core: 7.5 YR N7 (light gray)	18
	e		Jar rim / Iron Age II	Ext. Feel: rough Int. Feel: rough Hardness: hard Texture: irregular	Abundant, poorly sorted, sub-angular shale, 0.5–3.5 mm in size, with infrequent, poorly sorted, sub-rounded limestone, 1.3–1.9 mm in size, and infrequent, poorly sorted, sub-rounded quartz, 0.5–1.1 mm in size.	Int.: 7.5 Y/R 6/4 (light brown) Ext.: 10 YR 8/3 (very pale brown) and 5 YR 7/3 (pink) Core: 10 YR 7/2 (light gray)	20
	f		Jar rim / Iron Age II	Ext. Feel: smooth Int. Feel: smooth Hardness: soft Texture: irregular	Frequent, well-sorted, sub-angular quartz, 0.3–0.4 mm in size, with frequent, poorly sorted, angular shale, 1.1–2.1 mm in size, and infrequent, poorly sorted, sub-angular limestone, 0.4–1.9 mm in size.	Int.: 5 YR 8/4 (pink) Ext.: 5 YR 8/4 (pink) Core: 10 YR 7/2 (light gray)	12
	g		Jar rim / Iron Age II	Ext. Feel: rough Int. Feel: rough Hardness: soft Texture: fine	Abundant, well-sorted, sub-rounded quartz, 0.2–0.3 mm in size, with frequent, medium sorted, sub-rounded shale, 0.3–0.8 mm in size.	Int.: 5 Y 8/3 (pale yellow) Ext.: 5 Y 8/3 (pale yellow) Core: 10 YR 7/2 (light gray) and 5 YR 8/4 (pink)	24

Fig.	No.	Site	Form / Date	Characteristics	Dominant Temper	Color / Decoration	Diam. (cm)
2	h	Mis'ar	Bowl/Jar rim / Iron Age II	Ext. Feel: smooth Int. Feel: rough Hardness: hard Texture: irregular	Abundant, poorly sorted, angular shale, 0.8–1.6 mm in size, with infrequent, poorly sorted, sub-rounded limestone, 0.3–1.8 mm in size, and very infrequent, sub-rounded, burnt out organic inclusions, 1.9–2.1 mm in size.	Int.: 5 YR 8/4 (pink) Ext.: 5 YR 8/3 (pink) Core: 7.5 YR N7 (light gray)	16
	i		Jar rim / Iron Age II	Ext. Feel: harsh Int. Feel: harsh Hardness: hard Texture: irregular	Abundant, poorly sorted, sub-rounded quartz, 0.2–1.1 mm in size, with infrequent, sub-angular shale, 0.9–1.7 mm in size.	Int.: 10 YR 8/3 (very pale brown) Ext.: 7.5 YR 8/4 (pink) Core: 5 YR 7/6 (reddish yellow)	24
	j		Holemouth jar rim / Iron Age II	Ext. Feel: rough Int. Feel: rough Hardness: soft Texture: irregular	Frequent, poorly sorted, angular shale fragments, 0.3–0.9 mm in size.	Int.: 5 YR 8/3 (pink) Ext.: 5 YR 8/4 (pink) Core: 7.5 YR 7/2 (pinkish gray)	36
	k		Bodysherd / Late Byzantine	Ext. Feel: harsh Int. Feel: harsh Hardness: very hard Texture: irregular	Abundant, well-sorted, sub-angular quartz, 0.1–0.3mm in size, with rounded, infrequent, well-sorted limestone, 0.4–0.5mm in size.	Int.: 5 Y 8/3 (pale yellow) Ext.: 5 Y 8/3 (pale yellow) Core: 2.5 YR 5/6 (red) Decoration: two parallel rouletted bands	–
	l		Bodysherd / Late Byzantine	Ext. Feel: harsh Int. Feel: harsh Hardness: very hard Texture: irregular	Abundant, well-sorted, sub-angular quartz, 0.1–0.6mm in size.	Int.: 5 Y 8/3 (pale yellow) Ext.: 5 Y 8/3 (pale yellow) Core: 7.5 YR 6/4 (light brown) and 2.5 YR 6/6 (light red) Decoration: applied 'pie-crust' band	–
8	a	Umm el-Habaj	Bodysherd / 4th–6th Century AD	Ext. Feel: very smooth Int. Feel: very smooth Hardness: very hard Texture: very fine and dense	No visible inclusions.	Int.: 2.5 YR 5/8 (red) Ext.: 2.5 YR 5/8 (red) Core: 2.5 YR 5/8 red Int. Decoration: Stamped design in the center of the bowl.	–
	b		Jar rim / Late Roman	Ext. Feel: smooth Int. Feel: rough Hardness: hard Texture: fine	Abundant, well-sorted, angular shale, 0.4–0.5 mm in size.	Int.: 5 YR 8/4 (pink) Ext.: 10 YR 8/3 (very pale brown) Core: 5 YR 7/6 (reddish yellow) and 10 YR 6/3 (pale brown)	12
	c	Umm el-Habaj	Bodysherd / Early Islamic	Ext. Feel: rough Int. Feel: smooth Hardness: hard Texture: irregular	Frequent, well-sorted, sub-rounded quartz, 0.1 mm in size, with infrequent, poorly sorted, angular and rounded burnt out organic inclusions, 1.1 mm in size.	Int.: 5 YR 7/6 (reddish yellow) Ext. Slip: 10 YR 8/4 (very pale brown) Core: 5 YR 8/4 (pink) Ext. Decoration: Painted bands in reddish brown (2.5 YR 5/4)	–

Fig.	No.	Site	Form / Date	Characteristics	Dominant Temper	Color / Decoration	Diam. (cm)
8	d		Bodysherd / Late Byzantine	Ext. Feel: smooth Int. Feel: harsh Hardness: very hard Texture: very fine	Frequent, well-sorted, angular shale, 0.1 mm in size, with infrequent, poorly sorted, rounded limestone, 0.4–1.5 mm in size.	Int.: 2.5 YR 6/6 (light red) Ext.: 10 YR 6/2 (light brownish gray) Core: 10 YR 6/1 (gray) Ext. Decoration: Painted bands in very dark gray (2.5 Y N4)	–
	e		Bodysherd / Middle Islamic	Ext. Feel: powdery Int. Feel: rough Hardness: soft Texture: irregular	Infrequent, poorly sorted, angular shale, 0.6–0.9 mm in size, with abundant poorly sorted, burnt out chaff temper, 0.7–2.6 mm in size.	Int. Slip: 10 YR 8/3 (very pale brown) Ext. Slip: 7.5 YR 8/4 (pink) Core: 10 YR 7/1 (light gray) Ext. Decoration: Painted geometric designs in very dark gray (10 YR 3/1)	–
	f		Bodysherd / Middle Islamic	Ext. Feel: smooth Int. Feel: rough Hardness: soft Texture: irregular	Infrequent, poorly sorted, angular shale, 0.6–1.3 mm in size, with abundant, poorly sorted chaff temper, 1.1–2.6 mm in size, and frequent, poorly sorted, rounded, white inclusions, 0.3–1.6 mm in size.	Int. Slip: 2.5 YR 8/2 (white) Ext. Slip: 2.5 YR 6/6 (light red) Core: 10 YR 7/1 (light gray) Ext. Decoration: Painted geometric designs in very dark gray (10 YR 3/1)	–
	g		Bodysherd / Middle Islamic	Ext. Feel: very smooth Int. Feel: smooth Hardness: soft Texture: irregular	Frequent, poorly sorted, angular shale, 0.5–0.9 mm in size, with frequent, poorly sorted chaff temper, 0.6–2.3 mm in size, and infrequent, poorly sorted, sub-angular basalt, 0.5–1.6 mm in size, and infrequent limestone, 0.5 mm in size.	Int.: 5 YR 7/4 (pink) Ext.: 5 YR 7/6 (reddish yellow) Core: 7.5 YR 7/2 (pinkish gray) Int. Decoration: Painted bands in weak red (10 R 4/4) Ext. Decoration: Painted bands in red (10 R 4/6) and dark reddish gray (10 R 4/1)	–
	h		Bodysherd / Late Byzantine	Ext. Feel: rough Int. Feel: rough Hardness: very hard Texture: irregular	Frequent, poorly sorted, sub-rounded quartz, 0.4–1.1 mm in size.	Int.: 10 YR 7/1 (light gray) Ext.: 10 YR 7/1 (light gray) Core: 10 YR 7/1 (light gray) Decoration: Wavy band combing	–
	i	Umm el-Habaj	Bowl rim / Early Islamic	Ext. Feel: rough Int. Feel: smooth Hardness: very hard Texture: very fine	Frequent, well-sorted, sub-rounded quartz, 0.1–0.2 mm in size.	Int. Slip: 2.5 Y 8/2 (white) Ext.: 10 YR 7/2 (light gray) Core: 7.5 YR 7/4 (pink) and 5 YR 7/6 (reddish brown) Int. Decoration: Painted motif in weak red (10 R 5/4) on a white (2.5 Y 8/2) slip Ext. Decoration: Painted motif in weak red (10 R 5/4) on a white (2.5 Y 8/2) slip	18

APPENDIX E: DESCRIPTION OF CERAMICS COLLECTED IN TEST EXCAVATIONS

Fig.	No.	Site	Form	Diam. (cm)	Interior Surface	Exterior Surface	Fabric (Munsell)
20	a	Lejjun	Holemouth jar rim	12	Smoothed 10YR7/4	Smoothed 7.5YR7/4	7.5YR7/4
	b		Holemouth jar rim	–	Smoothed, blackened	Smoothed, blackened	2.5YR6/4–10R5/6
	c		Holemouth jar rim	–	Smoothed	Smoothed, blackened	2.5YR6/3–5YR7/4
	d		Holemouth jar rim	12	Smoothed 5YR7/3	Smoothed, blackened 5YR5/3	7.5YR6/2
	e		Holemouth jar rim	14	Smoothed	Smoothed	2.5YR6/4–10R5/6
	f		Holemouth jar rim	17	Smoothed 5YR7/4	Smoothed 7.5YR7/4–7.5YR7/6	5YR7/4
	g		Holemouth jar rim	14	Smoothed	Smoothed	2.5YR6/3–5YR7/4
	h		Holemouth jar rim	12	Smoothed	Smoothed, blackened	2.5YR6/4–10R5/6
	i		Holemouth jar rim	22	Smoothed, blackened 2.5YR5/6	Smoothed, blackened 10YR6/3	10R6/8
	j		Jar rim	8	Smoothed	Smoothed	5YR8/2
	k		Jar rim	10	Smoothed 10R6/3	Smoothed 10R6/3	10R6/3
	l		Jar rim	–	Smoothed 7.5YR7/4	Smoothed 2.5YR7/6	7.5YR7/4
	m		Bowl rim (reused as lamp after broken)	12	Red slipped 7.5YR5/4	Red slipped 5YR5/4	7.5YR7/7
	n		Bowl rim (lamp)	–	Smoothed, soot on lip	Smoothed, soot on lip	–
	o		Platterbowl rim	30	Red slipped and burnished 7.5YR6/4	Red slipped and burnished 7.5YR7/3	10YR6/3
	p		Base	18	Smoothed 5YR7/4	Smoothed 5YR6/6	5YR6/6
	q		Base	24	Smoothed, blackened Gley N6	Smoothed, blackened Gley N5	Gley N4
	r		Ledge handle	–	–	Smoothed	–
	s		Ledge handle	–	–	Smoothed 5YR6/6	5YR7/6
25	a	Minsahlat	Holemouth jar rim	36	Smoothed 7.5YR6/6	Red slipped 2.5YR4/4	7.5YR7/6
	b		Holemouth jar rim	–	Smoothed	Incised with dots below rim (decoration around entire rim, or potter's mark?)	–
	c		Holemouth jar rim	–	Smoothed 2.5YR7/6	Smoothed, blackened 7.5YR7/3	10R6/3
	d		Holemouth jar rim	–	Smoothed, blackened 5YR6/6	Smoothed, blackened 5YR3/1	5YR5/4
	e		Holemouth jar rim	–	Smoothed 7.5YR7/4	Smoothed 7.5YR6/4	7.5YR5/4
	f		Holemouth jar rim	22	Smoothed	Smoothed	–
	g		Holemouth jar rim	–	Smoothed	Smoothed with incised, diagonal lines below rim	–
	h		Jar rim	4	Smoothed 5YR6/4	Smoothed 2.5YR6/4	2.5YR6/2

Fig.	No.	Site	Form	Diam. (cm)	Interior Surface	Exterior Surface	Fabric (Munsell)
25	i	Minsahlat	Jar rim	7	Smoothed 5YR7/6	Smoothed 2.5YR7/6	7.5YR7/4–7.5YR7/6
	j		Jar rim	3	Smoothed 5YR7/6	Smoothed 2.5YR7/6	5YR7/6
	k		Jar rim	–	Smoothed 2.5YR7/4	Smoothed 5YR6/4	5YR6/4
	l		Jar rim	8	Smoothed	Red slipped	–
	m		Jar rim	8	Smoothed 5YR6/3	Smoothed 10YR8/2	5YR4/3
	n		Jar rim	–	Smoothed 10YR7/4	Smoothed 10YR7/4	10YR7/4
	o		Jar rim	12	Smoothed 10YR8/2	Smoothed 5YR7/4	2.5YR7/8
	p		Jar rim	14	Smoothed 2.5YR7/6	Smoothed 5YR8/4	2.5YR7/8
	q		Jar rim				
	r		Jar rim	18	Smoothed 2.5YR7/6	Combed lightly 2.5YR6/6	2.5YR7/8
	s		Ledge handle	–	–	Smoothed (pierced before firing, folds closed)	–
	t		Ledge handle	–	–	Smoothed (folds closed)	–
26	a	Minsahlat	Bowl rim	16	Smoothed 10YR8/2	Smoothed 10YR7/4	10YR4/1
	b		Bowl rim and base	13/8	Smoothed	Smoothed	–
	c		Bowl rim	23	Red slipped and burnished 2.5YR5/4	Smoothed 7.5YR7/4	7.5YR7/1
	d		Bowl rim	32	Smoothed	Smoothed	–
	e		Bowl rim	32	Red slipped and burnished 5YR6/3	Red slipped and burnished 5YR4/4	7.5YR6/2
	f		Bowl rim	30	Smoothed 10YR8/4	Smoothed 10YR8/3	10YR7/4
	g		Bowl rim	30	Smoothed 5YR7/6	Smoothed with ledge handle 5YR7/4	5YR7/6
	h		Bowl rim	34	Smoothed	Smoothed	–
	i		Bowl rim	–	Smoothed, blackened	Smoothed, blackened	–
	j		Bowl rim	30	Smoothed7.5YR7/4	Smoothed 7.5YR6/4	7.5YR6/3
	k		Vat rim	26	Smoothed 10YR7/3	Smoothed 10YR7/3	Gley N4
	l		Vat rim	–	Smoothed	Smoothed	–
	m		Basin rim	40	Smoothed	Smoothed	–
	n		Basin rim	36	Smoothed 2.5YR7/4	Smoothed with appliqué band below rim 2.5YR7/6	5YR7/4

APPENDIX F: DESCRIPTION OF ILLUSTRATED CHIPPED STONE ARTIFACTS AND SMALL FINDS

Fig.	No.	Site	Object
21	a	Khirbet el-Minsahlat	Bone needle
	b		Polished bone object fragment
	c	Lejjun	Shaped gazelle horn core
	d		Polished bone bead
	e		Polished bone bead
	f		Polished, shaped and pierced shell
	g		Basalt groundstone object
27	a	Lejjun	Tabular scraper
	b		Tabular scraper
	c		Bifacial Chisel
	d	Khirbet el-Minsahlat	Tabular Fanscraper
	e		Sickle Blade
	f		Retouched Blade

REFERENCES

Amiran, R., and Gophna, R.

1989 Urban Canaan in the EB II and EB III Periods: Emergence and Structure. Pp. 109–16 in *L'Urbanisation de la Palestine a l'Âge du Bronze Ancien*, ed. P. de Miroschedji. Oxford: British Archaeological Reports.

Bar-Oz, G., and Dayan, T.

2002 "After 20 years": A Taphonomic Re-evaluation of Nahal Hadera V, an Epipaleolithic Site on the Israeli Coastal Plain. *Journal of Archaeological Science* 29: 145–56.

2003 Testing the Use of Multivariate Inter-site Taphonomic Comparisons: The Faunal Analysis of Hefzibah in its Epipaleolithic Cultural Context. *Journal of Archaeological Science* 30: 88–90.

Bartosiewicz, L.

1998 Interim Report on the Bronze Age Animal Bones from Arslantepe (Malatya, Anatolia). Pp. 221–32 in *Archaeozoology of the Near East III*, eds. H. Buitenhuis, L. Bartosiewicz, and A. M. Choyke. Groningen: Centre for Archeological Research and Consultancy.

Bending, J.

2002 Report on the Paleobotanical Analysis of Materials Collected in the 2001 Season of Test Excavations at Lejjun and Khirbet el-Minsahlat, Jordan. Ms. in possession of author.

Brown, R. M.

1991 Ceramics from the Kerak Plateau. Pp. 169–280 in *Archaeological Survey of the Kerak Plateau*, ed. M. Miller. Atlanta: Scholars.

Chesson, M. S.

2003 Households, Houses, Neighborhoods, and Corporate Villages: Modeling the Early Bronze Age as a House Society. *Journal of Mediterranean Archaeology* 16.1: 79–102.

Chesson, M. S., and Philip, G.

2003 Tales of the City? 'Urbanism' in the Early Bronze Age Levant from Mediterranean and Levantine Perspectives. *Journal of Mediterranean Archaeology* 16.1: 3–16.

Clutton-Brock, J.

1979 The Mammalian Remains from the Jericho Tell. *Proceedings of the Prehistoric Society* 45: 135–57.

Davis, S. J.

1976 Mammal Bones from the Early Bronze Age City of Arad, Northern Negev, Israel: Some Implications Concerning Human Exploitation. *Journal of Archaeological Science* 3: 153–64.

1988 The Mammal Bones: Tel Yarmouth 1980–83. Pp. 143–49 in *Yarmouth I: Rapport sur les trois premières campagnes de fouilles à Tel Yarmouth*, ed. P. de Miroschedji. Editions Recherche sur les Civilisations Mémoire no. 76. Paris: CNRS.

Dechert, B.

1995 The Bone Remains from Hirbet ez-Zeraqon. Pp. 79–87 in *Archaeozoology of the Near East*, eds. H. Buitenhuis and H. P. Uerpmann. Leiden: Bachhys.

Dornemann, R. H.

1990 Preliminary Comments on the Pottery Traditions at Tell Nimrin, Illustrated from the 1989 Season of Excavations. *Annual of the Department of Antiquities of Jordan* 34: 153–81.

Ducos, P.

1968 *L'Origine des animaux domestiques en Palestine*. Publications de l'Institut de Préhistoire de l'Université de Bordeaux, Mémoire 6. Bordeaux: Institut de Préhistoire de l'Université de Bordeaux.

Esse, D. L.

1991 *Subsistence, Trade, and Social Change in Early Bronze Age Palestine*. Chicago: Oriental Institute of the University of Chicago.

Fellmann Brogli, R.

1996 Die Keramik aus den Spätrömischen Bauten Pp. 219–81 in *Petra, Ez Zantur I, Ergebnisse der Schweizerisch-Liechtensteinischen Ausgrabungen 1988–1992*, eds. A. Bignasca, N. Desse-Berset, R. Fellmann Brogli, R. Glutz, S. Karg, D. Keller, B. Kolb, C. Kramar, M. Peter, S. G. Schmid, C. Schneider, R. A. Stucky, J. Studer and I. Zanoni. Mainz: von Zabern.

Finnegan, M.

1984 Faunal Remains from Bab edh-Dhra and Numeira. Pp. 177–80 in *The Southwestern Dead Sea Plain Expeditions: An Interim Report of the 1977 Season*, eds. W. E. Rast and R. T. Schaub. Annual of the American Schools of Oriental Research 46. Cambridge: American Schools of Oriental Research.

Genz, H.

1993 Zur bemalten Keramik der Frühbronzezeit II–III in Palästina. *Zeitschrift des Deutschen Palästina-Vereins* 109: 1–19.

2003 Cash Crop Production and Storage in the Early Bronze Age Southern Levant. *Journal of Mediterranean Archaeology* 16.1: 59–78.

Grant, A.

1982 The Use of Tooth Wear as a Guide to the Age of Domestic Ungulates. Pp. 91–108 in *Ageing and Sexing Animal Bones From Archaeological Sites*, eds. B. Wilson, C. Grigson, and S. Payne. British Archaeological Reports, British Series 109. Oxford: British Archaeological Reports.

Greenberg, R.

2003 Early Bronze Age Megiddo and Bet Shean: Discontinuous Settlement in Socio-political Context. *Journal of Mediterranean Archaeology* 16.1: 17–32.

Greenfield, H.

2002 Preliminary Report on the Faunal Remains from the Early Bronze Age site of Titriş Höyük in Southeastern Turkey. Pp. 251–60 in *Archaeozoology of the Near East V*, eds. H. Buitenhuis, A. M. Choyke, M. Mashkour, and A. H. al-Shiyab. Groningen: Centre for Archeological Research and Consultancy.

Grigson, C.

1987 Shiqmim: Pastoralism and Other Aspects of Animal Management in the Chalcolithic of the Northern Negev. Pp. 219–41 in *Shiqmim I: Studies Concerning Chalcolithic Societies in the Northern Negev Desert, Israel (1982–1984)*, ed. T. E. Levy. British Archaeological Reports, International Series 356. Oxford: British Archaeological Reports.

1995 Plough and Pasture in the Early Economy of the Southern Levant. Pp. 245–67 in *The Archaeology of Society in the Holy Land*, ed. T. E. Levy. London: Leicester University.

Harrison, T. P.

1997 Shifting Patterns of Settlement in the Highlands of Central Jordan during the Early Bronze Age. *Bulletin of the American Schools of Oriental Research* 306: 1–37.

Harrison, T. P., and Savage, S.

2003 Settlement Heterogeneity and Multivariate Craft Production in the Early Bronze Age Southern Levant. *Journal of Mediterranean Archaeology* 16.1: 33–57.

Hayes, J. W.

1972 *Late Roman Pottery*. London: British School at Rome.

Hellwing, S. and Gophna, R.

1984 The Animal Remains from the Early and Middle Bronze Ages at Tel Aphek and Tel Dalit: A Comparative Study. *Tel Aviv* 11: 48–59.

Henry, D. O.

1995 *Prehistoric Cultural Ecology and Evolution*. New York: Plenum.

Horwitz, L. K., and Tchernov, E.

1989 Animal Exploitation in the Early Bronze Age of the Southern Levant: An Overview. Pp. 276–96 in *L'Urbanisation de la Palestine à l'Âge du Bronze ancien*, ed. P. de Miroschedji. British Archaeological Reports, International Series 527(II). Oxford: British Archaeological Reports.

Johns, J.

1993 The Rise of Middle Islamic Hand-Made Geometrically-Painted Ware in Bilad al-Sham (11th–13th Centuries A.D.). *Textes Arabes et Études Islamiques* 36: 65–93.

Kareem, J.

2001 The Pottery from the First Season of Excavations at Khirbet Nakhil. Pp 77–93 in *La Céramique Byzantine et Proto-Islamique en Syrie-Jordanie (IVe–VIIIe Siècle apr. J.-C.), Actes du Colloque Tenu à Amman les 3, 4 et 5 Décembre 1994*, eds. E. Villeneuve and P. M. Watson. Bibliothèque Archéologique et Historique. Beirut: Institut Français D'Archéologique du Proche-Orient.

Khairy, N.

1982 Fine Nabataean Ware with Impressed and Rouletted Decorations. *Studies in the History and Archaeology of Jordan* 1: 275–83.

Lernau, H.

1978 Faunal Remains. Pp. 83–113 in *Early Arad*, ed. R. Amiran. Jerusalem: Israel Exploration Society.

Levy, T. E.

1992 Transhumance, Subsistence, and Social Evolution in the Northern Negev Desert. Pp. 69–92 in *Pastoralism in the Levant: Archaeological Materials in Anthropological Perspectives*, eds. O. Bar-Yosef and A. Khazanov. Madison, WI: Prehistory.

Lyman, R. L.

1994 *Vertebrate Taphonomy*. Cambridge: Cambridge University.

Mattingly, G.

1983 Nelson Glueck and Early Bronze Age Moab. *Annual of the Department of Antiquities, Jordan* 27: 481–89.

1984 The Early Bronze Age Sites of Central and Southern Moab. *Near Eastern Archaeology: Bulletin of the Near East Archaeological Society* 23: 69–98.

McConaughy, M.
1979 Formal and Functional Analysis of Chipped Stone Tools from Bab edh-Dhra. Unpublished Ph.D. Dissertation, University of Pittsburgh.

Miller, J. M., ed.
1991 *Archaeological Survey of the Kerak Plateau.* Atlanta: Scholars.

Palmer, C.
2002 Milk and Cereals: Identifying Food and Food Identity among Fallahin and Bedouin in Jordan. *Levant* 34: 173–95.

Palumbo, G.
1991 *The Early Bronze Age IV in the Southern Levant: Settlement Patterns, Economy, and Material Culture of a 'Dark Age'.* Contributi e Materiali di Archaeologia Orientale 3. Rome: Università degli studi di Roma "La Sapienza".
2001 The Early Bronze Age IV. Pp. 233–70 in *The Archaeology of Jordan*, eds. B. MacDonald, R. Adams, and P. Bienkowski. Sheffield: Sheffield Academic.

Parker, S. T.
1987a The Pottery. Pp. 525-619 in *The Roman Frontier in Central Jordan*, ed. S.T. Parker. British Archaeological Reports, International Series, 340 (ii). Oxford: British Archaeological Reports.

Parker, S. T., ed.
1987b *The Roman Frontier in Central Jordan.* British Archaeological Reports, International Series, 340 (ii). Oxford: British Archaeological Reports.

Payne, S.
1972 Partial Recovery and Sample Bias: The Results from some Sieving Experiments. Pp. 49–64 in *Papers in Economic Prehistory*, ed. E. S. Higgs. Cambridge: Cambridge University.
1973 Kill-off Patterns in Sheep and Goats: The Mandible from Asvan Kale. *Anatolian Studies* 23: 281–303

Philip, G.
2001 The Early Bronze I–III Ages. Pp. 163–232 in *The Archaeology of Jordan*, eds. B. MacDonald, R. Adams, and P. Bienkowski. Sheffield: Sheffield Academic.
2003 The Early Bronze Age of the Southern Levant: A Landscape Approach. *Journal of Mediterranean Archaeology* 16.1: 103–32.

Philip, G., and Baird, D., eds.
2000 *Ceramics and Change in the Early Bronze Age of the Southern Levant.* Sheffield: Sheffield Academic.

Rosen, S.
1983 The Tabular Scraper Trade: A Model for Material Culture Dispersion. *Bulletin of the American Schools of Oriental Research* 249:79–86.
1997 *Lithics after the Stone Age: A Handbook of Stone Tools from the Levant.* New York: Altamira.

Sauer, J. A.
1982 The Pottery of Jordan in the Early Islamic Periods. *Studies in the History and Archaeology of Jordan* 1: 329–37.

Schaub, R. T., and Rast, W. E.
1989 *Bab edh-Dhra': Excavations in the Cemetery Directed By Paul W. Lapp (1965–1967).* Winona Lake, IN: Eisenbrauns.

Schmid, S. G.
1995 Nabataean Fine Ware from Petra. *Studies in the History and Archaeology of Jordan* 5: 637–47.

Silver, I. A.
1969 The Ageing of Domestic Animals. Pp. 283–302 in *Science in Archaeology*, 2nd edition, eds. D. Brothwell and E. S. Higgs. London: Thames and Hudson.

Steele, C.
1990 Early Bronze Age Socio-Political Organization in Southwestern Asia. *Zeitschrift des Deutschen Palästina-Vereins* 106: 1–33.

Stucky, R. A.; Gerber, Y.; Kolb, B.; and Schmid, S. G.
1994 Swiss-Liechtenstein Excavations at ez-Zantur in Petra 1993: The Fifth Campaign. *Annual of the Department of Antiquities of Jordan* 38: 271–92.

Von den Driesch, A.
1993 Faunal Remains from Habuba Kabira in Syria. Pp. 52–59 in *Archaeozoology of the Near East I*, eds. H. Buitenhuis and A. T. Clason. Leiden: Backuys.

Walmsley, A.
1995 Tradition, Innovation, and Imitation in the Material Culture of Islamic Jordan: The First Four Centuries. *Studies in the History and Archaeology of Jordan* 5: 657–68.

Two Early Alphabetic Inscriptions from the Wadi el-Ḥôl

New Evidence for the Origin of the Alphabet from the Western Desert of Egypt

John Coleman Darnell
Yale University

F. W. Dobbs-Allsopp
Princeton Theological Seminary

Marilyn J. Lundberg
WSR, University of Southern California

P. Kyle McCarter
The Johns Hopkins University

Bruce Zuckerman
University of Southern California

with the assistance of

Colleen Manassa
Yale University

Contents

ACKNOWLEDGMENTS

The fieldwork that led to the discovery of these inscriptions was carried out under the auspices of the Supreme Council for Antiquities in Egypt, and we thank that organization and all from the Egyptian antiquities service, police, and military, who have accompanied the Theban Desert Road Survey and aided in the recording of this material. We specifically would like to thank Dr. Zahi Hawass, General Secretary of the Supreme Council for Antiquities; Dr. Gaballa Ali Gaballa, former General Secretary of the SCA; Dr. Sabri Abd el-Aziz, General Director of Pharaonic Antiquities; Dr. Mohammed es-Saghir, former General Director of Pharaonic Antiquities; Mr. Attia Radwan, General Director for Desert Antiquities; Dr. Mohammed el-Bialy, former General Director of Qurna Antiquites; Mr. Hussein Afiuni, General Director of Antiquities for Qena and the Red Sea, and last but not least, Inspector Ramadan Ahmed Ali and Inspector Abd el-Fatah Abd el-Qadr, and Officer Ashraf Hassanein el-Ashmawi and Officer Madawan. J. C. Darnell gratefully acknowledges the financial support received from the National Endowment for the Humanities (an independent Federal agency), the Simpson Endowment for Egyptology at Yale University, the American and Swiss branches of the Michela Schiff Giorgini Foundation; he also thanks Anthony Leahy, Patricia Spencer, and the Egypt Exploration Society, London. Dobbs-Allsopp's participation in the 1999 photographic expedition to the Wadi el-Ḥôl was financially supported by a SBL Research Grant and an A. Whitney Griswold Faculty Research Grant (Yale University). Zuckerman and Lundberg, in collaboration with John M. Melzian, were supported by the West Semitic Research Project (University of Southern California) and especially The Ahmanson Foundation for the photographic expedition in 1999.

The first announcement of these inscriptions appeared in J. C. Darnell and D. Darnell, "The Luxor–Farshût Desert Road Survey," *OIAR* (1994–95) 46–47: "We also discovered and copied two inscriptions written in the Proto-Sinaitic script." The vertical inscription appears in one of Winkler's photographs now stored in the office of the Egypt Exploration Society in London. No one appears to have recognized the significance of the inscriptions, and a search through the records of the Mond expedition (also stored at the Egypt Exploration Society office) failed to reveal any discussion or even mention of such an inscription. J. C. Darnell first presented these inscriptions to the public at the British Museum (at the invitation of Vivian Davies, Keeper of Egyptian Antiquities), in a lecture with the title, "New Discoveries in the Western Desert: the World's Oldest Alphabetic Inscriptions," on July 12, 1999. A general presentation by the authors of the present volume followed at a joint session of the Annual Meetings of the Society for Biblical Literature and the American Schools of Oriental Research, entitled "The Early Alphabetic Inscriptions in the Wadi el-Ḥôl: the Oldest Alphabetic Inscriptions, and the Egyptian Origins of the Alphabet," on November 22, 1999. Subsequent preliminary presentations of these materials include Dobbs-Allsopp, "The Wadi el-Ḥôl and Alphabetic Origins" (general lecture and graduate seminar at the University of Wisconsin, Madison, co-sponsored by the Madison Biblical Archaeology Society; May 1, 2002).

The authors wish to extend a special word of thanks to Gordon J. Hamilton of Huron University College, who has been a constant conversation partner over the last several years and who has generously shared with us his own ongoing research on the paleography of early alphabetic writing.

Epigraphic Note

All carved texts have an aspect of depth to the incised lines; since an epigraphic drawing exists in only two dimensions, the epigrapher has the choice of representing either the outer edges of the carved lines, the deepest portion of the lines, or an amalgam of the two. All rock inscriptions made as incised lines thus have upper, outer edges of the cut and a lower base cut. The bottom, deeper cut represents where the carving tool exerted the greatest pressure on the stone and is typically more representative of the original intent of the author. The author of the early alphabetic inscriptions was carving a linear script and any variation in thickness of the individual lines is almost certainly accidental. In order to record the greatest amount of information with the maximum of clarity, we present for each inscription a copy of the base line of the carving (figs. 2:a, 16:a) as well as a drawing of the upper, outer edges of the cut (figs. 2:b, 16:b). The drawings of the deepest portions of the carving should naturally take precedence in paleographic considerations, and it is these we present in the paleographic charts.

Most of the photographs in the present publication result from the assistance of Bruce Zuckerman and Marilyn J. Lundberg. Due to the uneven natural surfaces on which rock inscriptions are carved, a certain amount of foreshortening and other distortions are inevitable in the photographs. Thus, we must caution against any paleographic commentary based solely on the photographs. The facsimile drawings included in this volume are based on careful tracing and collation in the presence of the original inscriptions, and represent the most accurate possible rendering of the inscriptions in two dimensions.

List of Figures

List of Plates

Two Early Alphabetic Inscriptions from the Wadi el-Ḥôl

New Evidence for the Origin of the Alphabet from the Western Desert of Egypt

by John Coleman Darnell, F. W. Dobbs-Allsopp, Marilyn J. Lundberg, P. Kyle McCarter and Bruce Zuckerman with the assistance of Colleen Manassa

The Egyptian Western Desert, now a virtually deserted wasteland, once teemed with economic and military activity. Much of the pharaonic desert traffic transiting through the Western Desert concentrated on a series of tracks linking the Upper Egyptian Thebaïd with points much farther to the west and south. On the main Theban road into the Western Desert, at the midpoint of the portion of this route crossing the desert filling the Qena Bend of the Nile, is the Wadi el-Ḥôl, a site of hundreds of rock inscriptions and depictions, and the location of major archaeological deposits of stratified caravansary debris.[1] Although T. Gray and H. Winkler photographed a few inscriptions at the site during the 1930s, and M. Drower was able to examine rubbings of some of the inscriptions at the same time,[2] the vast majority of the material and its significance remained unknown until the Theban Desert Road Survey rediscovered the site and placed it in the proper context of the pharaonic road system.[3] Unlike the other textual inscriptions at the Wadi el-Ḥôl,[4] the two rock inscriptions published here (discovered during the 1994–95 field season of the Theban Desert Road Survey) are not legible Egyptian. Rather, they appear to be alphabetic in nature and are directly comparable to the small corpus of known early alphabetic writings.[5] This initial publication of the Wadi el-Ḥôl early alphabetic inscriptions presents a description and paleographic analysis of these inscriptions, an assessment of their date (in conjunction with other Egyptian inscriptions at the Wadi el-Ḥôl), and some preliminary thoughts about their significance for understanding the origins of the alphabet.[6]

THE WADI EL-ḤÔL

The Wadi el-Ḥôl site is located approximately halfway between Luxor (ancient *W3s.t*; Thebes) and Hou (ancient *Ḥw.t-sḫm*) along the so-called Farshût Road—a track crossing the tongue of the Western Desert filling the Qena Bend of the Nile (fig. 1). The Wadi el-Ḥôl site occupies one of the strategically and economically important passes through which desert roads ascend and descend the high desert plateau—"the narrow doors of the desert" of the ancient Egyptians, often the objects of police patrols and the sites of military garrisons. As a result of the military and economic importance of the routes through the Western Desert, much of the rich archaeological and epigraphic evidence from these desert sites dates to periods of instability and conflict in the Nile Valley; al-

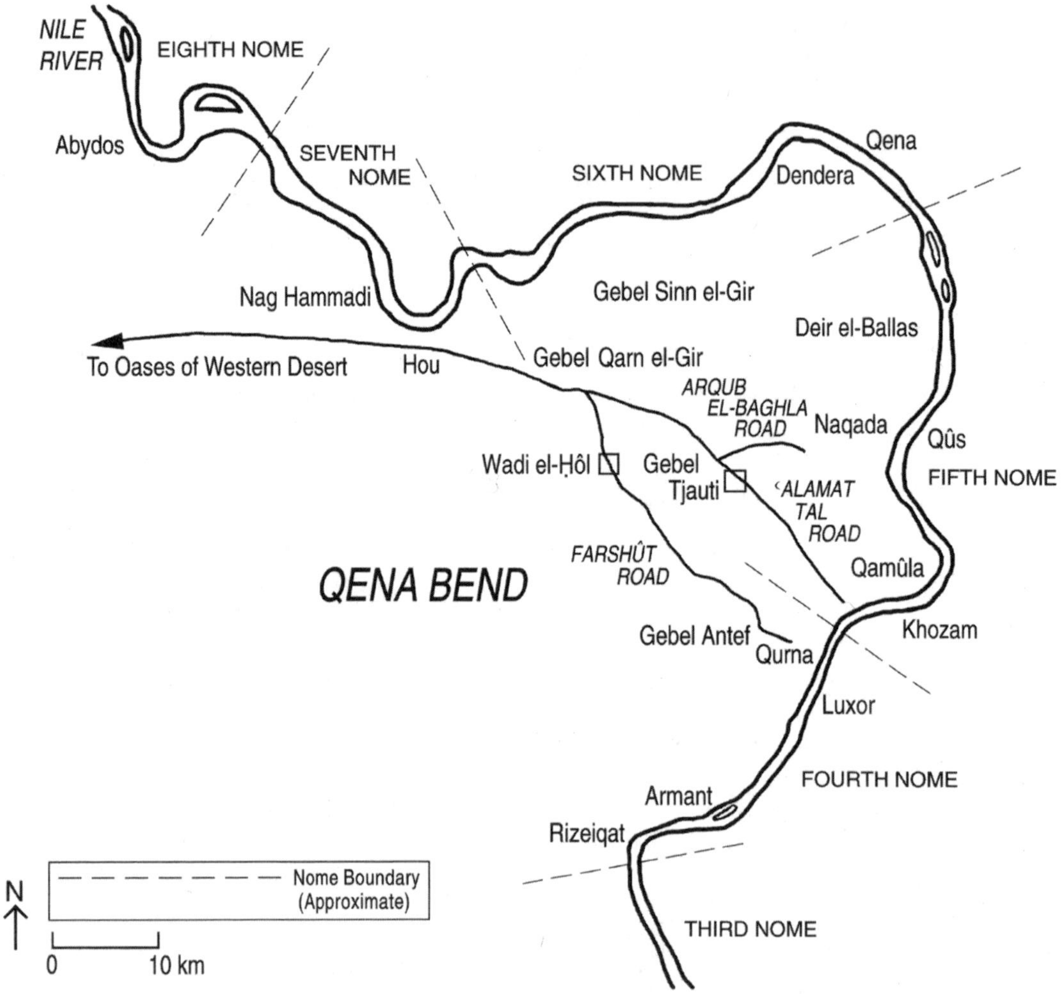

Fig. 1. *Map of the Qena Bend (from J. C. Darnell 2002a: pl. 1).*

though inscriptions at the Wadi el-Ḥôl range in date from the earliest Predynastic through the early Islamic periods, the great bulk of the inscriptions date between the early Middle Kingdom (mid-11th Dynasty) and the beginning of the New Kingdom, approximately 2050–1550 B.C.E. A large number of the dated inscriptions belong to the late 12th and early 13th Dynasties.

Despite the isolation and general barrenness of its contemporary setting, the Wadi el-Ḥôl was not a remote and secluded site during the height of pharaonic antiquity, but rather the bustling center of a great desert highway, connecting Thebes with Hou and Abydos in the north, and with the oases of Kharga and Dakhla in the Western Desert. As an ancient traveler along the Farshût Road descended or ascended at the Wadi el-Ḥôl on his (or her)[7] way to any one of these locations, he (or she) would have passed a stratum of soft limestone, fractured into large, flat surfaces ideal for carving—probably with the ubiquitous flint nodules that litter the desert surface.[8] The rock inscriptions and depictions carved at the Wadi el-Ḥôl range from hastily executed sketches to names of individuals and their relations, to elaborately carved literary texts.[9] In addition to a site of intense economic activity,[10] the Wadi el-Ḥôl was also a center for religious observance, mostly centered on the worship of the goddess Hathor, as evidenced by the "spending the day on holiday" inscriptions,[11] depictions of the goddess in her bovine manifestation, and representations of musical celebrants.[12]

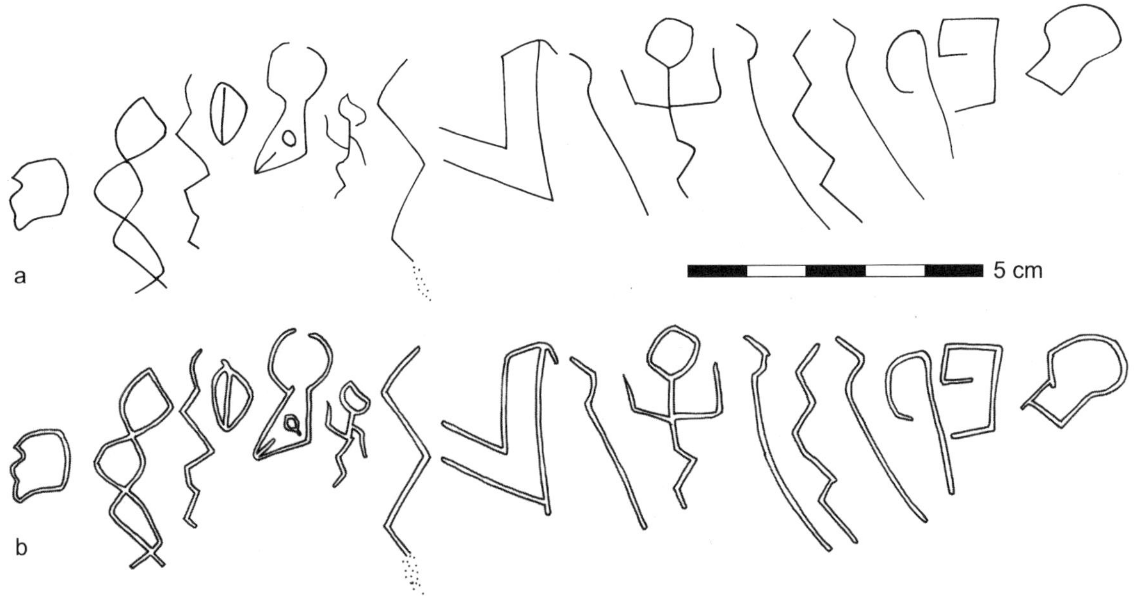

Fig. 2. Wadi el-Ḥôl Alphabetic Inscription 1; the Horizontal Inscription. a) facsimile of the base of the incised lines; b) facsimile of the outer edges of the incised lines.

Due to the strategic location of the Wadi el-Ḥôl, many of the inscriptions relate to soldiers and military activity. By the reign of Amenemhat III, Theban troops appear to have garrisoned the Wadi el-Ḥôl,[13] and the desert outpost continued to serve as a military base into the Second Intermediate Period,[14] guarding the back door to Thebes, while giving access to the Theban base at Abydos[15] and a Theban outpost between the Nile and Kharga Oasis.[16] Through the late second millennium, the Wadi el-Ḥôl and its associated tracks were a thoroughfare for military units, often supplemented with foreign auxiliaries, who in times of peace ensured safe passage for travelers—be they traders, pilgrims, or priests—and in times of war used those same routes for strategic maneuvers.[17] It is into this complex conjunction of activities in a militarized setting that the two early alphabetic inscriptions fit.

THE EARLY ALPHABETIC INSCRIPTIONS

These two inscriptions do not write any recognizable form of Egyptian, in either *Normalschrift* or cryptography, and palaeographically the signs belong to the small corpus of early alphabetic inscriptions recovered most especially from Sinai (the so-called "Proto-Sinaitic" inscriptions from Serabit el-Khadim and its environs).[18] They are located toward the left portion of Section C in the Wadi el-Ḥôl (pls. I.1–II; the site itself contains four major concentrations of rock inscriptions), the section of the site closest to the main ascending and descending track, with a general southwesterly exposure. The Egyptian inscriptions spatially closest to the early alphabetic inscriptions are the names of Egyptian scribes, apparently of Middle Kingdom date, but none of these are so close as to suggest some definite association of the inscriptions. The surfaces on which the Wadi el-Ḥôl early alphabetic inscriptions were carved are otherwise uninscribed, flat facets of soft limestone in fairly prominent locations. The lines forming the signs of these two inscriptions are relatively thin, most of no more than ¼ millimeter thickness (.013 microns); the thickest line in either inscription is the horizontal of the second mark sign (*tāw*) in the vertical inscription (Waḍi el-Ḥôl Early Alphabetic Inscription 2), a line of almost 1 millimeter thickness (.04 microns).

The texts appear to read from right to left. Unlike Egyptian texts,[19] most of the signs—compare the ox head (1.12) and seated man (2.5)—face in the direction of the writing,[20] that is to say to the left. However, there are some notable exceptions, such as the sign of the seated man with his arms raised (1.7), which appears from the initial angle of his legs to be facing right, and the eye, which also appears to be facing right (2.6). This mixture suggests that one cannot be absolutely dogmatic about the stance of alphabetic signs in this early period. Like Egyptian, the early alphabetic script accommodates both horizontal and vertical arrangement, but for the most part, the signs appear to be written one after another in a line (be it horizontal or vertical), without any use of sign groups of the sort most common for formal hieroglyphic inscriptions.[21]

The Horizontal Inscription (Wadi el-Ḥôl Early Alphabetic Inscription 1)

The first inscription, oriented horizontally, is approximately 20 (19.985) cm long and exhibits sixteen letters (pl. III–IV; fig. 2). The characters are for the most part well-executed, deeply and crisply carved, especially on the rightmost half of the inscription. The depth of the lines becomes increasingly shallow towards the left, due to the abutting rock face on the left-hand side of the inscription, because of which the scribe probably found it difficult to execute the various strokes of the individual signs. As a consequence, the signs on the left-hand side of the inscription are more poorly executed, lacking the precision and depth of the signs on the right-hand side. The physical layout of the rock face strongly suggests that the direction of the writing (and reading) is from right to left.

Paleographic Observations

1.1. *Head* = *rêš*. The first sign is the outline of a head in profile—while its stance is vertical, it gives the impression of being tilted back at an angle. Although the overall shape of the sign is round, the lower portion of the sign consists of angular cuts. Two other head signs appear in the Wadi el-Ḥôl alphabetic inscriptions (1.16; 2.4), and both are of a similar form, but neither is so well-executed as the first sign in the horizontal inscriptions (see pl.

Fig. 3. *Human head (D1). a) Möller 1927a: no. 79, Abusir and Elephantine examples; b) James 1962: I/16 and VII/15.*

V.1–2). Initially, one might be tempted to interpret the pronounced angles of these signs as exaggerated facial features;[22] although one might expect to see more clearly indicated hair to the back of the head, such "close-cropped" hieroglyphic heads do appear, especially during the First Intermediate Period.[23] The apparent backwards tilt of the heads does not fit well, however, with hieroglyphic Egyptian prototypes.[24] On closer inspection, the angles of the possible front of the head appear more probably to derive from the angles of the back of the head in early Middle Kingdom hieratic (see fig. 3).[25] Interpreted on the basis of hieratic prototypes, the head would not be tilted back, and its stance is vertical (like all the other signs in this inscription), facing right; the bottom point is in essence the neck, the sign representing a reasonable facsimile of the hieratic version of the sign of the human head.[26] The sign of the head here represents an angular, lapidary hieratic derivation of the more cursive hieratic head. Such a lapidary hieratic origin of the head sign gains plausibility in light of the several other signs in these inscriptions clearly derived from hieratic models (see below) and explains the otherwise unique backwards-tilted appearance of the head sign in the inscriptions.

The head signs in the Wadi el-Ḥôl early alphabetic inscriptions add to the variety of head signs already in evidence at Serabit el-Khadim.[27] Of the twelve to seventeen occurrences of the head sign at Serabit, most appear to derive from the hieroglyph of the head in profile (Gardiner D1). In its execution this sign reveals a great deal of variation—some face left (Sinai 349) and some face right (Sinai 346, 376); some indicate eyes (Sinai 346, 376), others do not (Sinai 376). Sass entertains the possibility that several of the head signs at Serabit (e.g., Sinai 364, 367) derive from Gardiner D2, the hieroglyph of the head shown frontally;[28] in both instances, however, alternative interpretations of the signs in question are possible.[29] Two of the Serabit forms exhibit potential flourishes more characteristic of hieratic (Sinai 349, 357), though given the variation of forms and the basic trajectory towards simplification already prominent in the Egyptian prototypes of the hieroglyph D1, it is often difficult to discern a strong distinction between hieroglyphic and hieratic influence. The head signs in the Wadi el-Ḥôl offer the best exemplars of hieratically derived head signs in the early alphabetic corpus.

1.2. *House* = *bêt*. This is a courtyard-styled house plan with the bottom left part of the courtyard remaining open (see pl. VI.1), a shape deriving from the Egyptian courtyard house sign (Gardiner O4). This is one of the more important forms in these inscriptions, because at last it provides us with the obvious precursor of the West Semitic linear *bêt*.[30] While the house sign at Serabit—for the most part consisting of a closed rectangular form—has usually been assumed to derive from the standard Egyptian hieroglyphic form of a house, the *pr*-sign (Gardiner O1),[31] other evidence raises questions about such an identification. The *pr*-sign in Egyptian hieroglyphs, unlike its assumed derivations at Serabit, invariably has an opening for a door,[32] most akin perhaps to the odd forms in Sinai 346 and 359,[33] although without the "entrance hall" appearance. In Egyptian hieratic of the late Middle Kingdom and Second Intermediate Period, the courtyard house sign (Gardiner O4) can have an entirely closed form;[34] this feature may well point to an origin in the hieratic of the courtyard house (Gardiner O4) for the standard Serabit house sign.[35] This would be consistent with one of the more characteristic features of the Wadi el-Ḥôl early alphabetic inscriptions, since the signs in evidence frequently derive from hieratic prototypes (see below). In either case, the Serabit forms of the house sign, with or without entrances, whatever their specific origin(s), clearly are not the precursors to the *bêt* that eventually prevails in the West Semitic linear scripts. Based on the form of the courtyard type of *bêt* that appears in the Lachish bowl fragment and in the St. Louis/Goetze Seal, F. M. Cross predicted that a courtyard house form of the *bêt*, a form such as that in the Wadi el-Ḥôl, should be in evidence in early alphabetic inscriptions.[36] The only possible candidate is the double box form of the otherwise obscure "house" sign in Sinai 375, which Hamilton believes derives from a hieratic form of the courtyard house sign.[37] The derivation of the Wadi el-Ḥôl house sign from a courtyard house model is beyond dispute and now shows Cross' intuition to have been correct after all. The courtyard-styled house form does indeed exist, and nicely matches the form of the *bêt* on the Lachish bowl fragment and the St. Louis/Goetze Seal.

The combined corpus of early alphabetic inscriptions from Egypt (i.e., Wadi el-Ḥôl, Serabit) now attests at least two different forms of the house sign—and perhaps yet a third is evidenced in Sinai 363 (based on Gardiner O6 or O20).[38] The Egyptian courtyard house model (Gardiner O4), common in Egyptian as a uniliteral phonetic sign (*h*), is the prototype for the house sign in the Wadi el-Ḥôl early alphabetic inscriptions, and this form is what eventually becomes stylized as the *bêt* of the later West Semitic linear alphabetic scripts.

1.3. *Coil of rope* = *lāmed*. The third sign is likely intended to depict a coil of rope, the object which the sign Gardiner V1 represents. The carving suggests that the sign was made in two strokes—the first stroke probably began at the left and lowest part of the head and curved around through the head; there is a brief gap, and then a downward stroke completed the tail. As with most of the signs in these inscriptions, it is crisply made, and the angularity of an expected rounded sign is due to the difficulty of incising the rock surface. The sign also appears in the vertical inscription (2.12), although the "head" there is at the bottom and on the left, with the tail moving upwards. The stance of this sign is similarly variable at Serabit.[39] However, the placement of the "head" at the bottom, as in the Wadi el-Ḥôl vertical inscription, appears to be not otherwise attested at Serabit and suggests that the model for this sign is the coil of rope and not one of the other putative sources of the linear alphabetic *lāmed*.[40] In fact, of the possible Egyptian models for this early alphabetic sign, the coil of rope is the most commonly attested in Egyptian texts; the shepherd's crook (S39) is the least well-represented. The coil usually has a relatively tightly rolled "head" and a slightly recurved tail.[41]

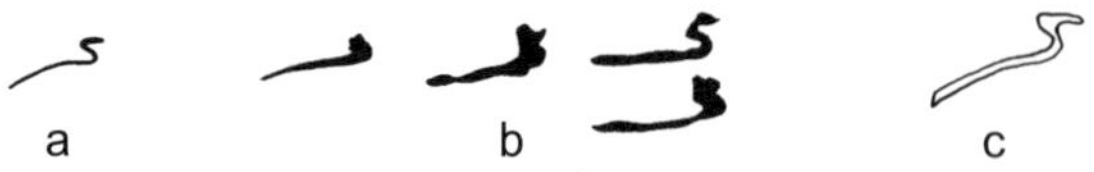

Fig. 4. Cobra Sign (I10). a) Möller 1927a: no. 250, Hatnub example (25,5); b) Roccati 1970: 50; c) Arnold et al. 1990: 111, N 24.2, l.2.

Fig. 5. Horned Viper (I9); Žába 1974: pl. 13.

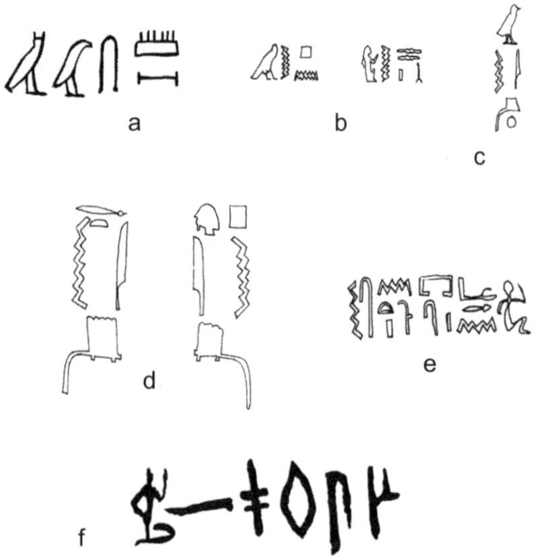

Fig. 6. Hieroglyphic examples of vertically oriented signs. a) Hall 1912: pl. 39, no. 226, l. 8; b) Obsomer 1993: 104 and 122; c) Simpson 1974: pl. 22; d) Boeser 1909: pl. 3; e) Limme 1979: 18 (Djari Stela); f) Hintze and Reineke 1989b: 101, no. 302.

1.4. *Serpent = nûn* (Ethiopic name: *naḥaš*). Three serpent signs appear in the horizontal inscription (1.4, 6, 8), each executed in the same basic fashion.[42] The head is abbreviated as a short diagonal line, incised from the top left-to-right; then a short downward stroke that moves back toward the left. Ultimately, this incision bends back to the right and down in a long bending curve. The general shape suggests that this sign derives from the *ḏ*-serpent ("cobra in repose," Gardiner I10) in its hieratic form (fig. 4).[43] The essentially straight body is, however, more in keeping with a derivation from the horned viper (Gardiner I9).[44] The stance of the sign is somewhat exaggeratedly vertical, a stance appearing in some hieratic inscriptions (fig. 5).[45]

The majority of the Serabit forms of the serpent-sign reveals a similar derivation from the cobra sign, although the Serabit serpent-signs appear to embody more the hieroglyphic (Gardiner I10) than the hieratic form of the sign;[46] additionally, the stance at Serabit is prevailingly horizontal.[47] Several of the Serabit forms, such as Sinai 363 (perhaps also Sinai 353, 357, 375), also appear to be based on the horned viper sign (Gardiner I9).[48] The horned viper and the cobra are alternative signs with the same alphabetic value, attesting to the existence of biforms in this early period of alphabetic development.

1.5. *Water = mêm*. There are three water signs in the horizontal inscription (1.5, 10, 14) and one in the vertical inscription (2.1). All three examples in this (horizontal) inscription are vertically oriented, while the one water sign in the vertical inscription is oriented horizontally. The first water sign is better executed than the other two—owing to the encroaching overhang of the rock face on the left.

Like its hieroglyphic model (Gardiner N35), the water sign in the early alphabetic inscriptions can have a variable number of angles; for example, the first water sign in the horizontal inscription has a total of five angles, while the other water signs vary from three to eight angles. The most significant feature of the water sign in the horizontal inscription (1.5, 10, 14) is its unique vertical orientation (all the water signs at Serabit are horizontal), shared by the vertical hobble-*ṯ* (2.2, 10) signs. These two signs have a normative (and natural) horizontal orientation that obtains throughout most of the life of the hieroglyphic script. Primarily in the hieroglyphic inscriptions of early Middle Kingdom date are a number of examples of normally horizontal signs set on end—against the nature of the object depicted in the sign—in order to fill a quadrant following a vertical sign (fig. 6). Both the water-*n* and hobble-*ṯ* signs in particular figure in these examples of vertically written horizontal signs.[49] The orientation of these signs is one of the many features that point toward an early Middle Kingdom date for the paleographical derivations of the two early alphabetic inscriptions at the Wadi el-Ḥôl.[50]

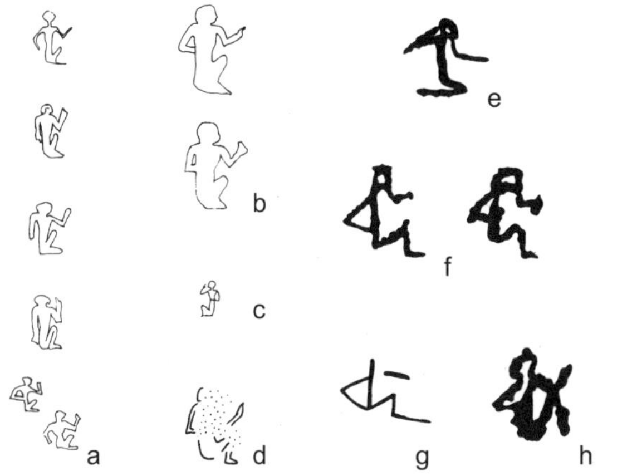

Fig. 7. Seated man (A1). *a) Fischer 1968: 80; b) Fischer 1964: 107; c) Fischer 1964: 109; d) J. C. Darnell 2002a: pl. 19; e) Žába 1974: no. A-1; f) Žába 1974: no. 195 (two seated men); g) Žába 1974: no. 60A (fig. 118); h) Žába 1974: no. 222 (fig. 358).*

1.6. *Serpent = nûn* (Ethiopic name: *naḥaš*). See discussion of 1.4 above.

1.7. *Seated man with raised arms = hê.* The figure (pl. VI.2) is well executed, and the incised lines are all clear and crisp (cf. the related figures [1.11, 2.5] which are not as well carved). The human figure, which can have an odd, abbreviated appearance in the Serabit inscriptions,[51] is much more complete and elaborated in the Wadi el-Ḥôl early alphabetic inscriptions. The odd, doubled angle of the lower portion of the sign (the zigzag flourish that gives the appearance of a "man on skis") makes clear that this is not the standard seated man of the average hieroglyphic sign list (Gardiner A1). This sign appears to show a male figure seated, with the feet forward (rather than kneeling with one foot forward and the other tucked behind), a pose uncommon for standard Egyptian paleography, but well attested from the First Intermediate Period and the early Middle Kingdom (fig. 7),[52] with sporadic examples occurring already in the Old Kingdom (fig. 8).[53]The legs and feet of the Wadi el-Ḥôl sign appear to derive specifically from the hieratic representation of feet-forward signs, most apparent in certain hieratic versions of seated male signs (particularly the sign of the seated soldier) from the First Intermediate Period/

Fig. 8. Seated man signs from the Old Kingdom. a) "prospector figure" *(Hintze and Reineke 1989b: 258–59, nos. 599, 598, and 597; b) man with pouring vessel* *(Dobrev1996: 118; paleography, A6B).*

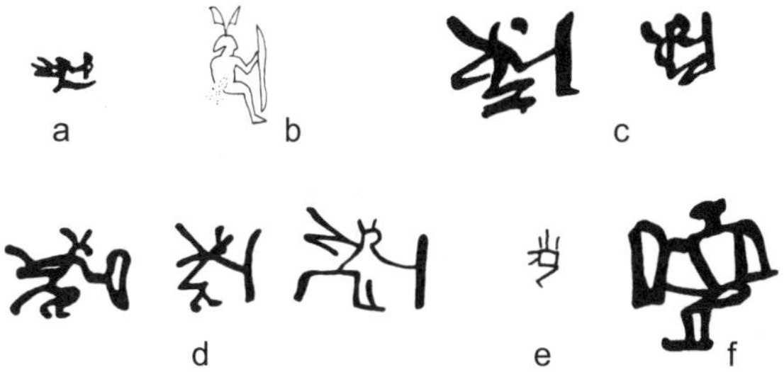

Fig. 9. Seated soldier *(A12). a) normal hieratic appearance (Möller 1927a: 4, no. 44); b) Sainte Fare Garnot 1937: pl. 14, fig. 2, l. 6; c) Goedicke 1988: 2a, Sharuna and Elephantine examples; d) Lopez 1966: 24–25 and 28; e) Goyon 1957: 180, no. 64, l. 2; f) Žába 1974: no. 170 (fig. 292).*

early Middle Kingdom, in which the lower legs are differentiated from the upper legs, resulting in a figure that appears to sit upon a nonexistent chair (attested in both hieroglyphic and hieratic forms; see fig. 9).[54] A comparison of the bottom of the soldier sign in the Hekanakht letters[55] with the legs of the hieratic sign for the child in Turin N. 54003[56] shows that the hieratic zigzag of the legs indeed represents this peculiarity of the legs and feet (fig. 10). This form of the child sign survives sporadically thereafter in hieratic (fig. 10: d),[57] but is not as common as earlier.[58] The zigzag differentiation of the upper and lower legs in the signs discussed here recalls the representation of the legs, forward placed, in the *šps*-sign (Gardiner A50 /A51 ; fig. 11). These orthographic peculiarities suggest an origin for the script during the Middle Kingdom.[59]

In the Serabit material the exultant man at times appears to be seated on an invisible chair (e.g., Sinai 345, 353, 374). Other versions of the sign appear to show the man as standing (Sinai 350, 354, 379), as we might expect from the standard

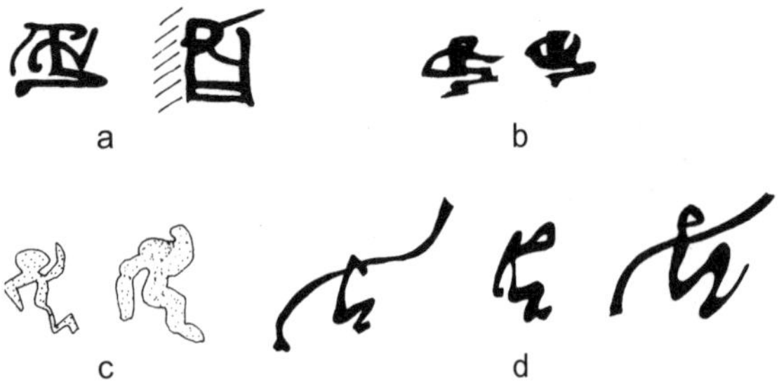

Fig. 10. *Comparison of soldier and seated child (A17). a) James 1962: IX/1 and XVI/1; b) Roccati 1970: 47; c) Edel 1980: nos. 199 and 588; d) Marciniak 1974: 180, 9,5; 3,16; 67,2.*

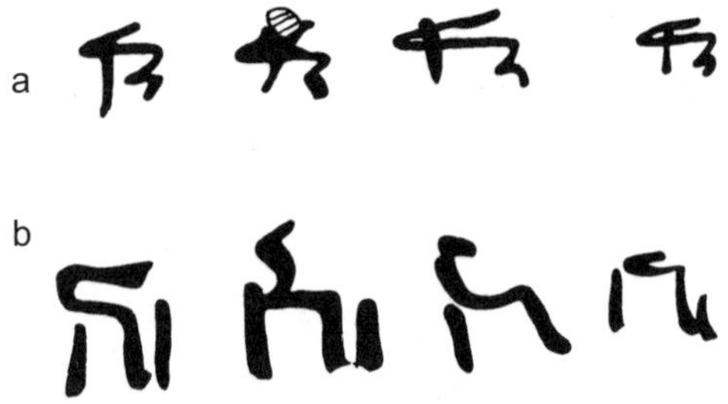

Fig. 11. *Seated noble (A51). a) Simpson 1965: 49; b) Edel 1980: pls. 3–8 (select examples).*

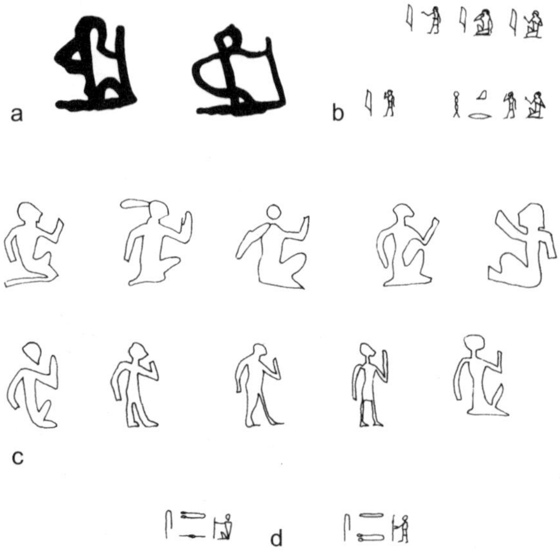

Fig. 12. *Interchange of standing and seated signs in Middle Kingdom hieratic and hieroglyphic texts. a) Standing official (A21) written as seated man holding staff (Žába 1974: no. 56, l. 5, figs. 110–11; no. 126, fig. 234); b) Seated man with hand to mouth (A2) written as standing man with hand to mouth (A84; Fischer 1968: 77, n. 325); c) Seated man with hand to mouth (A2) written as standing man with hand to mouth (A84; Fischer 1976: 153–54); d) Seated man grasping stick alternates with standing man grasping stick as determinative of sṯs (Fischer 1968: 77, n. 325).*

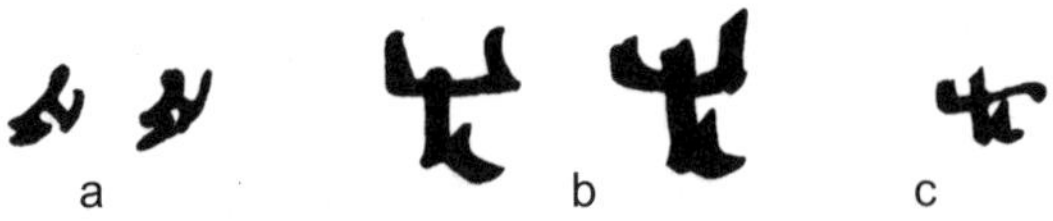

Fig. 13. *"Seated" appearance of standing signs in Old Kingdom hieratic (Posener-Kriéger and De Cenival 1968: paleography, pl. 1). a) Striking man (A24); b) Exultant man (A28); c) Dancing man (A32).*

hieroglyphic version of the exultant man (e.g., Gardiner A28). Rather than showing two signs, one derived from the standard standing, jubilant man, the other derived from the kneeling *ḥḥ*-figure (Gardiner C11), the versions of the man in the Serabit inscriptions preserve an interchange of standing and seated sign forms not uncommon for Middle Kingdom hieratic and hieroglyphic texts (figs. 12–13).[60]

Though the development of this sign into the *hê* of the linear alphabetic scripts is certain, the acrophone underlying the association between the pictograph and its alphabetic value remains obscure.[61]

1.8. *Serpent* = *nûn* (Ethiopic name: *naḥaš*). See discussion of 1.4 above.

1.9. *Corner* = *pê*. Of the two corner signs attested in these inscriptions (1.9, 2.9), the example in the horizontal inscription is more angular. This sign (Gardiner O38) appears rather late in Archaic hieroglyphic texts with the value *qnb.t* "corner."[62] The appearance of the sign in the Wadi el-Ḥôl inscriptions is similar to what one would expect for a derivation from hieratic[63]—closed and rounded to one end (see fig. 14).[64]

The corner sign appears a half-dozen times at Serabit, where its alphabetic value (*pê*) and underlying reconstructed acrophone (*pi*ʾ*t* "corner") were recognized as early as 1931 by Sprengling and was eventually accepted by Albright.[65] While Sass remains skeptical, writing that the *pê* is "still not definitely identified" and that "there is scarcely a

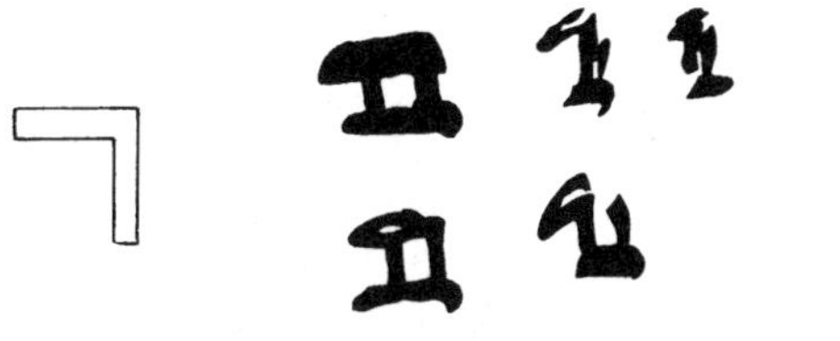

Fig. 14. *Corner sign (O38; Möller 1927a: 45, no. 478).*

single certain example of *pê*,"[66] all of the possible examples cited in his chart clearly appear in the photographs (Sinai 353, 355, 357, 375). Although the decipherment of the sign is not certain in all contexts, the signs themselves and their Egyptian prototype are unambiguous, and the two additional exemplars from the Wadi el-Ḥôl should lay to rest the debate over the pictographic origin of the linear alphabetic *pê*.[67]

1.10. *Water* = *mêm*. The second water sign is less well executed than the first (1.5), with three clear angles (cf. Sinai 365a). The clumsier carving results from the rougher surface and the encroaching rock face to the left (for other details, see the discussion of 1.5 above).[68]

1.11. *Seated man with one arm lowered and one arm raised* = *hê* (?). This sign is executed at a somewhat smaller scale than the surrounding signs. Like the preceding water sign and all succeeding signs, its execution is generally hampered by the rough surface of the stone and the encroaching wall face. The sign portrays a human figure, like 1.7, but rather than having both arms raised to either side, this sign shows a man with one arm raised in front and the other lowered behind (pl. VI.3). The vertical inscription has a similar—though better incised—figure (2.5). The exaggerated angle of the forward arm and the clearly-carved hand in the vertical inscription's exemplar suggest that this sign more specifically represents the Egyptian seated man with hand to mouth (Gardiner A2), although it could also conceivably derive from the sign of the seated child (fig. 10:c).[69] The sign itself faces left, as the upraised arm—always on the side in which the figure is facing in the Egyptian models—most conspicuously demonstrates; the leftward slant of the final zigzag and the perceptible attempt to show the face of the figure in left profile in the vertical inscription also suggests that the sign faces left. No similarly portrayed figures are found at Serabit or in other early alphabetic inscriptions.[70]

The difference in arm gesture between 1.11 and 2.5 (one arm raised and one lowered), on the one hand, and 1.7 (both arms raised), on the other, raises the question of whether the two different seated figure signs—definitely deriving from distinct Egyptian models—should have two distinct alphabetic values, or whether they are biforms with a common alphabetic value (presumably *hê*). A third possibility may also be considered, namely, that the writing in these earliest of alphabetic texts in fact may not be wholly alphabetic but may also employ signs similar to determinatives in Egyptian. Without a conclusive decipherment of these inscriptions, however, the question must remain open.

1.12. *Ox head* = *ʾālep*. This is one of those signs whose alphabetic development is well known.[71] The sign portrays an ox head in profile facing left; given the amount of detail—eye, line for mouth, and horns—the sign as portrayed probably derives from the similarly richly detailed hieroglyphic form of the sign (Gardiner F1). Indeed, its nose is especially reminiscent of earlier forms of this sign.[72] Another ox head occurs in the vertical inscription (2.11), having the same basic features, including the pointed nose, which, if anything, is more explicit. The stance of the sign gives the impression that the head rests on a diagonal axis.[73] Both ox heads face in the direction of writing, right to left. The Serabit forms of the ox head are more schematized in two respects: they typically have no mouth or eye. Only Sinai 345, 376, and 377 have dots for an eye, and they are still far more schematized than the "square" eyes of the Wadi el-Ḥôl inscriptions. Sinai 377 has by far the most complex form in comparison to the rest of the Serabit ox heads, exhibiting long horns, an ear, indented jaw, and eye.

1.13. *Sun* = *šin* (?). This sign has a circular shape, slightly flattened at the top, with a vertical line running just to the right of center (pl. VI.4); later alphabetic scripts provide no clear parallel for

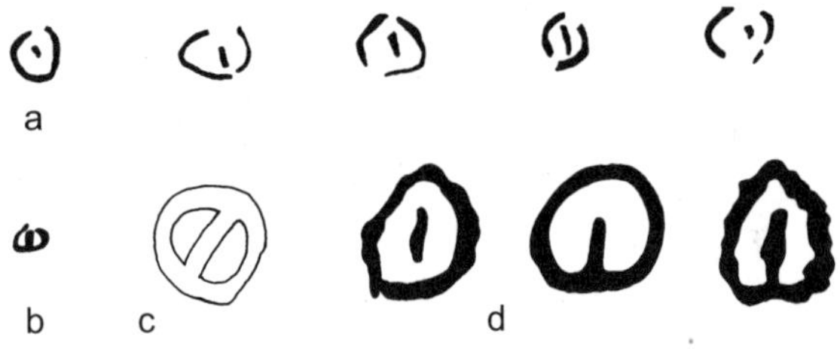

Fig. 15. Sun disk (N5). a) Verner 1992: LXV; b) James 1962: 7 (I/14); c) Arnold et al. 1990: 88, W59; d) Žába 1974: palaeography (N5), nos. 105–106, 103.

such a sign, and the lack of an obvious successor in the developed alphabetic scripts suggests that the sign in the Wadi el-Ḥôl inscription may represent a biform that ultimately did not evolve. Without additional exemplars, the shape of the sign provides the best clue to its potential range of alphabetic values, which could derive from several possible Egyptian models. At first glance, this sign suggests a rather naturalistic rendition of the vulva (listed by Gardiner under the substitutes N41 and N42). However, that sign consistently has a horizontal top in Egyptian writing;[74] even in very abbreviated hieratic versions, apparently made with a continuous stroke of the pen, the sign of the vulva is horizontal at top.[75] Another possible origin for the sign 1.13 is the hieratic form of the city sign (Gardiner O49)[76]—a circular circumvallation with a cross-street within—which can sometimes appear as a circle with only a single interior line.[77] However, from an Egyptian perspective the sign is most likely a version of the sun disk (Gardiner N5), the internal dot not infrequently appearing as a vertical line (fig. 15), as here.[78] If the circle-shaped sign in the Wadi el-Ḥôl alphabetic inscription indeed derives from the Egyptian sun disk, the sign may perhaps represent the Semitic phoneme *šin*, with **šamšu* or the like as the appropriate acrophone.

A sign for *šin* otherwise occurs once at Serabit (Sinai 357). Albright identified the leftmost horizontal sign in Sinai 357 as a *šin*,[79] his reasoning being that such a value for the sign fits his decipherment, and the sign in question was one of the few remaining unidentified signs. Albright may well have been correct, although his reasoning is suspect. The sign in Sinai 357 is more likely a version of the Egyptian *ḫʿ*-sign (Gardiner N28), a depiction of the rays of the sun rising over the hill; the two angling vertical strokes in Sinai 357 are presumably a representation of the sun's rays.[80] The sign in the Wadi el-Ḥôl horizontal inscription (1.13) then may reflect an alternative sun sign, yet another biform.[81]

If one looks to the developed alphabetic traditions, two further possibilities for the identity of the sign in 1.13 suggest themselves: either an abbreviated form of the *ṭêt* sign, which Hamilton derives from the Egyptian "city" sign (Gardiner O49),[82] or the precursor to the sign that comes to represent *wāw* in the South Semitic traditions. As with the former suggestions, one cannot propose either of these possibilities with full confidence.

1.14. *Water = mêm*. This is the third water sign in the horizontal inscription. It has seven angles and possibly nine strokes (for other details, see the discussion of 1.5 above).

1.15. *Twisted flax = ḫa* (Ethiopic name: *ḫarm*). The twisted flax sign appears as the penultimate sign in the horizontal inscription. Although poorly incised, its three twisted and intertwined loops are clear (see pl. VI.5). The hieroglyphic sign (Gardiner V28) is often the model for this sign in Nubian rock inscriptions, "even in inscriptions where hieratic forms predominate."[83] With the exception of Sinai 376, all the twisted flax signs at Serabit have only a double twist. No obvious continuation of this sign appears in the linear scripts (though compare the strikingly similar alphabetic cuneiform representation of *ḫ* at Ugarit).

The generally accepted alphabetic value for this sign, *ḫ* (as opposed to its use in Egyptian to represent *ḥ*), is deduced from the name of the sign preserved in Ethiopic (*ḫarm*, "loops of rope, netting").[84] Albright read *ʾrḫt*, "wild cow," at Serabit (Sinai 353, 365b, 375), lending his substantial authority to this construal.[85]

1.16. *Head = rêš*. The last sign in the horizontal inscription is another head sign, similar in execution to the first sign in the inscription, though more faintly inscribed because of the difficulty in accessing the rock face (for details, see discussion of 1.1 above).

Fig. 16. Wadi el-Ḥôl Alphabetic Inscription 2; the Vertical Inscription. a) facsimile of the base of the incised lines; b) facsimile of the outer edges of the incised lines.

The Vertical Inscription (Wadi el-Ḥôl Early Alphabetic Inscription 2)

The second alphabetic inscription at the Wadi el-Ḥôl—measuring 11 cm in length—has a vertical orientation, slanting towards the left on a slight diagonal towards the bottom, consistent with a right-to-left orientation (pl. VII–VIII; fig. 16). The twelve signs of this inscription are on the whole executed on a somewhat smaller scale than those in the horizontal inscription. The surface of the rock face is fairly smooth, especially in the middle of the inscription; a number of extraneous lines are present, but none are associated directly with the early alphabetic inscription. The signs appear to face both left (ox head, 2.11; seated man, 2.5) and right (eye, 2.6), and are written one after another in a vertical line; as with the horizontal inscription there is no stacking of signs in quadrants.

To the left of the vertical inscription is an *ʿnḫ*-sign, the hieroglyphic representation of "life," apparently carved at the same time as the vertical inscription. As with the early alphabetic inscriptions, the "scribe" who carved the *ʿnḫ*-sign worked from right to left: the horizontal arms are a separate element, made with one continuous line, beginning in the upper right with a line descending to the lower left, angling up to form the left side, crossing to the lower right, and then angling up to end just below and to the left of where the line began. The bottom vertical apparently began at the upper right, went down to the bottom, and angled to the left; the left side of the bottom vertical was then made as a separate element. The upper loop is a continuous curve, joining the tops of the sides of the lower vertical element. The element is not common in the Egyptian texts from the Wadi el-Ḥôl, but a large ʿnḫ-sign featuring prominently in a possible memorial inscription does have Middle Kingdom Egyptian parallels.[86]

Paleographic Observations

2.1. *Water* = *mêm*. The first sign in the vertical inscription is a water sign, deeply incised like the first water sign in the horizontal inscription; yet the water sign in the vertical inscription is oriented horizontally and is more uniformly formed than the water signs in the horizontal inscription. Because the surface of the rock is rough here, the writer made almost every stroke individually; nevertheless, the form is well executed, consisting of four more or less uniform crests and troughs—nine slanting strokes in all (for other details, see the discussion of 1.5 above).

2.2. *Hobble* = *ṯa* (?). The second and tenth signs down in the vertical inscription (pl. IX.1) derive from the Egyptian hobble-*ṯ* sign (Gardiner V13); both exhibit an odd vertical orientation (see discussion of 1.5 above).The sign itself is clear and unambiguous, although shortened from its normal length in Egyptian texts.[87] Its occurrence twice in the Wadi el-Ḥôl inscriptions indicates that the sign is deliberately and consistently made, but short of a completely compelling decipherment of these inscriptions, any alphabetic value assigned to this sign will remain hypothetical. One may propose that the hobble sign represents the Semitic voiceless interdental fricative, the phoneme *ṯ*, based principally on the sign's strong resemblance to the *ṯ* in the South Semitic scripts.[88] If this equation is correct, the sign in Wadi el-Ḥôl early alphabetic inscription 2.2 and 2.10 would lend further support to Cross' contention that the Proto-Arabic script tradition branched off from the alphabetic traditions relatively early,[89] suggesting that the South Semitic *ṯ* sign was not secondarily derived, as is usually assumed.[90] The hobble sign may well be evidence of yet another pair of biforms in the early alphabetic traditions, since the symbol for the composite bow, which eventually evolves into the sign for *šin* in the later linear scripts, presumably represents the phoneme *ṯ* at Serabit.[91]

2.3. *Mark* = *tāw*. The mark sign (a simple cross) occurs again as the eighth sign in the vertical inscription.

2.4. *Head* = *rêš*. This head sign, though deeply incised and similar in general appearance to the head signs in the horizontal inscription, appears squat and compressed, almost as if it were smashed together, probably the result of the coarseness of the rock surface here. In appearance the sign (2.4) is most similar to the second of the two head signs (1.16) in the horizontal inscription (for other details, see discussion of 1.11 above).

2.5. *Seated man with one arm lowered and one arm raised* = *hê* (?). This is the better carved of the two figures representing a seated man with hand to mouth—indeed the hand itself is clearly represented in this version (see pl. VI.2; for details, see discussion of 1.11 above.)

2.6. *Eye* = *ʿayin*. This detailed eye sign is unique to the Wadi el-Ḥôl alphabetic inscriptions; while it appears to face to the right, the canthus is much longer and the back corner much less elongated than we expect from hieroglyphic writing (Gardiner D4). This emphasized canthus suggests ultimately a derivation of the outline of the sign from hieratic (fig. 17:a, e);[92] the emphasis on the inner canthus in hieratic and on the outer canthus in hieroglyphic script probably contributes to reversals of the eye in some rock inscriptions (fig. 17:b–d).[93] Most of the Serabit forms show evidence of more schematization: most are without a pupil, some have a dot (Sinai 345, 353, 354, 375), and two examples, Sinai 352 and 358, may have circular pupils—or at least pupils that are more than a dot. In Sinai 345 and once in 346 the eye sign is oriented vertically.

2.7. *Mace (?) / tent pole (?)* = *wāw*. The sign is traditionally derived from the Egyptian *ḥḏ*-sign (Gardiner T3), a mace with a pear-shaped head.[94] However, the "handle" of the early alphabetic sign is not oriented vertically, as in Egyptian script, but slants downward to the right with the "mace head" attached at the bottom; the horizontal[95] or only slightly slanted mace (Gardiner T2) appears

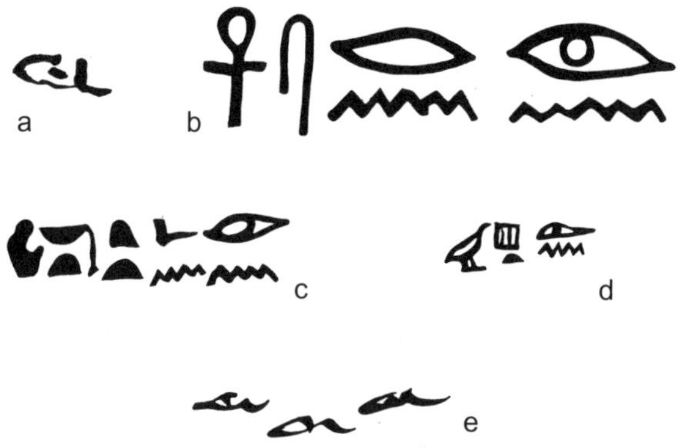

Fig. 17. *Eye sign (D4). a) Edel 1990: pl. 10, no. 583 (126); b) Hintze and Reineke 1989b: 171, no. 449; c) Hintze and Reineke 1989b: 139, no. 392; d) Hintze and Reineke 1989b: 158, no. 426; e) Möller 1927a: 7, no. 82 (Prisse, Illahun, and Sinuhe examples).*

only rarely elsewhere in Egyptian (fig. 18),[96] but is attested in early alphabetic inscriptions at Serabit (Sinai 351) and in the Gezer Sherd (though the slight opening of the head is a later paleographic feature).

However, considering the odd appearance of the sign in the early alphabetic inscriptions, and the vertical and horizontal orientations thereof, an origin of the *wāw* in the Egyptian sign representing a tent pole (Gardiner O29 ; phonetically *ʿ3*; see fig. 19) is perhaps more likely. Unlike the mace, the tent pole can routinely appear with either a horizontal or vertical orientation in normal hieroglyphic script; additionally, the tent pole would have been a common sight to Asiatic mercenaries in Egypt (such as those *ʿ3m.w* attested at the Wadi el-Ḥôl—see below), more common presumably than the mace, a predominantly ceremonial weapon of the royal regalia. Although the hieratic tent pole is usually a horizontal line with short crossing stroke,[97] lapidary hieratic versions of the sign can have a shape similar to that of the mace.[98]

2.8. *Mark* = *tāw*. See discussion of 2.3 above.

2.9. *Corner* = *pê*. This corner sign is more rounded than the one in the horizontal inscription (1.9) in two places: 1) at the inner joint connecting the leftmost horizontal and vertical strokes and 2) at the top of the leftmost vertical stroke as it bends to form the short top horizontal stroke. For other details, see discussion of 1.9 above.

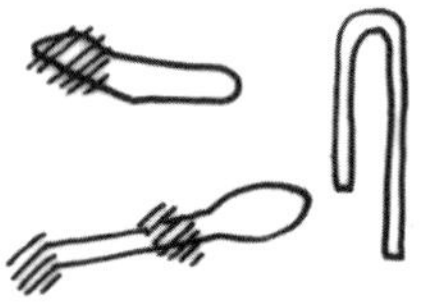

Fig. 18. *Slanting mace (T3); Gardiner et al. 1952, pl. 6.*

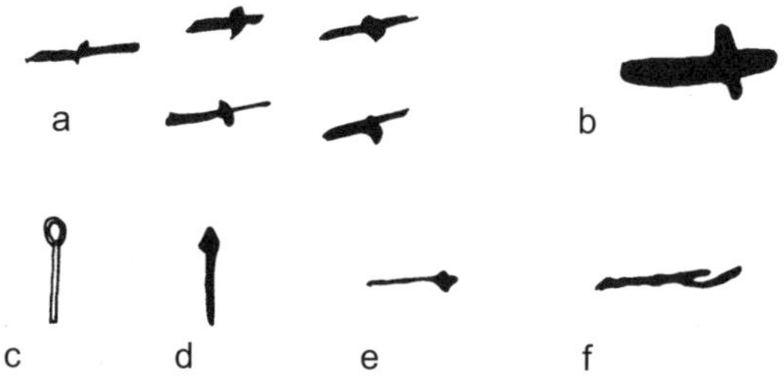

Fig. 19. *Tent pole sign or (O29). a) Möller 1927a: 34, no. 363 (Prisse, Illahun, and Sinuhe examples); b) Žába 1974: no. 148, l. 3; c) J. C. Darnell 2002a: no. 21, l. 1; d) Hintze and Reineke 1989b: 160, no. 429, l. 1; e) Hintze and Reineke 1989b: 219, no. 524, l. 3; f) Žába 1974: no. 158.*

2.10. *Hobble* = *ṯa* (?). See discussion of 2.2 above.

2.11. *Ox head* = *ʿālep*. This ox head generally resembles the one in the horizontal inscription (for details, see discussion of 1.12 above). As in 1.12, the middle portion of the forward (left) horn is slightly straight, as opposed to the uniform curve of the rear (right) horn.

2.12. *Coil of rope* = *lāmed*. Unlike the coil of rope in the horizontal inscription (1.3), here the "head" of the coil is at the bottom and on the left, with the tail moving upwards (for details, see discussion of 1.3 above).

DECIPHERMENT AND ALPHABETIC QUALITY

No definite and compelling decipherment of these two inscriptions can yet be offered. As with any similarly brief, archaic, and highly opaque inscription, multiple and various readings can be forced, should one make sufficient effort.[99] Aside from *rb* / *rab* / "chief" at the beginning of the horizontal inscription and perhaps *ʾl* / *ʾil(u)* / "god, El" (either as independent noun or as theophoric element in a name) in the vertical inscription, no other sequence of signs is transparently decipherable; and thus our reluctance to speculate more specifically on possible decipherments at this time. In a more positive vein, the inscriptions themselves are complete and their alphabetic character—the lack of an obvious decipherment notwithstanding—is patent. First, these inscriptions are not legible Egyptian of any sort, normal or cryptographic. Second, they employ a radically abbreviated number of graphemes, the *sine qua non* of alphabetic writing. Third, most of the signs bear a very close resemblance to—or exhibit clear continuity with—the various signs in the emergent alphabetic tradition as it appears at Serabit, the handful of early alphabetic inscriptions from Palestine, and the later linear (non-pictographic) alphabetic script traditions. The ox head (ʾ), jubilant man (*h*), eye (ʿ), coil of rope (*l*), head (*r*), house (*b*), serpent (*n*), water (*m*), corner (*p*), twisted flax (*ḥ*), tent pole (*w*), and mark (*t*) signs are recognizable and continuous with their pictographic and/or linear counterparts. Fourth, the acrophones that one may reconstruct for these signs are broadly consistent with those known from later alphabetic traditions.[100]

DATING THE INSCRIPTIONS

Dating rock inscriptions of the kind found at the Wadi el-Ḥôl can be a tricky matter, and no single paleographic feature or aspect of carving associated with these inscriptions incontrovertibly certifies their date. However, a number of features, when considered together, point strongly and consistently (if not indisputably) to a general Middle Kingdom milieu for our inscriptions. First, as noted above, although earlier and later inscriptions and depictions occur in the Wadi el-Ḥôl, the bulk of the texts, and certainly the more elaborate ones, are of late Middle Kingdom and Second Intermediate Period date. The prominent location of the alphabetic inscriptions and the superior quality of the rock surfaces on which they were carved are consistent with an earlier rather than later carving date during this general period—otherwise these surfaces would probably have been filled with other inscriptions before some of the less desirable areas near them.

Second, and most substantially, the emerging paleographic profile of the script (as detailed above) points to a Middle Kingdom date for these inscriptions. Since Gardiner, scholars have generally appreciated (although to greater and lesser degrees) the informing influence the various Egyptian paleographies and orthographic traditions played on the graphic shapes of the individual signs in the emerging alphabetic script tradition. What is most striking about the alphabetic texts from the Wadi el-Ḥôl is how so many of the signs appear to reflect features and peculiarities best known from the paleographic, orthographic, and lapidary hieratic traditions of the early Middle Kingdom.[101] So, for example, several of the signs—the water (*m*), serpent (*n*), and hobble (*ṯ*) signs—that normally appear in a horizontal position are shown standing on end (vertical orientation). This practice, never common in Egyptian, does appear in a number of early Middle Kingdom inscriptions (see discussions of 1.5 and 2.2 above). Moreover, as observed above, the two Wadi el-Ḥôl early alphabetic inscriptions evidence a mixture of pictographic forms that appear to be derived both from hieroglyphic and hieratic prototypes. The forms that most clearly reflect hieroglyphic prototypes include the ox head, twisted flax, coil of rope, and water signs, while the signs modeled on hieratic forms include the serpent, seated man, corner, head, eye, mark, and sun(?) signs. The courtyard house sign potentially has good hieroglyphic and hieratic prototypes.[102] Such a mixture of forms with hieratic and hieroglyphic inspirations is most characteristic of Middle Kingdom lapidary hieratic—where the choice between using hieratic or hieroglyphic signs depends primarily on the ease of execution and recognition of a particular sign[103]—and hence is a significant feature for dating these inscriptions.[104] Lastly, there are other features peculiar to sign forms of the early Middle Kingdom as well. These would include, for example, the "zigzag" representation of the legs and feet of the seated figures (1.7, 11; 2.5), which finds its closest parallels in early Middle

Kingdom hieratic and hieroglyphic texts, and the apparent confusion of sitting and standing figures—the origin behind the seated "exultant" man in Serabit early alphabetic texts, also more common in the early Middle Kingdom than any other period. In sum, whether the individual signs in these inscriptions reflect hieratic or hieroglyphic prototypes, their paleographic peculiarities point solidly towards an early Middle Kingdom date for the time when the signs departed from the stream of Egyptian paleographic development.

A final consideration that argues for placing these inscriptions in a broadly Middle Kingdom milieu is the rise in contact between Egyptians and Asiatics that begins during the early part of this period, with much of this interaction taking place in the Nile Valley itself.[105] Some of this interaction between Egyptians and Western Asiatics occurred at the Wadi el-Ḥôl itself, as two late Middle Kingdom hieratic inscriptions at the site reveal. A large body of evidence attests to a significant Asiatic presence in Egypt during the Middle Kingdom. If the Prophecy of Neferti reflects the social conditions of the time it purports to predict, Western Asiatics infiltrated the Egyptian Delta during the First Intermediate Period.[106] During the nascent Middle Kingdom a number of texts refer to combat with Asiatics, and scenes of late First Intermediate Period/early Middle Kingdom date depict Egyptian and Nubian troops assaulting strongholds manned by Asiatics.[107] The Nubian warrior Tjehemau, in rock inscriptions south of the First Cataract at Abisko,[108] recounts his enlistment in the army of Monthuhotep II and subsequent war—perhaps during the reign of Monthuhotep II or that of Amenemhat I—against the Asiatics of the obscure locale Djati. An inscription of the early 12th Dynasty at Hatnub mentions roving bands of Egyptians, Nubians, and Asiatics menacing urban life at the beginning of the Middle Kingdom.[109]

Apparently during the reign of Amenemhat I at the beginning of the 12th Dynasty, the mercenaries—including Asiatics—who swelled the ranks of Egyptian armies during the First Intermediate Period and the 11th Dynasty became a serious threat to Egypt's stability. Asiatics continued to enter Egypt and Egyptian military service in significant numbers through the Middle Kingdom, some as prisoners of war.[110] During the early Middle Kingdom, Asiatic workers and their families also appear—at least occasionally—to have entered Egypt.[111] According to the famous story of Sinuhe, early during the reign of Sesostris I, at a time when many Asiatics had already entered Egypt in order to become in some way part of the pharaonic realm, some Egyptians—most perhaps criminals and *personae non gratae*—had fled Egypt into Syria-Palestine. Sinuhe's host Amuneshi assures the fugitive that he will hear the Egyptian language spoken in the Asiatics' domain (Sinuhe B 31–32), and a number of Egyptians, who vouch for Sinuhe, were already living in the Asiatics' tribal domain (B 33–34).[112]

That this Asiatic presence extended to the desert roads crossing the Qena Bend is apparent from two late Middle Kingdom hieratic inscriptions discovered at the Wadi el-Ḥôl. Near the main inscription sites in the Wadi el-Ḥôl is a small concentration of hieratic inscriptions, paleographically and onomastically of late Middle Kingdom (probably late 12th Dynasty) date (see figs. 20–21; pl. IX.3). Two of the texts in this concentration have a bearing on the presence of Asiatics in the Wadi el-Ḥôl, and appear to have been executed at roughly the same time.[113] The first and most important of the inscriptions is written within the depiction of a ship's sail and mast—apparently an allusion to the cool north wind. Although the inscriptions consist primarily of lists of names and titles, the first four lines of the first of these inscriptions are of great significance for the proper dating of the early alphabetic inscriptions in the Wadi el-Ḥôl, and for the correct understanding of the milieu in which the alphabet was born. These inscriptions are carved into a darkly patinated area of limestone, its surface marred by many closely spaced cracks. Although this now complicates the task of differentiating carved lines from cracks, when first carved the bright, white lines of the freshly scratched limestone would have contrasted markedly with the dark background. Fortunately, the lines of the first few columns of text in the second inscription are of sufficient width to make them stand out clearly from any interference due to natural blemishes in the stone.

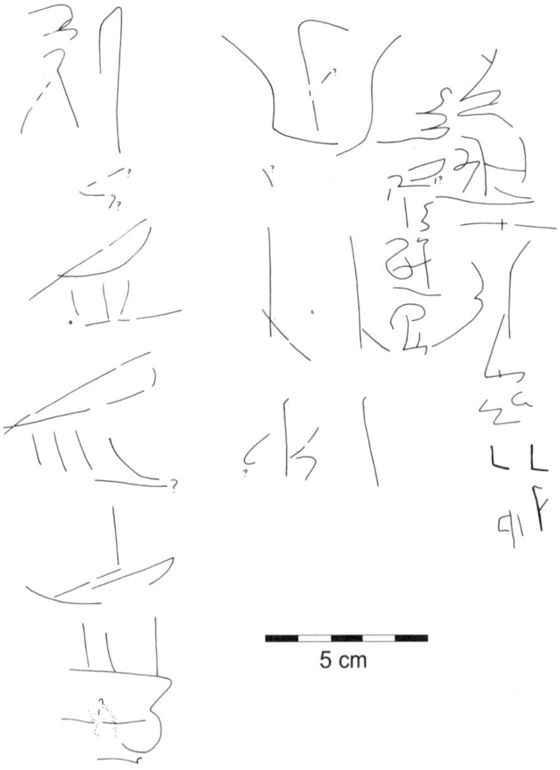

Fig. 20. Inscription of Bebi from the Wadi el-Ḥôl.

Fig. 21. Transcription of the Inscription of Bebi.

The first inscription consists of eleven vertical columns of text of differing lengths, carved within the irregular depiction of a ship's mast and unfurled sail. Of immediate importance for understanding the early alphabetic inscription of the Wadi el-Ḥôl are the first four lines of the text (for a treatment of the entire inscription, related texts, and text notes, see the Appendix, below):

[1] *ỉmy-rꜣ mšʿ n(y) ʿꜣm.w Bbi*

[2] *sꜣ.t=f Mʿꜣ.t-ḥr-ʿnḫ-n=ỉ*

[3] *wpw.ty-nsw.t Bbi*

[4] *sinw Ḥr-nb-ḫꜣst-m-sꜣ=f…*

[1] The general of the Asiatics, Bebi;

[2] his daughter Maatherankheni;

[3] the royal messenger Bebi;

[4] the express courier Hornebkhasutemsaf …

The first of the names in the inscription within the sail is that of the "general of the (Semitic speaking) Asiatics, Bebi" (*ỉmy-rꜣ mšʿ n(y) ʿꜣm.w Bbi*). The ancient Egyptians appear to have employed the term *ʿꜣm.w* as a general designation in Egyptian for Semitic speaking groups,[114] and elements of the *ʿꜣm.w* inhabited not only much of Southwestern Asia proper, but also roamed the northern portions of the Eastern Desert.[115] Some *ʿꜣm.w* also appear to have found their way much deeper into the pharaonic realm, even south thereof, originally perhaps as mercenaries,[116] later as household servants as well.[117] Bebi's title thus indicates that Western Asiatics constituted an important contingent under Bebi's charge; since Bebi writes the seated man and woman over plural strokes as the determinatives of *ʿꜣm.w*, "Asiatics," the group probably included soldiers and their families. Egyptian military units such as Bebi's group also included scribes,[118] and a "scribe of Asiatics" in fact appears in a Middle Kingdom papyrus.[119] This was probably neither an Asiatic scribe, nor an Egyptian writing an alphabetic script, but an Egyptian military scribe whose company consisted of Asiatic conscripts. Settlements of Asiatic troops appear to have existed near the Middle Kingdom

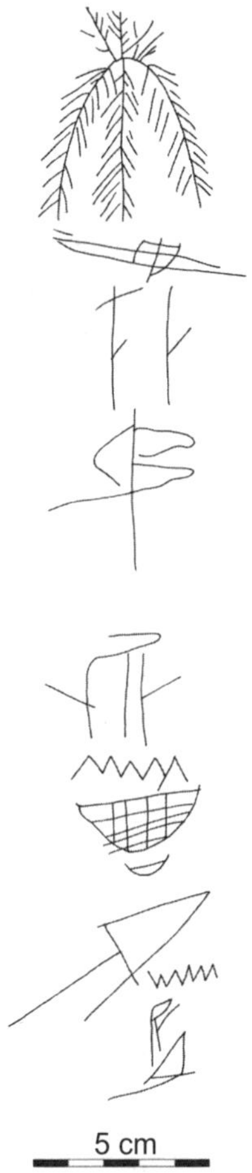

Fig. 22. *Inscription mentioning "Nebet-Kepenet" from the Wadi el-Ḥôl.*

Residence,[120] and the "scribe of the Asiatics" may have been attached to such a group. Such a man would know lapidary hieratic, and would have had occasion to write the names of the Asiatics in his unit. One should not, however, rule out the possibility that by the end of the Middle Kingdom Semitic language speakers, thoroughly Egyptianized, may have joined in further developing and even codifying a perhaps already nascent alphabetic script.[121]

The same inscription mentions various kinds of messengers, including a *wpwty-nswt*, "royal messenger," and others, such as *sin.w* "express couriers," may suggest that Bebi's group included a late Middle Kingdom courier service of sorts—mounted couriers travelled the Farshût Road in later periods.[122] The Asiatics associated with General Bebi and the couriers were perhaps soldiers with their families, assisting the Egyptian desert police, perhaps maintaining water depots, preparing food and shelter for the couriers and other patrols. The Asiatics who appear in inscriptions from Sinai are mostly of late 12th Dynasty date, and the relatively small numbers of these people suggest that they were a specialized group working for the Egyptians, rather than menial laborers or "slaves."[123] The Asiatics in the Egyptian scenes and inscriptions at Serabit el-Khadim often appear armed, and were apparently trusted members of the expeditions, perhaps even well integrated into Egyptian society.[124]

Associated with the Bebi inscription are several other hieratic texts of late Middle Kingdom date, including one that places Bebi and his associates in the reign of Amenemhat III (for translation and commentary to these inscriptions, see the Appendix, below). The names of the men who accompanied Bebi appear immediately above two inscriptions recording the name of the priest Kheperkare. This same priest wrote yet another inscription in Section B in the Wadi el-Ḥôl dated to year 26 of the reign of Amenemhat III during the late 12th Dynasty. The appearance of men with the same names and titles in this series of inscriptions, the last of which contains a regnal date, suggests that the General of the Asiatics, Bebi, and the men who most likely carved the early alphabetic inscriptions all visited the Wadi el-Ḥôl during the reign of Amenemhat III.

Another hieratic Egyptian inscription, just to the right of that of general Bebi and the like-named royal courier, mentions someone who may in some way be related to the Asiatics under Bebi's control: *Msy ms.n Nb.t-Kpn.t* "Mesy, born of Nebet-Kepenet" (fig. 22, a portion of a larger inscription). The name of Mesy's mother is Egyptian,[125] even though it alludes to the East Mediterranean port of Byblos, and there is no reason to assume that she herself was of Byblian origin.[126] The name, nevertheless, reveals an awareness of Byblos, and apparently some devotion to the goddess Hathor as Baalat-Gebel.[127] Paleographically the Nebet-Kepenet inscription is of late Middle Kingdom date as well.[128]

In sum, then, both internal and external evidence suggests a Middle Kingdom milieu for the

Wadi el-Ḥôl early alphabetic inscriptions. The external evidence—the hieratic inscriptions mentioning Bebi and "Mesy, born of Nebet-Kepenet," and the most prominent chronological grouping of texts preserved at the Wadi el-Ḥôl—isolates the late Middle Kingdom period as the likeliest time of actual inscription (late 12th to early 13th Dynasty, ca. 1850–1700 B.C.E.). The occurrence of the name of Kheperkare in association with the Bebi inscription suggests most probably a date late in the reign of Amenemhat III (ca. 1853–1809 B.C.E.). The Wadi el-Ḥôl early alphabetic inscriptions may themselves be the products of the people of Bebi, official visitors to the site during the late Middle Kingdom, most likely during the reign of Amenemhat III. At the time of the late Middle Kingdom, the Egyptians apparently employed the Asiatics to manage a mobile settlement in a desert environment—the Semitic language speakers were not slaves, but rather desert experts, working for the Egyptians. They would have learned what they knew of Egyptian writing not in schools attached to the temples, but from military scribes.[129] In such a scenario, the prominent influence of lapidary hieratic on the shape and execution of these early alphabetic inscriptions becomes most intelligible. The internal evidence—the specific paleographic models used for certain signs, the mixture of both hieratic and hieroglyphic models, and the vertical orientation of otherwise predominantly horizontally oriented signs—indicates the early Middle Kingdom as the probable period of alphabetic origins—or at least this is the probable time when the Egyptian hieratic peculiarities became fossilized in many of the signs in these inscriptions (early to mid-12th Dynasty, ca. 1900 B.C.E.).

CONCLUSION

The importance of these two short inscriptions for understanding the origins of alphabetic writing cannot be overstated. First, we may now, more confidently than at any time in the past century, push the origins of alphabetic writing back to the beginning of the second millennium, with the carving of the Wadi el-Ḥôl early alphabetic inscriptions dating more specifically to the latter part of the Middle Kingdom. The paleographic models from which the Wadi el-Ḥôl early alphabetic signs derive suggest an ultimate origin of early alphabetic script during the first half of the second millennium B.C.E. The late Middle Kingdom date for the time of the carving of the Wadi el-Ḥôl early alphabetic inscriptions is consistent with Gardiner's original dating of the Serabit alphabetic texts,[130] is supported most recently by Sass,[131] and goes beyond simply supporting Hamilton's thesis that the invention of the alphabet occurred during the late 12th Dynasty or early in the 13th Dynasty.[132] The Wadi el-Ḥôl alphabetic inscriptions provide paleographic evidence for the extraction of the alphabetic signs from the Egyptian paleographic tradition during the first half of the Middle Kingdom, although an alphabetic inscription from this nascent stage remains to be discovered. The Wadi el-Ḥôl texts, then, would be among the earliest (if not the earliest) specimen of alphabetic writing discovered to date.

Second, the likelihood that alphabetic writing began geographically in Egypt is now, in light of the Wadi el-Ḥôl texts, a thesis that deserves serious attention by scholars.[133] Previously, scholars have thought largely in terms of Palestine and the Sinai—the only two well-recognized find spots for early alphabetic inscriptions until now—as the most likely geographical setting for the origins of alphabetic writing, despite a longstanding awareness that the inventors of alphabetic writing drew their inspiration (*viz.*, the example of the uniliteral [uniconsonantal] signs, the acrophonic principle, the graphic shapes of individual signs) from Egyptian. However, now with the recovery of alphabetic writing from the Egyptian Western Desert, the fairly high degree of literacy in Egyptian (knowledge of hieratic, and a hybrid of hieratic and hieroglyphic scripts as well) presumed by these texts,[134] and the well known Asiatic presence within Egypt proper from the early Dynastic periods onwards, strongly suggest that it is to Egypt itself that we must look for the geographical home of alphabetic writing. More specifically, the Bebi inscription and its immediate neighbors offer tantalizing clues about the context in which Semitic-speaking Asiatics adopted and adapted certain aspects of the Egyptian writing system for the needs of their own language(s). The Egyptian military, known both to have employed Asiatics (as the Bebi inscription so wonderfully attests) and to have included scribes, would provide one likely context in which Western Asiatic Semitic language speakers could have learned and eventually adapted the Egyptian writing system. Indeed, the prominence of lapidary hieratic, the form of hieratic utilized by army scribes, as models for alphabetic forms at the Wadi el-Ḥôl (and at Serabit) makes such a hypothesis all the more attractive. Of course, any speculation about the precise context in which alphabetic writing first emerged should not be pressed too hard, given the paucity of early alphabetic texts and the still highly impoverished state of these texts' decipherment. What one may perhaps state more positively is 1) that the interaction between Asiatic mercenaries and Egyptian military scribes that may have been members of the kind of Egyptian expeditionary forces known to be present in Qena Bend during the Middle Kingdom provides the likeliest understanding of the setting in which the Wadi el-Ḥôl early alphabetic inscriptions emerged; and 2) that alphabetic writing likely emerged initially in a plurality of cultural contexts.[135]

Hamilton writes that the major conclusion of his study, completed already in 1985 and based on the Serabit texts and the other early alphabetic inscriptions known at that time from Palestine, "is that some letter forms derive from hieroglyphic prototypes, while others stem from hieratic precursors."[136] If anything, the mixed character of Egyptian prototypes used for alphabetic forms is more pronounced in the two Wadi el-Ḥôl graffiti, and thus spectacularly confirms Hamilton's conclusions. It has always been the general assumption—at least since Gardiner—that alphabetic writing derived (almost) solely from hieroglyphic models.[137] Although several nineteenth- and early twentieth-century proposals suggest a derivation of the Semitic alphabet specifically from hieratic (e.g., W. R. Taylor, F. de Rougé),[138] a view more recently investigated by W. Helck[139] and championed by K.-Th. Zauzich,[140] the equations posited or the specific models used for comparison make these theories unpersuasive. And most crucially, none of those scholars, whether supporting hieroglyphic or hieratic precursors, recognized that only a mixture of both types of Egyptian writing can comprehensively and compellingly account for the range and complexity of attested alphabetic forms. The Wadi el-Ḥôl inscriptions, as two of the earliest alphabetic inscriptions, thus provide the crucial link that conclusively proves the derivation of early alphabetic signs from both hieratic and hieroglyphic Egyptian writing. That hieratic, and especially lapidary hieratic traditions utilized for the carving of rock inscriptions, should prove to be so influential on the writer(s) of these two early alphabetic texts in particular is not surprising. Hieratic was the first script an ancient Egyptian student would have learned,[141] and some form of the cursive script was the primary medium for the letters, administrative documents and legal accounts of pharaonic Egypt. Knowledge of hieroglyphic shapes, and the ability to properly interpret hieratic into hieroglyphic and vice versa, was the mark of a higher level of education.[142] Knowledge that the hieroglyphic forms were more suited to official commemorative purposes, and an understanding of their greater adaptability to lapidary purposes, as opposed to the hieratic forms intended for pen and ink, led to the development of a lapidary hieratic sign list, most clearly in evidence for the military and mining expeditions of the Middle Kingdom.[143]

Finally one may note that the Wadi el-Ḥôl early alphabetic inscriptions contribute considerably to a clearer understanding of certain individual alphabetic letter forms, since their paleography attests to earlier Egyptian models than that apparent for most of the Serabit inscriptions. For example, the horizontal inscription provides the earliest attestation of the form of the house sign—the courtyard house—that eventually evolves into the *bêt* of the later linear alphabetic scripts in the West. These inscriptions add to the list of alphabetic signs with known biforms—single forms known to have multiple or alternative Egyptian models,[144] most notably the new (courtyard) house sign and, possibly, the two seated man signs. They also attest to at least two previously unknown signs: possibly a hieratic informed form of the sun sign (perhaps representing a Semitic *š*) and the hobble sign (perhaps indicating a Semitic *ṯ*). Finally, these inscriptions add significantly to the list of alphabetic signs that are modeled on hieratic prototypes: the serpent, seated man, corner, head, eye, mark, and possibly sun (?) signs.[145]

In summary, even without a definitive decipherment, the contribution of the two early alphabetic inscriptions from the Wadi el-Ḥôl to our understanding of the origins of alphabetic writing is substantial. They suggest that Tjekerbaal, ruler of Byblos during the early 21st Dynasty in Egypt, knew whereof he spoke when he told the Egyptian envoy Wenamun:[146]

> "Now it was in order to reach the place where I am that craftsmanship went out therefrom (from Egypt),
> and it was in order to reach the place where I am that learning went out therefrom."

NOTES

1. See provisionally the overviews in Cappers and Sikking 2001; J. C. Darnell 2002a: 91.
2. Winkler 1938: 8; for a history of work at the site, see J. C. Darnell 2002a: 89–90.
3. For overviews of the work of the Theban Desert Road Survey, see most conveniently J. C. Darnell 2002b: 104–21; 2002c: 132–55; D. Darnell 2002: 156–77; Darnell and Darnell 1993; 1994; 1995; 1996.
4. The first group of these inscriptions is now published in J. C. Darnell 2002a: 89–162.
5. This corpus consists of the so-called "Proto-Sinaitic" inscriptions (early alphabetic writings recovered from the turquoise mines and temple complex of Serabit el-Khadim and the nearby wadis) and the handful of other early alphabetic inscriptions from Palestine. For convenient treatments of these materials (with extensive bibliographies and references to earlier discussions), see Hamilton 1985 and forthcoming; Sass 1988.
6. For a preliminary overview of the Wadi el-Ḥôl early alphabetic inscriptions, in part based on a draft of the present article, see J. C. Darnell 2003a (note also the color photographs of the early alphabetic inscriptions, and the large reproduction of the horizontal inscription—Wadi el-Ḥôl Early Alphabetic Inscription No. 1—as the frontispiece to that volume). Tropper (2003: 173–75), although with reproduction of rough copies prepared from photographs, also recognizes the significance and implications of the Wadi el-Ḥôl inscriptions for the origin of the alphabet.
7. Cf. the inscription of the woman Ipenut at the Wadi el-Ḥôl (no. 9; J. C. Darnell 2002a: 119) and the evidence for women on long-distance missions cited therein; for select evidence of female literacy in ancient Egypt, see Baines and Eyre 1983: 81–85; see also Capel and Markoe 1996: 142, 209–10.
8. J. C. Darnell 2002a: 8; Vandekerckhove and Müller-Wollermann 2001: 347–48.
9. J. C. Darnell 2002a: 95–101 (WHRI [Wadi el-Ḥôl Rock Inscription] no. 4), and 107–19 (WHRI no. 8).
10. Cf. the inscriptions relating to divine offerings and grain accounting (J. C. Darnell 2002a: 92, 154–55).
11. J. C. Darnell 2002a: 129–37 (WHRI nos. 17–19).
12. J. C. Darnell 2002a: 93 (WHRI no. 3), 126–27 (WHRI, no. 15). For the social context that brought together religious worship, musical celebration, and possibly spontaneous poetic compositions, see Parkinson 2002: 61.
13. In fact, the Wadi el-Ḥôl may be synonymous with the Medjoy outpost *ꜥꜣ-bꜣ.w* (the Horus name of Amenemhat III) mentioned in an 18th Dynasty text (J. C. Darnell 2002a: 90). The Horus name of Amenemhat III is attested at the Wadi el-Ḥôl (WHRI no. 21), and his cartouche appears in another inscriptions at the wadi (WHRI no. 5; J. C. Darnell 2002a: 138).
14. Numerous inscriptions of *ꜥnḫ-n-niw.t* soldiers (cf. J. C. Darnell 2002a: 141 [more await publication in a future volume]), and the literary inscription referring to an embattled Theban ruler overseeing a military watch in the Wadi el-Ḥôl (J. C. Darnell 2002a: 107–19; for a brief analysis of the structure of the piece, although necessarily based on the preliminary publication thereof, see Kitchen 1999: 159–62) suggest such a use of the site. Military presence in the Wadi el-Ḥôl as early as the First Intermediate Period is indicated by an "overseer of recruits" of that date (J. C. Darnell 2002a: 123–24, WH no. 13).

15. See Snape 1994: 311–13.
16. On which see the preliminary notices in J. C. Darnell 2002c: 147–49; D. Darnell 2002: 169–72.
17. Cf. the Scorpion Tableau, the inscription of the nomarch Tjauti, and the mention of the "assault troops of the son of Re Antef" at Gebel Tjauti (J. C. Darnell 2002a: 18–19, 34–37, 39-46).
18. For inscriptions of a similar nature from Egypt (outside Sinai), compare Dijkstra (1990) and the reference to another such object, British Museum EA 70881, from el-Lahun (Parkinson 1999: 196, n. 24). Throughout we use "Serabit" as shorthand for the group of early alphabetic inscriptions that have been found in or around the Egyptian turquoise mining site at Serabit el-Khadim in the southern Sinai.
19. The dominant Egyptian practice is for the signs to face *against* the direction of reading (see Gardiner 1954: 25), though this is not monolithic (on reversals and retrograde orientation in Egyptian texts, see Fischer 1973: 21–23; 1977: 123). Attempts at retrograde writing in rock inscriptions (cf. Hintze and Reineke 1989b: 17, no. 23, the name Antef, with a mixture of orientations, in an attempt to write the name from left to right) probably—like the introduction of hieroglyphic forms—represent attempts to enter the realm of hieroglyphic script.
20. Cf. Hamilton 1985: 184–85; Cross 1954: 18; 2003: 310; Sass 1988: 107–8. Throughout our discussion of the paleography of these graffiti frequent reference will be made to Hamilton's study, by far the most thorough and reliable discussion of the paleography of early alphabetic inscriptions known to us (he is currently revising this important study for publication).
21. A lack of sign group quadrants (on which see conveniently Loprieno 1995: 21–22) is never common for Egyptian, but does occur, more often in hieratic and lapidary hieratic inscriptions. Hamilton (1985: 186–87) recognizes the relatively rare "single-file" writing attested in Egyptian texts, and cites a number of examples from Žába (1974). Note, however, that for most of his examples, the shapes and arrangements of the individual signs (so perhaps Žába 1974: Nos. 14, 60A, 77, 78, 88, 89, 93, 190, 193, 208 and 227), or the appearance of hieratic ligatures (so Žába 1974: No. 33 [*n*, *t*, and *f* are ligatured, even though in the hieroglyphic transcription this is not apparent]) dictated the single-file arrangement, rather than an avoidance of possible groupings. Note also that—contra Hamilton—the inscription Žába 1974: No. 15 does contain sign groups. Žába 1974: No. 69 is, however, a good example of single-file orthography where such was not dictated by the signs employed. There is in fact some suggestion that such a style of individual signs, one after the other, is more common during the early Middle Kingdom (cf. the remarks of Goedicke 1988: xxii: "the particular arrangement of narrow columns of single hieroglyphs appears to be typical for the period of the later Eleventh Dynasty"). A tendency to single-file orthography appears in a number of inscriptions, alongside occasional sign groups (cf. J. C. Darnell 2002a: pl. 93, WHRI 13, probably of First Intermediate Period date).
22. For similar graffiti-heads, with exaggerated chins and sharply rendered lips, apparently dating from the time of the construction of the pyramid of Sesostris III, see De Morgan 1903: 93–96, and figs. 137–40.
23. Compare Traunecker et al. 1981: 227 (note particularly figs. 76–77 and 81–82).
24. Hamilton accounts for the tilt by positing a rotation in stance away from Egyptian Prototypes (forthcoming).
25. Cf. particularly the Abusir and Elephantine examples from Möller (1927a: 7) and James (1962: I/16 and VII/15). The Wadi el-Ḥôl inscriptions again show a similarity to the hieratic prototype no longer so clearly discernable in the Serabit and Proto-Canaanite signs (cf. Hamilton 1985: 209, n. 113).
26. For the stance and appearance, and pointed neck as well, compare Shimy 1977: pl. 296, nos. 3870 and 3872.
27. Sass 1988: 131.
28. Sass 1988: 131.
29. As Sass himself notes regarding the sign in Sinai 364, which he compares to the square house sign in Sinai 359 (1988: 131; cf. Hamilton 2002: 37), and as Hamilton suggests for Sinai 367 (1985: 326).
30. Hamilton 1985: 219.
31. Sass 1988: 111.
32. Gardiner 1916: 14; Sass 1988: 111.
33. Cf. Hamilton 1985: 36.
34. Möller 1927a: 33 (no. 342), especially examples from the Mathematical Papyrus and Westcar.
35. So already Hamilton 1985: 36–37 (see now forthcoming). An *h*-like variant of the normal *pr*-sign, open to the lower right, closed to the lower left, but without the inner upturn of the lower line present in the *h*-sign, occasionally appears in Egyptian as well (see Meeks 2004: 146, §394).

36. Cross 1984: 72; 2003: 295. Hamilton (1985: 39) also thinks the double box form of the otherwise obscure "house" form in Sinai 375 derives from a Hyksos form of the courtyard house sign. He also now believes that the form of the *bêt* in Sinai 364 might also derive from the courtyard house (personal communication).
37. Hamilton 1985: 39.
38. See Hamilton's discussion (1985: 39–41).
39. See Hamilton 1985: 89–97, and Sass 1988: 123–25.
40. In the past, scholars have posited as many as four sources for the early (and linear) alphabetic *lāmed* (e.g., Driver 1976: 164), with the several crook signs (commonly termed an ox-goad in the literature) receiving the most attention, even though it is clear that the shape of Gardiner V1 ("coil of rope") stands behind most of the attested early alphabetic versions of this sign (so Hamilton 1985: 89–91; Sass 1988: 123–25; and especially now Hamilton forthcoming, who says quite straightforwardly, based on an earlier draft of the present examination of the Wadi el-Ḥôl early alphabetic inscriptions, "the letter *lāmed* has only one definite source in Egyptian writing: V1, coil of rope."). The Ethiopic letter name *lāwī*, while possibly exhibiting an etymology that is consistent with the notion of a coil (cf. Arabic *lawā*, "to turn, twist, wind, coil"), was likely created secondarily to rhyme with *wāwi* and *tāwi*. The suggestion by Wimmer and Wimmer-Dweikat (2001: 108) that the sign reflects a form of the ("figure eight") precursor of linear alphabetic *qōp* (e.g. Sinai 349, 351) may be doubted on graphic grounds.
41. However, a less tightly curved, more crook-like variant of the coil does occur (cf. Arnold et al. 1990: 44; Willems 1996: 125–26), particularly during the Middle Kingdom in the title *imy-r šnṯ* "sheriff." For the title see the references in J. C. Darnell 2002a: 63–64; for the particular crook-like coil in the title see specifically Fischer 1964: 107–10 (and 117, n. t; 112, fig. 16a; and pl. 37, for an 11th Dynasty form similar to several of the Proto-Sinaitic crook-like *waw*'s); 1998: 208. Such people functioned in the militarized world of the Wadi el-Ḥôl and its Semitic language-speaking troops and apparently carried as a badge of office a baton flail (Yoyotte 1952; Andreu 1980: 3, 7); note also the depiction at Gebel Tjauti of an apparent arrest, with a policeman carrying a flail baton (Darnell and Darnell 1995: 49–50, fig. 6d). This object also appears as a signaling device in the hands of naval officers, a substitute for a charioteer's whip, and a goad for plowing oxen. For the naval signal, see The Epigraphic Survey 1994: pl. 29, and the commentary volume, p. 15; for the charioteer's use of the object see Ockinga and al-Masri 1990: pl. 55; for the use in plowing compare the well-known scene of tilling in the fields of the beyond from the tomb of Sennedjem at Deir el-Medina (Andreu and Gombert 2002: 74–75); for additional discussion of these sources, and for other references, see the Epigraphic Survey 1994 commentary cited above. Such an object could easily bridge the gap between the designations "training instrument" and "coil." An origin of the *lāmed* sign in a coil of rope would suit the stance of the *lāmed* in Wadi el-Ḥôl Early Alphabetic Inscription 2—an "upside-down" rope makes more sense than an upside-down crook.
42. Contra Wimmer and Wimmer-Dweikat's identification as *wāw*'s (mace-signs; 2001: 108; their better instincts are recorded in n. 8).
43. Möller 1927a: nos. 248–49; compare also Anthes 1928: no. 26/8; Roccati 1970: 50.
44. Some ambiguity between Gardiner I9 and I10 can exist (Willems 1996: 429, n. h).
45. Cf. Žába 1974: figs. 22–23 (pl. 13; *f* in *ḏꜣ=f* in the name Djafantef). For a truly vertical orientation of normally horizontal signs compare the discussion of the water (1.5, 10, 14) and hobble-*ṯ* (2.2, 10) signs below.
46. Compare the head of the serpents in the horizontal inscription at the Wadi el-Ḥôl, which is abbreviated as a short diagonal line, with the more rounded head of most of the Serabit serpents (e.g., Sinai 349, 352). There are, of course, exceptions, like Sinai 374, which appears more hieratic in form.
47. Sass 1988: 125–26.
48. This alternative form is scarcely due to "carelessness" (so Sass 1988: 125). Hamilton (1985: 107) correctly recognizes the derivation of these signs from the horned viper sign.
49. Cf. Budge 1912: pl. 39, no. 226 [362], l. 8 (*ṯ* in *Mnṯw* on end); compare the stela of Nesumonthu (Obsomer 1993: 104, 122); note also the 12th Dynasty stela British Museum E567 (Simpson 1974: pl. 22, no. 13.2), the 3rd vertical line of text in front of the figure of the man, a water-*n* is placed on end immediately after a reed leaf, in order to fill a block of space with the reed leaf; Boeser 1909: pl. 3: *in* with vertical *n* in the vertical bands of text at each side of the stela. On this "Zeichendrehung," see Schenkel 1962: 29–31; Brovarski 1989: 900–901, n. 276; recognized, albeit as a "curiosité" on the

sole basis of Leiden V6, in Traunecker et al. 1981: 180, 238, no. 1183. See also the Brussels stela of Djari (Clère and Vandier 1982: 14, §19, l. 3; Limme 1979: 18). Gardiner (1954: 490) notes the rare vertical orientation of the water-*n*; see also Hamilton 1985: 101. In Hintze and Reineke (1989b: 101, no. 302), both the mouth-*r* and the bolt-*s* of the name Senwosret have an unusual vertical orientation, whereas the following water-*n* of the same name retains the common horizontal orientation. They (1989a: 78) recognize this to represent "die für das frühe MR typische Senkrechtstellung ursprünglich liegender Zeichen"; they also compare no. 218 (1989b: 71, no. 218; vertical mouth-*r*). In no. 279, the normally horizonal or slightly diagonally angled *mr*-hoe (Gardiner U6) appears in an unusual, vertical orientation (Hintze and Reinecke 1989b: 92, no. 279). Of possible late Middle Kingdom date is an unusual example of a vertical sign (F32) in the name of the deity *Ḫnty-ḫty* (Hein and Satzinger 1989: 53–54, ÄS 136=Wien 4).

50. There is also some evidence of vertically written horizontal signs in the Serabit material. Note especially the eye sign in Sinai 345 and the fish sign in Sinai 376. All of this suggests that we may need to reconsider whether the 90 (and 180) degree rotation of the signs that is typically posited for the later linear scripts (cf. Cross 1954: 18–19; 2003: 310–11) also obtains in early alphabetic inscriptions, such as these or those from Serabit (so also Sass 1988: 108).
51. For example, the head is sometimes represented with a simple vertical line, cf. Sinai 350, 353, 354, 374.
52. See Fischer 1964: 109 n. (h), 115 n. (i); 1968: 79–82, 169; J. C. Darnell 2002a: 32 n. k, pl. 19 (end of l.2); compare also the comments of Schenkel, 1962: 112–13. The two basic forms of seated man figures—"squatting" and "kneeling"—appear together in Fakhry 1952: 23, fig. 18, and pl. 7B (far right).
53. In the Old Kingdom "prospector" signs in Hintze and Reineke (1989b: 258–59) nos. 597, 598 and 599, more normal legs (no. 599) contrast with differentiated upper and lower legs (no. 598, similar to the legs on human figures in our inscriptions). For the zigzag of the legs, compare also the feet of the late Old Kingdom sign of the kneeling man with pouring vessel in Dobrev 1996: 121, fig. 1; 140, photo 3.
54. Cf. the versions from Edfu (Sainte Fare Garnot 1937: pl. 14, fig. 2, l.6 [vertical]), Sharuna (Goedicke 1988: 2a), Elephantine (Goedicke 1988: 2a; Möller 1927a: 44, Elephantine example [P10523(E)186]), the Khor el-Aquiba in Nubia (López 1966: 24–25, 28, pls. 15–17), Wadi Hammamat in the Eastern Desert (Goyon 1957: 180, no. 64, l.2), and the region of Marîya in Lower Nubia (Žába 1974: 175–76; no. 170, fig. 292). For the more common appearance of the hieratic soldier, compare Möller 1927a: 44.
55. James 1962: IX/1 and XVI/1.
56. Roccati 1970: 47.
57. Cf. Marciniak 1974: 177.
58. Recognition of this similarity may have led those transposing from hieratic to hieroglyphic forms to introduce feet-forward seated signs into hieroglyphic texts.
59. In both the Wadi el-Ḥôl and Serabit early alphabetic inscriptions the arms of the signs representing human figures are clearly separated from the heads of the figures. If any of the inscriptions were based on Egyptian hieratic signs of later 17th Dynasty date, the time of the Hyksos occupation of the north, one might expect to see, at least sporadically, some occurrence of the arms coming out of the head area of the sign (Vernus 1980: 184–85).
60. Cf. Žába 1974: 80 (note to l.5 of inscription no. 56); compare also Fischer 1968: 77, n. 325; 79–82; 124–25; Osing 1982: 35, no. 32; pls. 7, 61. One should also note the use of the standing version of the man with hand to mouth during the Heracleopolitan Period due to confusion of the normal, kneeling version of that sign with the sign of the seated man (Gardiner A1; Fischer 1976: 153–54). These confusions could easily derive from the appearance of some standing signs in late Old Kingdom hieratic (Posener-Kriéger and De Cenival 1968: pal. pl. 1; Gardiner nos. 24, 28, and 32).
61. Hamilton (1985: 63–64) posits two possible acrophones: the onomatopoeic interjections **hiʾ* "Oh!" and **hōy* "Ah!" See also Cross and Lambdin 1960: 25.
62. See Kahl 1994: 646 and n. 1672.
63. Möller 1927a: no. 478.
64. According to Hamilton (1985: 208, n. 98), the hieratic of Gardiner O38 does not resemble the Proto-Canaanite *pê*; the corners in the Wadi el-Ḥôl alphabetic inscriptions do, however, preserve echoes of the hieratic originals.
65. Sprengling 1931: 44; Albright 1948: 21, n. 71; 1966: fig. 1.

66. Sass 1988: 128.
67. Hamilton (1985: 121–25) correctly recognizes the Egyptian antecedents of linear alphabet *pê*.
68. Given that the shape of this sign is significantly different from the other water signs—fewer and more elongated strokes—its identification as a more angular composite bow sign (*θann*; see the bow in Sinai 365a) perhaps should be entertained (such angularity comes to typify the later linear *šîn*s, see Hamilton 1985: 272–73).
69. Edel 1980: nos. 199, 588.
70. Hamilton (forthcoming) now compares the kneeling figure in Sinai 375a.
71. Hamilton 1985: 30–34.
72. Cf. Hamilton 1985: 32.
73. Cf. Hamilton 1985: 32.
74. Cf. the examples in Posener-Kriéger and De Cenival 1968: pl. 8; Möller 1927a: 98; James 1962: 7; Roccati 1970: 51; Žába 1974: N42.
75. Cf. Roccati 1970: 51 (rt. 21).
76. Möller 1927a: 339.
77. Cf. also Castel et al. 2001: 144, and some orthographies of the so-called "placenta" (Gardiner Aa1; see Žába 1974 paleography). In the probable Middle Kingdom rock inscription from Nubian Abu Sir in Hintze and Reineke (1989b: 83, no. 247), the round sign with internal vertical is of uncertain reading (compare Hintze and Reineke 1989a: 69). Hamilton (1985: 75–78), following Ullman (1927: 317), tentatively suggests that linear alphabetic *ṭêt* derives from this sign. Wimmer and Wimmer-Dweikat (2001: 108) propose construing the sign 1.13 as a hieratic version of the eye sign; as the eye appears much more successfully in Wadi el-Ḥôl Early Alphabetic Inscription 2 (2.6), such an identification of 1.13 is unlikely.
78. Verner 1992: LXV, especially the example from no. 234; James 1962: 7 (the example from I, vs. 14); Arnold et al. 1990: 88, W59. Examples particularly similar to our sign appear in Žába 1974: N5.
79. Albright 1948: 21, n. 77.
80. In hieratic the many solar rays of the *ḫʿ*-sign are more often simplified in Middle Egyptian hieratic, with a multiplicity of rays earlier and later (Möller 1927a: 29; 1927b: 28). An extremely abbreviated version of *ḫʿ* from the early Middle Kingdom appears in James 1962: 7; a relatively simplified, dual-rayed form, appears in Simpson 1963: 99. For other examples of the multi-rayed early form see Posener-Kriéger and De Cenival 1968: palaeography pl. 8; for additional later versions of the same form see Marciniak 1974: 215; Goyon 1957: 116.
81. Hamilton (1985: 86–89) likewise understands the sign in Sinai 357 as a representation of *šin*, although he proposes a derivation from the Egyptian "thorn"/"triangle" sign (Gardiner M44; Möller 1927a: 299, 567). However, he admits that such a derivation can be maintained only by excluding "marks that occur on or near" the form of the sign in question on Sinai 357 (Hamilton 1985: 87–88)—most crucially the leftmost line attached to the triangular shaped sun, which there seems little reason to dismiss (after consulting the original negatives).
82. Hamilton 1985: 75–78, following Ullman 1927: 317.
83. Žába 1974: 263. A single rock inscription may reveal both hieroglyphic and hieratic versions of the sign, cf. J. C. Darnell 2002a: 99 = WHRI 5, l.8 (hieroglyphic in *ḥnʿ*) and 1.9 (hieratic in *ḥs.t*).
84. Cross 1954: 24, n. 32; Cross and Lambdin 1960: 22, n. 1; Sass 1988: 118. Somewhat surprisingly, Wimmer and Wimmer-Dweikat (2001:108–9) reintroduce *h* as the presumed alphabetic value for this sign.
85. Albright 1948: 18; 1966: 21–22, 27–28. Of course, there is no real contextual warrant for Albright's reading, leaving us without a decipherable lexeme for which this sign is used in early alphabetic inscriptions. The complications surrounding the history of the pictographic (and non-pictographic) graphemes for *ḫ*, *ḥ*, and *ḏ* in the alphabetic traditions are well known. Hamilton's solution (1985: 49–54, 72–75) to construe all the putative *ḥêts* identified at Serabit (Sinai 362, 367, and 376) as "door" signs, derived most likely from hieratic models of Gardiner O31 (Early: Möller 1927a: 34; Roccati 1970: 51; James 1962: XVII/9; Later: Möller 1927b: 32; Marciniak 1974: 221), is generally attractive from an Egyptological perspective.
86. Compare Kitchen 1961: 10–18 (with parallels cited on p. 13).
87. However, short hobble-*ṯ*s do appear in rock inscriptions (Hintze and Reineke 1989a: 87, no. 258).
88. See Diringer 1948: 155, fig. 13.1. So construed, the sequence *m-ṯ* is the only obvious sequential overlap exhibited between the Wadi el-Ḥôl and the Serabit inscriptions (cf. Sinai 351, 360). Albright (1966: 41–42), followed by others (e.g., Sass 1988: 48–49), interprets *mṯ* and *mṯt* at Serabit as "lord" and "lady" respectively, principally on the evidence of the tile *mṯt ḥry* "Lady Huraya" at Ugarit (e.g., *CTU* 1.14.III.39). The etymology of the Ugaritic

lexeme is unclear, however; and, with the growing unlikelihood that the (whole of the) Serabit inscriptions are to be dated to the New Kingdom period (see below), it is not so obvious how this sequence of signs should be construed.

89. Cross 1954: 22; 1967: 19*; 2003: 312, 325.
90. Cross 1954: 22; 1967: 19*, n. 68.
91. On *šin* (< **θann-* "composite bow"), see Hamilton 1985: 143–48.
92. Cf. Edel 1980: pl. 10, particularly no. 583 (126). This Wadi el-Ḥôl inscription thus provides a reference to the hieratic form of the eye apparently unknown in the other early alphabetic inscriptions (see Hamilton 1985: 207, n. 92).
93. Cf. Hintze and Reineke 1989a: 171, no. 449; cf. also 139, no. 392; 158, no. 426.
94. For details, see Hamilton 1985: 65–69.
95. Note the relatively rarely attested sign of the mace with discoidal head (Gardiner T1).
96. The suggested reading of T2 with horizontal orientation in a possible ideographic writing of *dꜣr* or *sḳr* in the first of the rock inscriptions of Tjehemau (see fig. 18), composed during the early 12th Dynasty (the sign appears in No. 1, l.3; see J. C. Darnell 2003b: 35, text note c), is actually a *d*-hand in the word *dp.t*, "to taste, experience"; a revised and expanded discussion of Tjehemau's inscriptions will be forthcoming in J. C. Darnell, *The Birth of Victorious Thebes*. The sign T2 is common only in the labels to "smiting scenes" (Gardiner et al. 1952: pls. 2–3 [no. 7], 5 [no. 8], 6 [no. 10], and 8 [nos. 14 and 16]).
97. Compare Möller 1927a: 34; Žába 1974: paleography (O29).
98. Compare J. C. Darnell 2002a: WHRI 21, l.1, WHRI 4, l.2 and references p. 138 n. b; Hintze and Reineke 1989b: 160, no. 429, l.1; 219, no. 524, l.3 (vertical line of text immediately in front of the figure); Hein and Satzinger 1989: 143, 146–47 (l.2); ÄS 191=Wien 4. Such an origin makes the often cited but still problematic *wāwîm*, "pegs, pins, nails, hooks," a more intriguing candidate for this signs' putative acrophone, but see the discussion in Hamilton 1985: 68–69.
99. Neither of the published attempts at decipherment (Wimmer and Wimmer-Dweikat 2001; Altschuler 2002) inspire great confidence, as they entail misreadings of signs, recourse to emendation, dubious linguistic analyses, and/or questionable assumptions about content.
100. Perhaps an additional indicator of alphabetic quality comes in the nature of the few lexemes, apparently West Semitic, that are immediately recognizable, a feature that would be consistent with the geographical area in which alphabetic writing eventually takes hold.
101. Most previous efforts to identify possible Egyptian hieratic prototypes for early alphabetic signs were hampered by misidentifications of the relevant Egyptian signs and the positing of anachronistic correspondences between the hieratic forms and their alphabetic derivatives (Hamilton 1985 is the notable exception; Sass 1988: 161).
102. Cf. Hamilton's analysis of the Serabit material (1985: 178–79).
103. For the mixing of hieroglyphic forms into otherwise hieratic texts, note the remarks of Žába 1974: 261.
104. Note in particular the Nubian rock inscriptions (Žába 1974: 263; see also Smith 1972: 51). H. E. Winlock (1941: 146) characterized the authors of Theban rock inscriptions during the Middle Kingdom as having "affected a minute, cramped, practically hieroglyphic hand which is far less likely to attract attention than the flowing hieratic of Ramesside scribes." Hamilton (1985: 180, 192) notes that this pre-New Kingdom feature "gives another clue ... regarding the origin of the alphabet." Although the mixed paleography persists in some New Kingdom inscriptions, the percentage of inscriptions alternating between hieratic and hieroglyphic orthographies appears to peak during the Middle Kingdom. Compare the observations of Ali 2002: 12–35; based on his analysis of several limited corpora of texts, approximately 40% of all Middle Kingdom rock inscriptions utilize a mixed hieratic-hieroglyphic orthography, compared to approximately 12% of such texts from the New Kingdom. See also the comments of Fischer 1979: 43–44. Note that the brief discussion of incised hieratic in McDowell (1995: 223–24) appears greatly to underestimate the number and significance of hieratic rock inscriptions.
105. For convenient overviews of the literature concerning Egyptian and Syro-Palestinian relations during the Middle Kingdom and Second Intermediate Period, see Bárta 2003: 139–95; Richards 2001: 13–29; Cohen 2002: 33–50; Ryholt 1997: 84–90, 105–16, 130–48, 176–83, and *passim*.
106. The Prophecy of Neferti describes Asiatics overrunning the Nile Delta (Helck 1970: 27–29; Blumenthal 1982: 4 and *passim*). For a bibliography and brief overview of the date of the text's composition, see Parkinson (2002: 303–304).

107. See Vandersleyen 1995: 29; Willems 1983–84: 97–98 (citing Schulman 1982; Jaroš-Deckert 1984: 37–47, pls. I [c] and 14). The fragment of a possible scene of Egyptians battling Asiatics in Russmann (2001: 87, no. 17) probably depicts Libyans rather than Asiatics, however. For such scenes already during the late Old Kingdom see Quibell and Hayter 1927: frontispiece and 25 (the editors suggested that the enemies of the Egyptians were Libyans); Petrie and Griffith 1898: 5–7 and pl. 4.
108. See Roeder 1911: vol. 1, 103–11; vol. 2, pls. 106–108; For Tjehemau's inscriptions, a discussion of their historical implications and a brief examination of the role of Nubian and Asiatic mercenaries in Egypt during the early Middle Kingdom, see now J. C. Darnell 2003b; 2004.
109. Hatnub inscription No. 16 (Anthes 1928: no. 16; Willems 1983–84: 95) refers to battle between the local governor and bands of Upper Egyptians, Lower Egyptians, Medjay Nubians, Wawat Nubians, Nehesy Nubians, and *ꜥꜣm.w*-Asiatics.
110. A number of people with Asiatic names appear in the records of the Great Prison at Thebes (Papyrus Brooklyn 35.1446; Hayes 1955). Although Egyptologists were often wont to view the Middle Kingdom as relatively inactive in Syria-Palestine (compare Hayes 1955: 99 and n. 363), relying on the northeast Delta "Wall of the Ruler" (on which see conveniently Quirke 1989: 261–75) for defense against potential Asiatic threats, ample evidence exists for military raids into the area. Although activity in the northeast during the reign of Amenemhat I may have been limited to the Delta fringe (Ward 1969: 215–16), and the location and exact date of the military activity of Nesumonthu remain uncertain (Arnold 1991: 18–20; for an overview of dating possibilities Obsomer 1995: 54–81), a Memphite inscription of Amenemhat II (Altenmüller and Moussa 1991: 1–48; Malek and Quirke 1992: 13–18) now complements the more personal and perhaps equivocal evidence of the stela of Khusobek (Baines 1987: 43–61).
111. Compare the Beni Hasan scene of Abishai and his people. For a convenient list of some of the more fully argued views on the purpose of the visit of Abishai's group, see Cohen 2002: 45; Aufrère 2002: 207–14.
112. Koch 1990: 24, ll. 8–14; 25, ll. 8–14; on Sinuhe's relationship with Amuneshi, see *inter alia* Derchain 1985.
113. Full publication of these inscriptions here would contain much commentary unrelated to the early alphabetic texts; for this reason, an appendix with preliminary editions of these rock inscriptions will appear here, and a complete treatment of these inscriptions will be forthcoming in J. C. Darnell, *Rock Inscriptions at the Wadi el-Ḥôl Part 2*.
114. Hayes 1955: 92 and n. 347; Redford 1986: 126–27; 1992: 32; Ryholt 1997: 293–94; Schneider 2003: 5 and *passim*. The term appears to be synonymous with *Sty.w* "Asiatics" in the texts of Kamose's war against the Hyksos (Smith and Smith 1976: 62); note also the probable "linguistic" use of the term Tjemehou (Manassa 2003: 83–84, n. 3). Supposed use of the term *ꜥꜣm* to refer to Libyans (recently repeated by Vandersleyen 1995: 27–28, 86) originate in ancient labeling errors and nothing more (J. C. Darnell 1995: 68, n. 114). References to Syria in texts accompanying a scene at Karnak of the presentation of Libyan prisoners and booty (Seti battle reliefs; Richardson 1999: 155–56) probably allude to the trade route sources of some of the booty captured in Libya.
115. The *ꜥꜣm.w* appear in the Eastern Desert as far south as the Wadi Hammamat Road (Koenig 1990: 107, n. a to §B; J. C. Darnell 1995: 68–69, n. 114; Murray 1935: 14). Meeks (1998: no. 77.0580) refers to *ꜥꜣm.w* of Punt, but that is based on his misunderstanding of the toponym *ꜥm* / *ꜥmm* (Zibelius 1972: 99) as *ꜥꜣm*. Redford (1986: 128–29) disputes the existence of *ꜥꜣm.w* in the Eastern Desert. Murnane and Brovarski (1969: 13, n. 11) imprecisely refer to *ꜥꜣm.w* as a designation of "the inhabitants of the eastern desert between the Nile Valley and the Red Sea"; the term refers not to Eastern Desert dwellers as such, but can include the *ꜥꜣm.w* groups living north of the Wadi Hammamat. Vandersleyen (1995: 31, n. 2), based primarily on an erroneous interpretation of the expedition of Pepynakht during the reign of Pepy II, also appears to assume a presence of *ꜥꜣm.w* in the south during the late Old Kingdom. Goyon (1957: 169 and pl. 50) may show an encounter between an Egyptian and a bearded *ꜥꜣm*-desert dweller, if the one figure indeed wears a goatee-like beard.
116. An inscription in the Wadi el-Hudi (Sadek 1980: 56–57, No. 31, and n. 212) depicts "overthrowing the *ꜥꜣm*." The inscriptions of Tjehemau at Abisko refer to war against the *ꜥꜣm.w* of Djaty, an obscure but apparently southern location, during the early Middle Kingdom (see above n. 108).

117. Compare the remarks of Hayes (1955: 99): "Perhaps the most surprising circumstance associated with these Asiatic servants is that an Upper Egyptian official of the mid-Thirteenth Dynasty should have had well over forty of them in his personal possession."

118. Compare Chevereau 1987: 43–44; 1991: 82–84; 1992: 34; see also Te Velde 1986: 258.

119. See Kaplony-Heckel 1971: 3, 5–6.

120. Posener 1971: 542, citing Fischer 1959: 263–64 (a Kahun papyrus reference to an *ʿ3m*-Asiatic from a *wn.t*-settlement, perhaps a walled settlement of Asiatics, of the sort mentioned in the earlier, 6th Dynasty inscriptions of Weni), and Posener 1957: 151–52. In P. Berlin 10037 ro. 16–20 a writer requests *corvée* workers, but asks that "the Asiatics" not be sent (see Luft 1998: 28–29).

121. Van Seters (1966: 88 n. 3) notes that a "chief lector priest, priest and scribe, the Asiatic Werkherephemut" appears in Sinai inscription No. 123B, and Hamilton (1985: 192) suggests that such a person might have been the inventor of the alphabet. Van Seters follows the reading in Gardiner et al. 1955: 128, supported by the plate Gardiner et al 1952: pl. 46; Valbelle and Bonnet (1996: 138) refer to the man and his titles, omitting *ʿ3m*, although no reason is apparent; R. Giveon (1978: 156) follows Gardiner et al. Such a priest was perhaps the source of the Northwest Semitic magical texts in an Egyptian papyrus discussed in Steiner 1992: 191–200 and Morenz 1997: 198 n. 42. The style of Egyptian script from which the alphabet derived, and the time of that derivation, may suggest a more military background for the people involved, as in the Wadi el-Ḥôl alphabetic inscriptions. Note, however, that the alphabet deriving from Egyptian is not a simplification of the Egyptian system (so Hamilton 1985: 193), but a rather small and simplistic derivation from the Egyptian system.

122. For the Farshût Road we know of the presence of mounted couriers during the late 17th Dynasty and the New Kingdom, attested by the depiction of a horse and rider in the Wadi el-Ḥôl (J. C. Darnell 2002c: 137, fig. 5), the signature of a Ramesside stable master from the same location (J. C. Darnell 2002a: 139), and a series of 21st Dynasty stelae referring to the Farshût Road as the "Road of Horses" (for a preliminary publication, see J. C. Darnell 2002c: 132–36; the final publication will be forthcoming in J. C. Darnell, *Gebel Antef and the Road of Horses*). Only on this road occur enormous mounds of organic debris, intermixed with ceramic material; an association of these mounds with the couriers, the two unique features of the Farshût Road, is probable. In fact, the modest beginnings of the debris mounds of the Farshût Road date to the late Middle Kingdom.

123. See Valbelle and Bonnet 1996: 34; compare the remarks of Giveon (1978: 131–35), who suggests that the associates of the Egyptians were "a special and a specialized group; their skill may be connected with their knowledge of land and people, of language and region and their expertise in fitting out and organizing caravans." Giveon suggests that rather than being local bedouin, they came either from the north, or from positions already within the pharaonic realm. O'Connor (1996: 90), without providing justification for the statement, says of the men employed at Serabit el-Khadem that "the workers were prisoners of war from southwestern Asia."

124. See Gardiner et al. 1955; 19, 206 (but note that the man on the donkey holds an axe rather than an "adze"). A close-up of an Asiatic with shield and battle axe appears in Valbelle and Bonnet 1996: 147, fig. 171 (not "des objets difficiles à identifier" [p. 147]); see also Valbelle and Bonnet 1996: 34–35.

125. This name appears in Hein and Satzinger 1993: 448–49 (ÄS 111, late Dynasty XII–Dynasty XIII); 7, 61–63 (ÄS 129, there misread [7, 61] as *Nb.t-sny*; the *kpn*-sign has the same appearance as in the graffito in the Wadi el-Ḥôl); Budge 1912: pl. 8, no. 320 [248]; pl. 41 (no. 300 [905]); on a seal from Mirgissa (Gratien 1991: 102). For further references to this name, see Schneider 2003: 109.

126. At least one 13th Dynasty ruler—Khendjer—probably has a West Asiatic name (Ryholt 1997: 220–21; note, however, the suggestion of a possible Egyptian etymology in Quirke 1991: 131), although that does not assuredly indicate a Western Asiatic origin for the ruler or his family. The suggested Asiatic origin of the name of Wegaf is unlikely to be correct (Ryholt 1997: 219–20). The patronymic of the ruler Sahornedjheritef, son of a man apparently named Qemaw, is sometimes read as "son of the Asiatic," although this is unlikely (Scandone Matthiae 1997: 418 and discussion 214 n. 737).

127. Scandone Matthiae 1987: 119, 123–25 and references therein; note also Espinel 2002: 103–4. The appearance of this name at the Wadi el-Ḥôl may also provide further evidence for Second Intermediate Period activity, because following an appar-

ent hiatus in Egyptian and Byblian relations for approximately three decades after the end of the reign of Amenemhat IV, penultimate ruler of the 12th Dynasty, the 13th Dynasty maintained at least sporadic relations with Byblos, at least between the reigns of Sehetepibre Sewesekhtawy and Wahibre Ibiaw (Ryholt 1997: 294, 297).

128. For the over-elaboration of the *ms*-sign, and the cross-hatched infilling of the *nb*-sign, compare Hein and Satzinger 1989: 158–61 (ll. 1 and 3; ÄS 198=Wien 4).

129. We may assume that scribes were the organizers behind all Egyptian military units; at least Papyrus Chester Beatty IV 4, 1–3 explicitly says this (Gardiner 1935: pl. 19).

130. Gardiner 1916: 13–14; cf. Ullman 1927: 325. Since at least the early 1960s scholars have generally agreed in dating the Serabit texts to ca. 1500 B.C.E. (see *inter alia* Briquel-Chantonnet 1998: 56–60), a dating based almost solely on the strength of the presumed date of the little sphinx bearing Sinai 345, now in the British Museum (EA 41748), to the time of Hatshepsut (Leibovitch 1963: 201–3; Albright 1963: 203–5). Petrie (1906: 129–31) already associated the sphinx loosely with a type of stone used during the reign of Thutmosis III, and with memorial works of Hatshepsut. The little sphinx more likely comes from the Middle Kingdom (Sass 1988: 135–37; cf. Gardiner et al. 1955: 202; Parkinson 1999: 181–82 ["... a date in the Middle Kingdom (c. 1800 BC) now seems certain"]; Healey 1998: 210–11 [dating the sphinx to ca. 1700 B.C.E.]). Stylistically the Sphinx owes much to the statuary of the late Middle Kingdom; for the sloping forehead and lack of beard note Evers 1929: 9, 29; for the concavities to the upper sides of the headdress, see Evers 1929: 14; for the sharp angle between the cheeks and the flat planes slanting out below the eyes, compare Fay 1996; and the face is most suggestive of royal iconography from the second quarter of the 13th Dynasty (compare Neferhotep I in Evers 1929: pl. 143; Khendjer in Jéquier 1933: pl. 5, figs. B and C). This accords with Hamilton's more recent dating (2002: 40 n. 5) in contrast with his earlier assignment of the sphinx to ca. 1500 B.C.E. on paleographic grounds (1985: 145–46). The Wadi el-Ḥôl texts constitute a compelling reason for rethinking the question of date for the Serabit texts and it is now not unlikely that at least some of the Serabit early alphabetic material (if not all!) dates to the Middle Kingdom period.

131. Sass 1988: 135–44.

132. Hamilton 1985: 193.

133. This revives an option raised by Ullmann (1927: 325–26) and Hamilton (2002: 40), the latter on the basis of the Wadi el-Ḥôl texts.

134. See nn. 7, 141–43.

135. So, for example, Hamilton imagines a more specifically religious context (see n. 121). Whether or not his specific thesis proves compelling (especially now given the need to rethink the date of the Serabit early alphabetic inscriptions), it illustrates the plausibility of imagining various contexts for the development of alphabetic writing.

136. Hamilton 1985: 178.

137. So most recently Sass (1988: 106).

138. Taylor 1930a: 10, 17; 1930b: 79–81; 1931: 27–28; de Rougé 1874.

139. Helck 1972: 41–45.

140. Zauzich 2003: 183–89 (overview), 189, n. 15 (references to earlier works).

141. Williams 1972: 214–21.

142. For scribes able to read and write hieratic, but confused by hieroglyphic forms, see De Garis Davies and Gardiner 1920: 8, 27–28, pls. 35–35A, nos. 2 and 3. Interesting confusions appear in the annotations of the tomb of Amenemhat at Deir el-Medina (No. 340), where a "scribe" appears to have composed in a pseudo-alphabetic manner: "il resort que celui-ci [l'auteur] connaissait seulement les signes hièroglyphiques unilitères (l'alphabet, en quelque sorte), auxquels il ajoutait quelques bilitères réduits par acrophonie à leur consonne initiale ..." (Cherpion 1999: 54–55).

143. Interestingly, Hamilton (1985: 180–81) recognizes the apparent combined hieratic and hieroglyphic origins of the early alphabetic signs. He notes that Žába's Nubian rock inscriptions provide an excellent set of parallels to many of the alphabetic signs, and notes that "its vogue before the New Kingdom gives another clue (nothing more) regarding the date of the origin of the alphabet." He cites Žába for the suitability of such hybrid script to sandstone, noting that sandstone was the surface employed at Serabit el-Khadim. Hamilton (1985: 211, n. 128) then states, "however, such would not account for the Proto-Canaanite texts from Palestine that have mixed antecedents on other media." The derivation of the alphabetic signs from lapidary hieratic, itself not restricted in Egyptian inscriptional evidence to sandstone, does not mean that the derived script would have to be restricted to any of the original

media for which the original signs were developed. His conclusion (Hamilton 1985: 192), "the early alphabet's constitution as a 'mixed' script of hieratic and hieroglyphic signs has its closest analogue in a style of writing from Nubia that was particularly common in Egypt's Middle Kingdom," is nevertheless essentially correct, especially if we understand "from lapidary hieratic" for "from Nubia." We would caution, however, that though we have spoken throughout of Egyptian "models" and "prototypes" for the emerging early alphabetic syllabary, we remain cognizant that the manner in which the Egyptian forms—hieroglyphic and hieratic—influenced and inspired the early alphabetic forms was anything but straightforward or simplistic. Part of the appeal and eventual development of alphabetic writing surely came in the convenience and ease of drawing common objects and exploiting them acrophonically. What seems likely, at least given the present evidence, is that the specific shapes of these common objects in the cultural area of writing have a pre-history, as it were, in the Egyptian syllabary, and it is to this "pre-history" that we mean to point when speaking of Egyptian "models" and "prototypes." Although the fact of Egyptian influence on the shapes of the specific alphabetic signs seems patent to us, we are content to leave it to others to debate the extent, degree, and ultimate nature of how this influence was exercised.

144. Hamilton (1985: 175) lists the following biforms in his study: "*b*, (possibly *g*), *d*, *y*, *l*, *n*, *q*, and *ṣ*/*ẓ*" (*r* should perhaps be added to this list).

145. Cf. Hamilton 1985: 179.

146. Note the first proper rendition of the passage in Nims 1968: 163–64 (quoting his translation here), although not quite the hyperbolic statement he suggests. For the "scribal" and cultural significance of Tjekerbaal's statement, see Te Velde 1986: 255.

APPENDIX: THE INSCRIPTIONS OF BEBI AND HIS ASSOCIATES IN THE WADI EL-ḤÔL

The following three inscriptions from the Wadi el-Ḥôl, located in Section B (Inscription 3) and on the rock face across the wadi from Section B (Inscriptions 1 and 2), date to the late Middle Kingdom. The titles of the men within the first two inscriptions relate to Asiatic troops and the royal courier service stationed at the Wadi el-Ḥôl. The General Bebi, his daughter, and the royal messenger Bebi only occur in the first inscription, but the express courier Hornebkhasutemsaf, his father the priest Hornebkhasutemsaf, the butler Nedjem, and the soldier Monthuemsaf are common to the first two texts. The priest Kheperkare, who commissioned the only dated inscription of the three, appears in both the second and third inscriptions. The close associations between these three texts provide the strongest evidence for dating the General Bebi, and probably the two early alphabetic inscriptions, specifically to the reign of Amenemhat III.

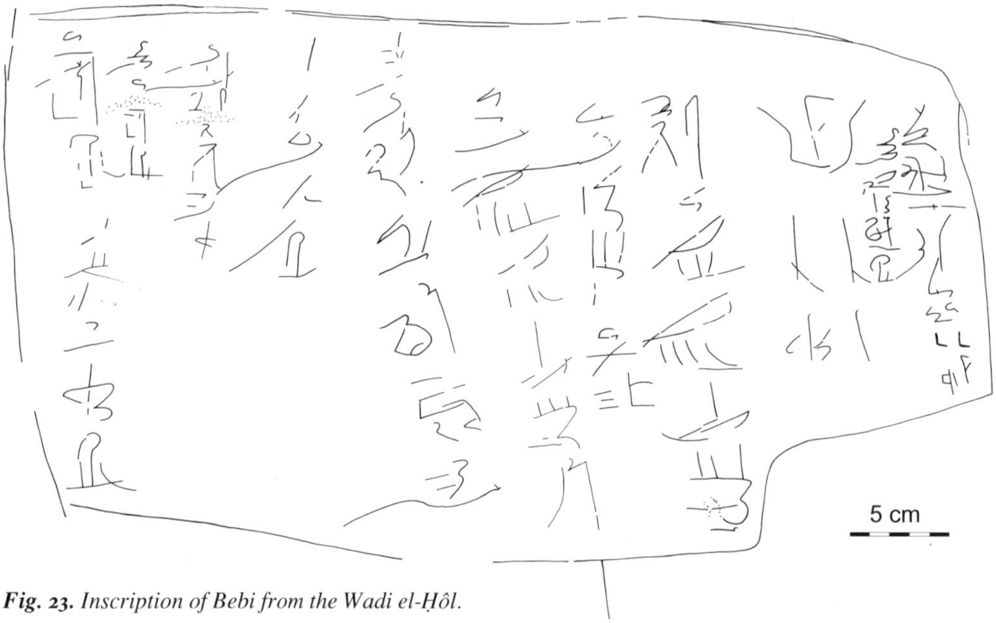

Fig. 23. Inscription of Bebi from the Wadi el-Ḥôl.

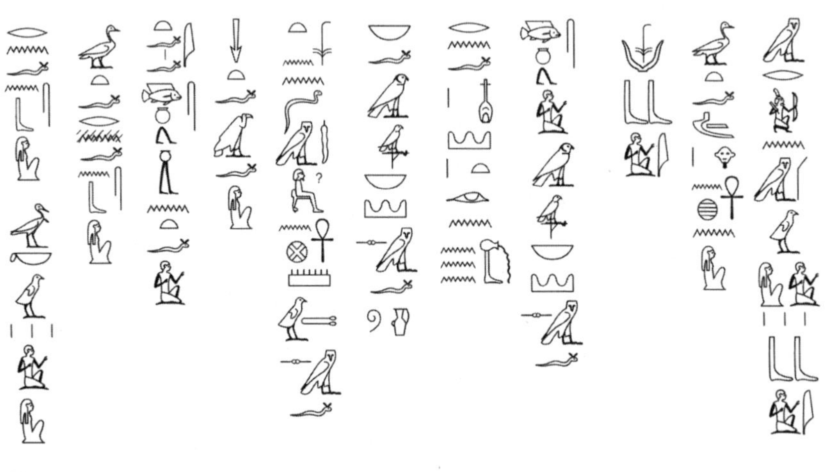

Fig. 24. Transcription of the Inscription of Bebi.

Inscription 1: The Bebi Inscription (figs. 23–24)

[1]*imy-rꜣ mšꜥ n(y) ꜥꜣm.w Bbi*
[2]*sꜣ.t=f Mꜣꜥ.t-ḥr-ꜥnḫ-n=i*
[3]*wpw.ty-nsw.t Bbi*
[4]*sinw Ḥr-nb-ḫꜣs.t-m-sꜣ=f*
[5]*rn=f nfr Ḫꜣs.t ir.n wꜥb* [6]*nb=f Ḥr-nb-ḫꜣs.t-m-sꜣ=f*
wdpw [7]*nsw.t Nḏm ir.n ꜥnḫ n niw.t Mnṯw-m-sꜣ=f*
[8]*sn.t=f mw.t=f*
[9]*it=f sinw Intf*
[10]*sꜣ.t=f Rn=f-snb*
[11]*Rn=f-snb bꜣk.w*

[1]The general of the Asiatics[a], Bebi;
[2]his daughter Maatherankheni;[b]
[3]the royal messenger Bebi;
[4]the express courier[c] Hornebkhasutemsaf,[d]
[5]whose nickname is Khasut, born of the priest [6] of his lord Hornebkhasutemsaef;
the royal butler [7]Nedjem, born of the soldier Monthuemsaf;
[8] his sister and his mother;
[9]his father, the express courier Antef;
[10]his daughter Renefseneb;
[11]Renefseneb, and the servants.

[a] The title "general of the Asiatics" appears on a Middle Kingdom papyrus, P. Berlin 10004 (unfortunately that general's name does not survive; see Ward 1982: 29, no. 206; Chevereau 1991: 56, no. 105; Kaplony-Heckel 1971: 3-4); the references to the *mšꜥ* of Asiatics in *Wb.* II 155, 8 are all to formations of enemy Asiatics. A general Bebi of the 13th Dynasty is attested (Chevereau 1991: 49, no. 38; Leiden stele 11), although he is unlikely to be the same as our Bebi since his title—*imy-r mšꜥ n pr-nsw.t*, "general of the palace"—differs from that of General Bebi in the Wadi el-Ḥôl. Quirke (1990: 186, n. 68) suggests reading *qmꜣ.w* for *ꜥꜣm.w* in the title in P. Berlin 10004—"overseer of harvestworkers;" the context of the Wadi el-Ḥôl inscriptions, the early alphabetic inscriptions nearby, the runner with Bebi, the "prince" in the probably associated inscription, and his "Byblian" mother (see above), support reading *ꜥꜣm.w* in the Wadi el-Ḥôl inscription of Bebi, and suggest that the title in P. Berlin 10004 is indeed to be read "general of the Asiatics" (see also Luft 1998: 29, n. 202).

[b] The first element in the daughter's name (the reading of which is somewhat uncertain) appears to be the name of the goddess *Mꜣꜥ.t*, never common in personal names (Ranke 1935–52: 144–45). For the roughly horizontal lower portion of the *mꜣꜥ*-sickle compare the example from P. Bulaq 18:43, 1, 5 (Möller 1927a: 44); Simpson 1963: 101; and the Middle Kingdom examples in Žába 1974.

[c] The *in*-fish sign in its lapidary hieratic simpification has a somewhat archaic appearance (and is closer to standard hieratic than the forms in Žába 1974). On the militaristic associations of couriers, their use during the First Intermediate Period, and the presence of foreign couriers in the Middle Kingdom execration texts, see Posener 1987: 41–42.

[d] The name Hornebkhasutemsaf is not otherwise attested, but represents a common late Middle Kingdom name formation with a well-known epithet of the god Horus. For a number of other references to Horus, lord of the foreign lands, see J. C. Darnell 2002a: 100, notes. g and h, and Leitz and Budde 2002: 710. The writing of *sꜣ* as the *z*-bolt is not uncommon in Middle Kingdom hieratic (Möller 1927a: 51 n. 2). The length of his name and the fact that his father also shared the same name may have led to his nickname "Khasut," otherwise unattested.

Inscription 2: The Associates of Bebi (figs. 25–26)

Vertical Columns:

[1]*sš šnʿ ḥꜣty-ʿ Sꜣ-wp-wꜣw.t*
[2]*sinw Ḥr-nb-ḫꜣs.t-m-sꜣ=f*
[3]*rn=f nfr Ḫꜣs.t ir.n*
wʿb [4]*nb tꜣ.wy Ḥr-nb-ḫꜣs.t-m-sꜣ=f*
wdpw [5]*Nḏm ir.n ʿnḫ n niw.t Mnṯw-m-sꜣ=f*

[1]The scribe of the storehouse of the mayor,[a] Sawepwaut;
[2]the express courier Hornebkhasutemsaf,[b]
[3]whose nickname is Khasut, born of
the priest of [4]the lord of the two lands[c] Hornebkhasutemsaf;
the butler [5]Nedjem,[d] born of the soldier Monthuemsaf.

Horizontal Lines:

[6]*mty <sꜣ> Mn* [7]*Sꜣ-in-ḥr.t*
[8]*sꜣ=f wʿb Ḫpr-kꜣ-rʿ*
[9]*sn=f Imn-ḥtp*
[10]*ḥm.t=f mw.t=f it.w*
[11]*wʿb Ḫpr-kꜣ-rʿ*

[6]Controller of the phyle of Min, [7]Saonuris;
[8]his son, the priest, Kheperkare;
[9]his brother Amunhotep;
[10]his wife, his mother, and the forefathers;[e]
[11]the priest Kheperkare.

[a] The "scribe of the storehouse" is a rare title (Ward 1982: 166 no. 1439; uncertain), and this is the sole example where it is further specified. The mayor in question is most likely that of Hou (ancient *Ḥw.t-sḫm*) or Thebes (ancient *Wꜣs.t*), the two end-points of the Farshût Road passing through the Wadi el-Ḥôl.

[b] This express courier also appears in Line 4 of the Bebi Inscription.

[c] The title "priest of the Lord of the Two Lands" is not listed by Ward (1982) but several similar titles lend support to this reading: *wʿb nswt* "priest of the king" (no. 671), *wʿb n ḥqꜣ* "priest of the ruler"(no. 680), and *wʿb n Sḥtp-ib-rʿ* "priest of Sehetepibre" (no. 684).

[d] The title here is the simple *wdpw*; the same man bears the title *wdpw-nsw.t*, "royal butler," in the Bebi Inscription (Appendix Inscription 1, lines 6–7).

[e] These three filiations may have been intended as headings for names that were not written. However, they closely resemble the mention of "servants" at the end of the Bebi inscription, and may simply refer to these people in general without individual names.

The *wʿb*-priest Kheperkare, who appears twice in this inscription, is probably the same man as the lector priest Kheperkare, who appears in an inscription in Section B of the Wadi el-Ḥôl dated late in the reign of Amenemhat III (Inscription 3). The *wʿb*-priest Kheperkare is possibly the same man as the *wʿb*-priest Kheperka of WHRI 4 (J, C. Darnell 2002a: 95, pls. 74–79). That man appears to be the addressee of the letter of Dedusobek, WHRI 5 (J. C. Darnell 2002a: 97–101, pls. 74–82), itself dated to regnal year 30 of Amenemhat III.

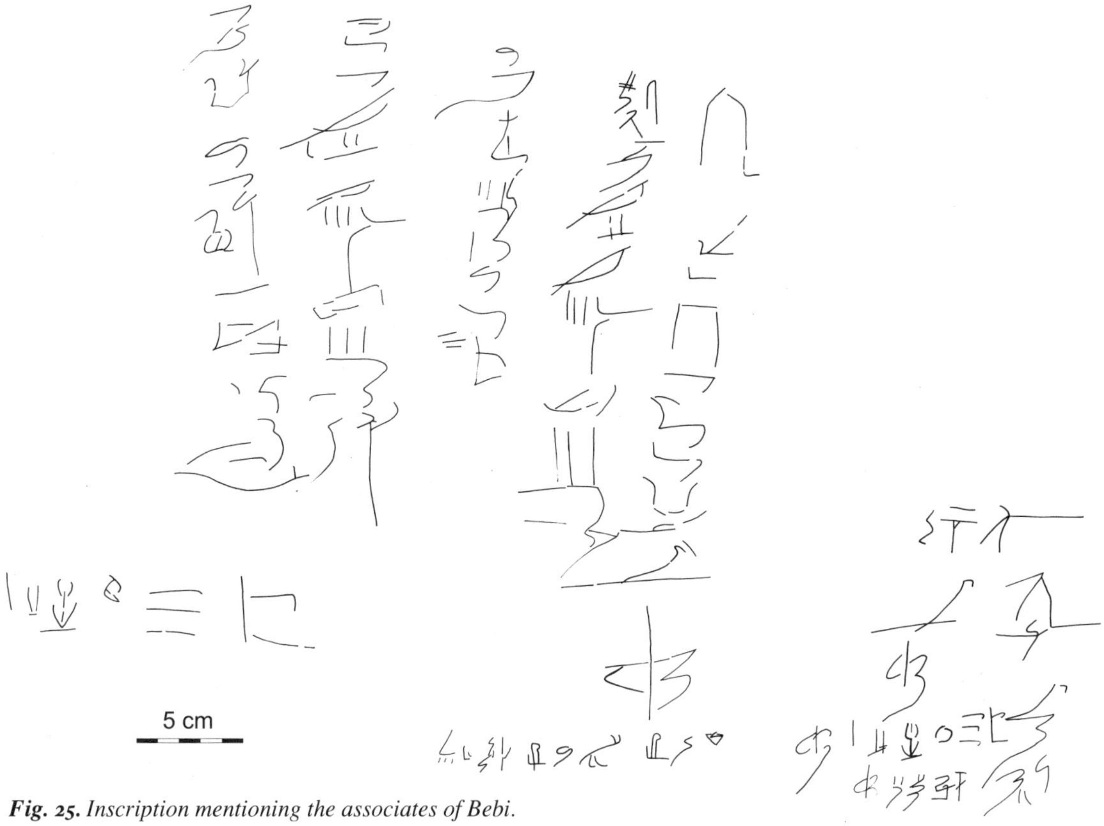

Fig. 25. *Inscription mentioning the associates of Bebi.*

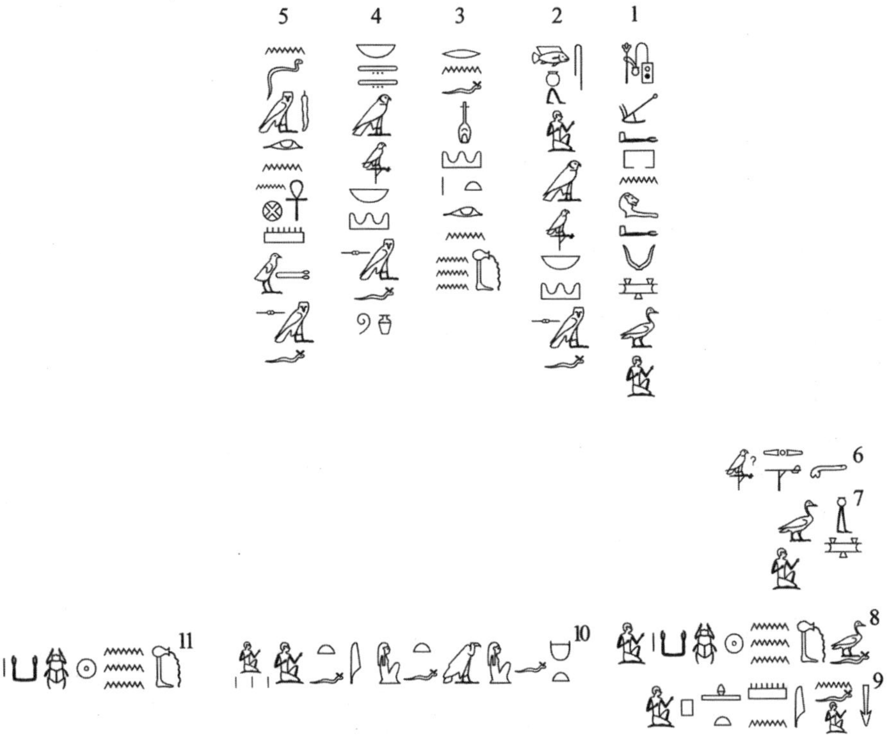

Fig. 26. *Transcription of the inscription of the associates of Bebi.*

Inscription 3: The Inscription of the Priest Kheperkare (fig. 27)

The inscription of Kheperkare as well as the text naming his son appear to be accompanied by images of the owners of the inscriptions. The representations of the two men are carrying *ḫrp*-scepters and tall staves and are shown standing on bases as though they are not simply depictions of the people, but images of statues of the people. Both men wear long kilts reaching below the knee with sashes across their chests. Kheperkare also wears a collar with drop-beads, anklets, and at least one bracelet.

[1]*ḥsb.t 26 ꜣbd 3 šmw*
ḫ<r> ḥm n nswt-bity Ni-mꜣʿ.t-rʿ ʿnḫ ḏ.t
[2]*bꜣk=f mꜣʿ n s.t ib=f*
irr ḥss.t=f nb.t m [3]ẖr.t hrw n.t rʿ nb
ẖry-ḥb n Ḥw.t-sḫm Ḫpr-kꜣ-rʿ nb imꜣḫ
[4]*sꜣ=f mry=f Sn.w-ʿnḫ*

[1]Regnal year 26, third month of Shomu,
under the majesty of the King of Upper and Lower Egypt Nimaatre,
living forever.
[2]His true and trusted servant,
who does all which he praises in [3]the course of every day,
the lector priest of Hut-sekhem, Kheperkare, posessor of veneration.
[4]His beloved son, Senuankh.[a]

[a] The name is well attested for the Middle Kingdom (Ranke 1935: 311. no. 7).

Fig. 27. Inscription of the Priest Kheperkare.

REFERENCES

Albright, W. F.

1948 The Early Alphabetic Inscriptions from Sinai and Their Decipherment. *Bulletin of the American Schools of Oriental Research* 110: 6–22.

1963 The Date of the Proto-Sinaitic Inscriptions. Additional Note. *Le Muséon* 76: 203–5

1966 *The Proto-Sinaitic Inscriptions and Their Decipherment*. Harvard Theological Studies 22. Cambridge, MA: Harvard University.

Ali, M. S.

2002 *Hieratische Ritzinschriften aus Theben*. Göttinger Orientforschung IV/34. Wiesbaden: Harrassowitz.

Altenmüller, H., and Moussa, A. M.

1991 Die Inschrift Amenemhet II. aus dem Ptah-Tempel von Memphis. Ein Vorbericht. *Studien zur altägyptischen Kultur* 18: 1–48.

Altschuler, E. L.

2002 Gloss of One of the Wadi el-Hol Inscriptions. *Ancient Near Eastern Studies* 39: 201–4.

Andreu, G.

1980 Sobek comparé à un policier. Pp. 3–7 in *Livre du Centenaire, 1880–1980*, ed. J. Vercoutter. Mémoires de l'Institut Français d'Archéologie Orientale 104. Cairo: Institut Français d'Archéologie Orientale.

Andreu, G., and Gombert, F.

2002 *Deir El-Médineh, les artisans de pharaon*. Paris: Réunion des musées nationaux.

Anthes, R.

1928 *Die Felsinschriften von Hatnub*. Untersuchungen zur Geschichte und Altertumskunde Ägyptens 9. Leipzig: Hinrichs.

Arnold, D.

1991 Amenemhat I and the Early Twelfth Dynasty at Thebes. *Metropolitan Museum Journal* 26: 5–48.

Arnold, F.; Arnold, D.; Edwards, I. E. S.; and Osing, J.

1990 *The South Cemeteries of Lisht II: The Control Notes and Team Marks*. New York: The Metropolitan Museum of Art.

Aufrère, S. H.

2002 The Deserts of the Fifteenth and Sixteenth Upper Egyptian Nomes during the Middle Kingdom. Pp. 207–14 in *Egypt and Nubia: Gifts of the Desert*, ed. R. Friedman. London: British Museum.

Baines, J.

1987 The Stela of Khusobek: Private and Royal Military Narrative and Values. Pp. 43–61 in *Form und Mass: Beiträge zur Literatur, Sprache und Kunst des alten Ägypten*, eds. J. Osing and G. Dreyer. Ägypten und Altes Testament 12. Wiesbaden: Harrasowitz.

Baines, J., and Eyre, C. J.

1983 Four notes on literacy. *Göttinger Miszellen* 61: 65–96.

Bárta, M.

2003 *Sinuhe, the Bible, and the Patriarchs*. Prague: Set Out.

Blumenthal, E.

1982 Die Prophezeiung des Neferti. *Zeitschrift für ägyptische Sprache und Altertumskunde* 109: 1–27.

Boeser, A. A.

1909 *Beschreibung der aegyptischen Sammlung des Niederländischen Reichsmuseums der Altertümer in Leiden, die Denkmäler der Zeit zwischen dem Alten und Mittleren Reich und des Mittleren Reiches*. Vol. 1. The Hague: Nijhoff.

Briquel-Chantonnet, F.

1998 Les inscriptions protosinaitiques. Pp. 56–60 in *Le Sinai durant l'antiquité et le moyen age*, eds. D. Valbelle and C. Bonnet. Paris: Editions Errance.

Brovarski, E. J.

1989 The Inscribed Material of the First Intermediate Period from Naga-Ed-Der. Unpublished Ph.D. Dissertation, University of Chicago.

Budge, E. A. W.

1912 *Hieroglyphic Texts from Egyptian Stelae etc. in the British Museum*. Vol. 3. London: British Museum.

Capel, A. K., and Markoe, G. E., eds.,

1996 *Mistress of the House, Mistress of Heaven*. New York: Hudson Hills.

Cappers, R. T. J., and Sikking, L.

2001 Eten in de woestijn: voedsel voor mens en dier op doortocht in de Westelijke woestijm van Egypte. *Paleoaktueel* 13: 100–106.

Castel, G.; Pantalacci, L.; and Cherpion, N.

2001 *Le mastaba de Khentika*. Vol. 1. Balat 5, Fouilles de l'IFAO 40. Cairo: Institut Français d'Archéologie Orientale.

Cherpion, N.
1999 *Deux tombes de la XVIIIe dynastie à Deir el-Medina*. Mémoires de l'Institut Français d'Archéologie Orientale 114. Cairo: Institut Français d'Archéologie Orientale.

Chevereau, P.-M.
1987 Contribution à la prosopographie des cadres militaires de l'Ancien Empire et de la Première Période Intermediaire. *Revue d'Égyptologie* 38: 13–48.
1991 Contribution à la prospographie des cadres militaries du Moyen Empire. *Revue d'Égyptologie* 42: 43–88.
1992 Contribution à la prosopographie des cadres militaires du Moyen Empire B. Titres nautiques. *Revue d'Égyptologie* 43: 11–34.

Clère, J. J., and Vandier, J.
1982 *Textes de la Première Période Intermédiaire et de la Xième Dynastie*. Bibliotheca Aegyptiaca 10. Brussels: Fondation égyptologique Reine Élisabeth.

Cohen, S. L.
2002 *Canaanites, Chronologies, and Connections: The Relationship of Middle Bronze Age IIA Canaan to Middle Kingdom Egypt*. Studies in the Archaeology and History of the Levant 3. Winona Lake, IN: Eisenbrauns.

Cross, F. M.
1954 The Evolution of the Proto-Canaanite Alphabet. *Bulletin of the American Schools of Oriental Research* 134: 15–24.
1967 The Origin and Early Evolution of the Alphabet. *Eretz-Israel* 8 (1967): 8*–24*.
1984 An Old Canaanite Inscription Recently Found at Lachish. *Tel Aviv* 11: 71–76.
2003 *Leaves from an Epigrapher's Notebook*. Winona Lake, IN: Eisenbrauns.

Cross, F. M., and Lambdin, T. O.
1960 A Ugaritic Abecedary and the Origins of the Proto-Canaanite Alphabet. *Bulletin of the American Schools of Oriental Research* 160: 21–26.

Darnell, D.
2002 Gravel of the Desert and Broken Pots in the Road: Ceramic Evidence from the Routes between the Nile and Kharga Oasis. Pp. 156–77 in *Egypt and Nubia: Gifts of the Desert*, ed. R. Friedman. London: British Museum.

Darnell, J. C.
1995 Hathor Returns to Medamûd. *Studien zur altägyptischen Kultur* 22: 47–94.
2002a *Theban Desert Road Survey in the Egyptian Western Desert I: The Rock Inscriptions of Gebel Tjauti in the Thebal Western Desert, Part 1, and the Rock Inscriptions of the Wadi el-Ḥôl, Part 1*. Oriental Institute Publications 119. Chicago: Oriental Institute, University of Chicago.
2002b The Narrow Doors of the Desert. Pp. 104–21 in *Inscribed Landscapes: Marking and Making Place*, eds. B. David and M. Wilson. Honolulu: University of Hawaii.
2002c Opening the Narrow Doors of the Desert: Discoveries of the Theban Desert Road Survey in the Egyptian Western Desert. Pp. 132–55 in *Egypt and Nubia: Gifts of the Desert*, ed. R. Friedman. London: British Museum.
2003a Die frühalphabetischen Inschriften im Wadi el-Hôl. Pp. 165–71 in *Der Turmbau zu Babel. Ursprung und Vielfalt von Sprache und Schrift 3A: Schrift*, ed. W. Seipel. Vienna: Kunsthistorisches Museum.
2003b The Rock Inscriptions of Tjehemau at Abisko. *Zeitschrift für ägyptische Sprache und Altertumskunde* 130: 31–48.
2004 The Route of Eleventh Dynasty Expansion into Nubia. *Zeitschrift für ägyptische Sprache und Altertumskunde* 131: 23–37.

Darnell, J. C., and Darnell, D.
1993 The Luxor-Farshût Desert Road Survey. Pp. 48–55 in *The Oriental Institute 1992–1993 Annual Report*. Chicago: Oriental Institute, University of Chicago.
1994 The Luxor-Farshût Desert Road Survey. Pp. 40–48 in *The Oriental Institute 1993–1994 Annual Report*. Chicago: Oriental Institute, University of Chicago.
1995 The Luxor-Farshût Desert Road Survey. Pp. 44–54 in *The Oriental Institute 1994–1995 Annual Report*. Chicago: Oriental Institute, University of Chicago.
1996 The Luxor-Farshût Desert Road Survey. Pp. 62–70 in *The Oriental Institute 1995–1996 Annual Report*. Chicago: Oriental Institute, University of Chicago.

De Garis Davies, N., and Gardiner, A. H.
1920 *The Tomb of Antefoḳer, Vizier of Sesostris I, and of his Wife, Senet (No. 60)*. Theban Tomb Series 2. London: Egypt Exploration Society.

De Morgan, J.
1903 *Fouilles à Dahchour en 1894–1895*. Vienna: Holzhausen.

Derchain, P.
1985 Sinouhe et Ammounech. *Göttinger Miszellen* 87: 7–13.

De Rougé, F.
1874 *Mémoire sur l'origine égyptienne de l'alphabet phénicien*. Paris: Imprimerie nationale.

Dijkstra, M.
1990 The So-called *Ahitub*-Inscription from Kahun (Egypt). *Zeitschrift des Deutschen Palästina-Vereins* 106: 51–56.

Diringer, D.
1948 *The Alphabet*. Vol. 2. New York: Hutchinson's Scientific and Technical Publications.

Dobrev, V.
1996 Les marques sur pierres de construction de la nécropole de Pépi Ier, étude prosopographique. *Bulletin de l'Institut Français d'Archéologie Orientale* 96: 103–42.

Driver, G. R.
1976 *Semitic Writing*. 3rd ed. London: Oxford University.

Edel, E.
1980 *Die Felsgräbernekropole der Qubbet el Hawa bei Assuan 2: Die althieratischen Topfaufschriften, Paläographie der althieratischen Gefässaufschriften aus den Grabungsjahren 1960 bis 1973*. Abhandlungen der rheinisch-westfälischen Akademie der Wissenschaften 66. Opladen: Westdeutscher Verlag.

The Epigraphic Survey
1994 *The Festival procession of Opet in the Colonnade Hall*. Reliefs and Inscriptions at Luxor Temple 1. Oriental Institute Publications 112. Chicago: Oriental Institute, University of Chicago.

Espinel, A. D.
2002 The Role of the Temple of Ba'alat Gebel as Intermediary between Egypt and Byblos during the Old Kingdom. *Studien zur altägyptischen Kultur* 30: 103–19.

Evers, H. G.
1929 *Staat aus dem Stein: Denkmäler, Geschichte und Bedeutung der ägyptischen Plastik während des Mittleren Reichs*. 2: *Die Vorarbeiten*. Munich: Bruckmann.

Fakhry, A.
1952 *The Inscriptions of the Amethyst Quarries at Wadi el Hudi*. Cairo: Government.

Fay, B.
1996 *The Louvre Sphinx and Royal Sculpture from the Reign of Amenemhat II*. Mainz: von Zabern.

Fischer, H. G.
1959 A Scribe of the Army in a Saqqara Mastaba of the Early Fifth Dynasty. *Journal of Near Eastern Studies* 18: 233–72.
1964 *Inscriptions from the Coptite Nome*. Analecta Orientalia 40. Rome: Pontificium Institutum Biblicum.
1968 *Dendera in the Third Millennium B.C. Down to the Theban Domination of Upper Egypt*. Locust Valley: Augustin.
1973 L'Orientation des textes. Pp. 21–24 in *Textes et langages de l'Égypte pharaonique I*. Bibliothèque d'Etude 64/1. Cairo: Institut Français d'Archéologie Orientale du Caire.
1976 Des chanteurs militaires à Gébélein et Hatnoub? *Revue d'Égyptologie* 28: 153–54.
1977 *The Orientation of the Hieroglyphs* Part 1: *Reversals*. Egyptian Studies 2. New York: Metropolitan Museum of Art.
1979 Archaeological Aspects of Epigraphy and Palaeography. Pp. 29–50 in *Ancient Egyptian Epigraphy and Palaeography*, eds. R. Caminos and H. G. Fischer. 2nd ed. New York: Metropolitan Museum of Art.
1998 *Varia Nova*. Egyptian Studies 3. New York: Metropolitan Museum of Art.

Gardiner, A.
1916 The Egyptian Origin of the Semitic Alphabet. *Journal of Egyptian Archaeology* 3: 1–16.
1935 *Hieratic Papyri in the British Museum, Third Series: Chester Beatty Gift*. London: British Museum.
1954 *Egyptian Grammar*. 3rd ed. Oxford: Griffith Institute.

Gardiner, A. H.; Peet, T. E.; and Černý, J.
1952 *The Inscriptions of Sinai* Part 1: *Introduction and Plates*. Egypt Exploration Society Excavation Memoir 36. London: Egypt Exploration Society.
1955 *The Inscriptions of Sinai* Part 2: *Translations and Commentary*. Egypt Exploration Society Excavation Memoir 45. London: Egypt Exploration Society.

Giveon, R.
1978 *The Stones of Sinai Speak*. Tokyo: Gakuseisha.

Goedicke, H.
1988 *Old Hieratic Paleography*. Baltimore: Halgo.

Goyon, G.
1957 *Nouvelles inscriptions rupestres du Wadi Hammâmât*. Paris: Imprimerie nationale.

Gratien, B.
1991 *Prosopographie des Nubiens et des Égyptiens en Nubie avant le Nouvel Empire*. Cahiers

de Recherches de l'Institut de Papyrologie et d'Égyptologie Lille, Supplément 3. Lille: Université Charles de Gaulle.

Hamilton, G. J.

1985 The Development of the Early Alphabet. Unpublished Ph.D. Dissertation, Harvard University.

2002 W. F. Albright and Early Alphabetic Epigraphy. *Near Eastern Archaeology* 65(1): 35–42.

Hayes, W. C.

1955 *A Papyrus of the Late Middle Kingdom in the Brooklyn Museum*. Brooklyn: Brooklyn Museum.

Healey, J. F.

1998 The Early Alphabet. Pp. 197–257 in *Reading the Past*. New York: Barnes and Noble.

Hein, I., and Satzinger, H.

1989 *Stelen des Mittleren Reiches I, einschliesslich der I. und II. Zwischenzeit*. Corpus Antiquitatum Aegyptiacarum 4. Mainz: von Zabern.

1993 *Stelen des Mittleren Reiches II, einschliesslich der I. und II. Zwischenzeit*. Corpus Antiquitatum Aegyptiacarum 7. Mainz: von Zabern.

Helck, W.

1970 *Die Prophezeiung des Nfr.tj*. Kleine ägyptische Texte. Wiesbaden: Harrassowitz.

1972 Zur Herkunft der sog. "phoenizischen" Schrift. *Ugarit-Forschungen* 4: 41–45.

Hintze, F., and Reineke, W. F.

1989a *Felsinschriften aus dem sudanesischen Nubien* 1. Berlin: Akademie.

1989b *Felsinschriften aus dem sudanesischen Nubien* 2. Berlin: Akademie.

James, T. G. H.

1962 *The Ḥeḳanakhte Papers and Other Early Middle Kingdom Documents*. New York: Metropolitan Museum of Art.

Jaroš-Deckert, B.

1984 *Das Grab des Jnj-jtj.f. Die Wandmalereien der XI. Dynastie*. Archäologische Veröffentlichungen 28. Mainz: von Zabern.

Jéquier, G.

1933 *Deux pyramides du Moyen Empire*. Cairo: Institut Français d'Archéologie Orientale du Caire.

Kahl, J.

1994 *Das System der ägyptischen Hieroglyphenschrift in der 0.–3. Dynastie*. Göttinger Orientforschung IV/29. Wiesbaden: Harrassowitz.

Kaplony-Heckel, U.

1971 *Ägyptische Handschriften* 1. Verzeichnis der Orientalischen Handschriften in Deutschland 19, ed. E. Lüddeckens. Stuttgart: Steiner.

Kitchen, K. A.

1961 An Unusual Stela from Abydos. *Journal of Egyptian Archaeology* 47: 10–18.

1999 *Poetry of Ancient Egypt*. Jonsered: Åström.

Koch, R.

1990 *Die Erzählung des Sinuhe*. Bibliotheca Aegyptiaca 17. Brussels: Fondation égyptologique Reine Élisabeth.

Koenig, Y.

1990 Les textes d'envoûtement de Mirgissa. *Revue d'Égyptologie* 41: 101–25.

Leibovitch, J.

1963 The Date of the Proto-Sinaitic Inscriptions. *Le Muséon* 76: 201–3.

Leitz, C., and Budde, D., eds.,

2002 *Lexikon der Ägyptischen Götter und Götterbezeichnungen*. Vol. 3. Orientalia Lovaniensia Analecta 112. Leuven: Peeters.

Limme, L.

1979 *Stèles égyptiennes*. Guides du Départment Égyptien 4. Brussels: Koninklijke Musea voor Kunst en Geschiedenis.

López, J.

1966 *Las inscripciones rupestres faraonicas entre Korosko y Kasr Ibrim*. Memorias de la Misión Arqueológica Española en Nubia 9. Madrid: Comité español de la UNESCO para Nubia.

Loprieno, A.

1995 *Ancient Egyptian: A Linguistic Introduction*. Cambridge, U.K.: Cambridge University.

Luft, U.

1998 The Ancient Town of El-Lâhûn. Pp. 1–41 in *Lahun Studies*, ed. S. Quirke. Reigate: SIA Publishing.

McDowell, A. G.

1995 An Incised Hieratic Ostracon (Ashmolean HO 655). *Journal of Egyptian Archaeology* 81: 221–25.

Malek, J., and Quirke, S.

1992 Memphis 1991: Epigraphy. *Journal of Egyptian Archaeology* 78: 13–18.

Manassa, C.

2003 *The Great Karnak Inscription of Merneptah: Grand Strategy in the 13th century* BC. Yale Egyptological Studies 5. New Haven: Yale Egyptological Seminar.

Marciniak, M.

1974 *Les Inscriptions hiératiques du Temple de Thoutmosis III*. Deir El-Bahari 1. Warsaw: PWN-Éditions scientifiques de Pologne.

Meeks, D.
1998 *Année lexicographique*, 3 vols. Paris: Cybele.
2004 *Les Architraves du Temple d'Esna, Paléographie*. Paléographie Hiéroglyphique 1. Cairo: Institut Français d'Archéologie Orientale.
Möller, G.
1927a *Hieratische Paläographie*. Vol. 1. 2nd ed. Leipzig: J. C. Hinrichs.
1927b *Hieratische Paläographie*. Vol. 2. 2nd ed. Leipzig: J. C. Hinrichs.
Morenz, L. D.
1997 (Magische) Sprache der 'geheimen Kunst'. *Studien zur altägyptischen Kultur* 24: 191–201.
Murnane, W., and Brovarski, E.
1969 Inscriptions from the Time of Nebhepetre Mentuhotep II at Abisco. *Serapis* 1: 11–33.
Murray, G. W.
1935 *Sons of Ishmael: a Study of the Egyptian Bedouin*. London: Routledge.
Nims, C.
1968 Second Tenses in Wenamun. *Journal of Egyptian Archaeology* 54: 161–64.
Obsomer, C.
1993 La Date de Nésou-Montou (Louvre C1). *Revue d'Égyptologie* 44: 103–40.
1995 *Sésostris Ier, étude chronologique et historique du règne*. Brussels: Connaissance de l'Égypte ancienne.
Ockinga, B., and al-Masri, Y.
1990 *Two Ramesside Tombs at El Mashayikh*. Part 2: *The Tomb of Anhurmose—the Inner Room, and the Tomb of Imiseba*. Sydney: Ancient History Documentary Research Centre.
O'Connor, M.
1996 Epigraphic Semitic Scripts. Pp. 88–107 in *The World's Writing Systems*, ed. P. T. Daniels. Oxford: Oxford University Press.
Osing, J.
1982 *Denkmäler der Oase Dachla aus dem Nachlass von Ahmed Fakhry*. Archäologische Veröffentilichungen 28. Mainz: von Zabern.
Parkinson, R.
1999 *Cracking Codes, the Rosetta Stone and Decipherment*. London: British Museum.
2002 *Poetry and Culture in Middle Kingdom Egypt, a Dark Side to Perfection*. New York: Continuum.
Petrie, W. M. F.
1906 *Researches in Sinai*. With C. T. Currelly. London: John Murray.
Petrie, W. M. F., and Griffith, F. L.
1898 *Deshasheh*. Egypt Exploration Fund 15. London: Egypt Exploration Fund.
Posener, G.
1957 Les Asiatiques en Égypte sous les XIIe et XIIIe dynasties. *Syria* 34: 145–63.
1971 Syria and Palestine, c. 2160–1780 B.C. Pp. 532–58 in *The Cambridge Ancient History*, eds. I. E. S. Edwards, C. J. Gadd, and N. G. L. Hammond. 3rd ed. Vol. 1, part 2. Cambridge, U.K.: Cambridge University Press.
1987 *Cinq figurines d'envoûtement*. Bibliothèque d'Etude 101. Cairo: Institut Français d'Archéologie Orientale.
Posener-Kriéger, P., and De Cenival, J. L.
1968 *The Abu Sir Papyri*. Hieratic Papyri in the British Museum, 5th Series. London: British Museum.
Quibell, J. E., and Hayter, A. G. K.
1927 *Excavations at Saqqara, Teti Pyramid, North Side*. Cairo: Institut Français d'Archéologie Orientale du Caire.
Quirke, S.
1989 Frontier or Border? The Northeast Delta in Middle Kingdom Texts. Pp. 261–75 in *The Archaeology, Geography and History of the Egyptian Delta in Pharaonic Times*, ed. A. Nibbi. Discussions in Egyptology Special Number 1. Oxford: Discussions in Egyptology.
1990 *The Administration of Egypt in the Late Middle Kingdom, the Hieratic Documents*. New Malden: SIA Publishing.
1991 Royal Power in the 13th Dynasty. Pp. 123–39 in *Middle Kingdom Studies*, ed. S. Quirke. New Malden: SIA Publishing.
Ranke, H.
1935–52 *Die ägyptischen Personnennamen* 1. Glückstadt: Augustin.
Redford, D.
1986 Egypt and Western Asia in the Old Kingdom. *Journal of the American Research Center in Egypt* 23: 125–43.
1992 *Egypt, Canaan, and Israel in Ancient Times*. Princeton: Princeton University.
Richards, F.
2001 *The Anra Scarab: an Archaeological and Historical Approach*, BAR International Series 919. Oxford: Archaeopress.
Richardson, S.
1999 Libya Domestica: Libyan Trade and Society on the Eve of the Invasions of Egypt. *Journal of the American Research Center in Egypt* 36: 149–64.

Roccati, A.
1970 *Papiro ieratico N. 54003, estratti magici e rituali del Primo Medio Regno.* Catalogo del Museo Egizio di Torino, Serie Prima, Monumenti e Testi 2. Turin: Edizioni d'Arte Fratelli Pozzo.

Roeder, G.
1911 *Debod bis Bab Kalabsche, Les temples immergées de la Nubie.* Cairo: Institut Français d'Archéologie Orientale du Caire.

Russmann, E. R., ed.
2001 *Eternal Egypt. Masterworks of Ancient Art from the British Museum.* London: British Museum.

Ryholt, K.
1997 *The Political Situation in Egypt during the Second Intermediate Period, c. 1800–1550 B.C.* Carsten Niebuhr Institute Publications 20. Copenhagen: Carsten Niebuhr Institute.

Sadek, A. I.
1980 *Wadi el-Hudi. The Amethyst Mining Inscriptions.* Vol. 1. Warminster: Aris and Phillips.

Sainte Fare Garnot, J. in B. Bruyère, et al.
1937 *Tell Edfou 1937.* Fouilles Franco-Polonaises Rapports 1. Cairo: Institut Français d'Archéologie Orientale du Caire.

Sass, B.
1988 *The Genesis of the Alphabet and Its Development in the Second Millennium B.C.* Ägypten und Altes Testament 13. Wiesbaden: Harrassowitz.

Scandone Matthiae, G.
1987 Una statuetta del Museo Egizio di Torino con dedica ad Hathor signora di Biblo. *Rivista di Studi Fenici* 15: 115–25.
1997 The Relations between Ebla and Egypt. Pp. 415–28 in *The Hyksos: New Historical and Archaeological Perspectives*, ed. E. D. Oren. University Museum Monograph 96. University of Museum Symposium Series 8. Philadelphia: University of Pennsylvania Museum.

Schenkel, W.
1962 *Frühmittelägyptische Studien.* Bonn: Orientalisches Seminar der Universitat Bonn.

Schneider, T.
2003 *Ausländer in Ägypten während des Mittleren Reiches und der Hyksoszeit.* Vol. 2. Ägypten und altes Testament 42. Wiesbaden: Harrassowitz.

Schulman, A. R.
1982 The Battle Scenes of the Middle Kingdom. *Journal for the Society for the Study of Egyptian Antiquities* 12: 167–76.

Shimy, M.
1977 *Graffiti de la montagne thébaine.* Volume 3, Fascicle 7. With P. du Bourguet. Cairo: Centre d'étude et de documentation sur l'ancienne Égypte.

Simpson, W. K.
1963 *Papyrus Reisner.* Vol. 1. Boston: Museum of Fine Arts.
1965 *Papyrus Reisner.* Vol. 2. Boston: Museum of Fine Arts.
1974 *The Terrace of the Great God at Abydos: The Offering Chapels of Dynasties 12 and 13.* Publications of the Pennsylvania-Yale Expedition to Egypt 5. New Haven: Peabody Museum of Natural History; Philadelphia: University Museum.

Smith, H. S.
1972 The Rock Inscriptions of Buhen. *Journal of Egyptian Archaeology* 58: 43–82.

Smith, H. S. and Smith, A.
1976 A Reconsideration of the Kamose Texts. *Zeitschrift für ägyptische Sprache und Altertumskunde* 103: 48–76.

Snape, S. R.
1994 Statues and Soldiers at Abydos during the Second Intermediate Period. Pp. 304–14 in *The Unbroken Reed*, eds. C. Eyre, A. Leahy, and L. M. Leahy. London: Egypt Exploration Society.

Sprengling, M.
1931 *The Alphabet, Its Rise and Development from the Sinai Inscriptions.* Chicago: University of Chicago.

Steiner, R. C.
1992 Northwest Semitic Incantations in an Egyptian Medical Papyrus of the Fourteenth Century B.C.E. *Journal of Near Eastern Studies* 51: 191–200.

Taylor, W. R.
1930 Recent Epigraphic Discoveries in Palestine: A New Gezer Inscription. *Journal of the Palestine Oriental Society* 10: 17.
1930 The New Gezer Inscription. *Journal of the Palestine Oriental Society* 10: 79–81.
1931 Some New Palestine Inscriptions. *Bulletin of the American Schools of Oriental Research* 41: 27–28.

Te Velde, H.
1986 Scribes and Literacy in Ancient Egypt. Pp. 253–64 in *Scripta Signa Vocis: Studies About Scripts, Scriptures, Scribes and Languages*

in the Near East, Presented to J. H. Hospers, eds. H. L. J. Vanstiphout and K. Jongeling. Groningen: Forsten.

Traunecker, C.; Le Saout, F.; and Masson, O.

1981 *La Chapelle d'Achôris à Karnak*. Recherches sur les grandes civilisations, Synthèse No. 5. Paris: Editions A.D.P.F.

Tropper, J.

2003 Die Erfindung des Alphabets und seine Ausbreitung im nordwestsemitischen Raum. Pp. 173–81 in *Der Turmbau zu Babel. Ursprung und Vielfalt von Sprache und Schrift*. Vol. 3A: *Schrift*. ed. W. Seipel. Vienna: Kunsthistorisches Museum.

Ullman, B. L.

1927 The Origin and Development of the Alphabet. *American Journal of Archaeology* 31: 311–28.

Valbelle, D., and Bonnet, C.

1996 *Le Sanctuaire d'Hathor maîtresse de la turquoise*. Paris: Picard.

Vandekerckhove, H., and Müller-Wollermann, R.

2001 *Die Felsinschriften des Wadi Hilâl* 1. Elkab 6. Turnhout: Brepols.

Vandersleyen, C.

1995 *L'Égypte et la vallée du Nil. 2: De la fin de l'Ancien Empire à la fin du Nouvel Empire*. Paris: Presses Universitaires de France.

van Seters, J.

1966 *The Hyksos*. New Haven: Yale University.

Verner, M.

1992 *Abusir II: Baugraffiti der Ptahschepses-Mastaba*. Prague: Universita Carolina Pragensis.

Vernus, P.

1980 Trois statues de particuliers attribuables à la fin de la domination Hyksôs. Pp. 179–90 in *Livre du centenaire, 1880–1980*, ed. J. Vercoutter. Mémoires de l'Institut Français d'Archéologie Orientale 104. Cairo: Institut Français d'Archéologie Orientale.

Ward, W.

1969 The Nomarch Khnumḥotep at Pelusium. *Journal of Egyptian Archaeology* 55: 215–16.

1982 *Index of Egyptian Administrative and Religious Titles of the Middle Kingdom*. Beirut: American University of Beirut.

Willems, H.

1983–84 The Nomarchs of the Hare Nome and Early Middle Kingdom History. *Jaarbericht van het Vooraziatisch-Egyptisch Genootschap* 28: 80–102.

1996 *The Coffin of Heqata (Cairo JdE 36418)*. Orientalia Lovaniensia Analecta 70. Leuven: Peeters.

Williams, R. J.

1972 Scribal Training in Ancient Egypt. *Journal of the American Oriental Society* 92: 214–21

Wimmer, S., and Wimmer-Dweikat, S.

2001 The Alphabetic Texts from Wadi el-Hol: A First Try. *Göttinger Miszellen* 180: 107–12.

Winkler, H.

1938 *Rock-Drawings of Southern Upper Egypt* I. London: Oxford University.

Winlock, H. E.

1941 Graffiti of the Priesthood of the Eleventh Dynasty Temples at Thebes. *American Journal of Semitic Languages and Literatures* 58: 146–68.

Yoyotte, J.

1952 Un corps de police de l'Égypte pharaonique. *Revue d'Égyptologie* 9: 139–51.

Žába, Z.

1974 *Rock Inscriptions of Lower Nubia (Czechoslovak Concession)*. Prague: Universita Karlova.

Zauzich, K.-Th.

2003 Unsere Buchstaben—ägyptische Hieroglyphen. Pp. 183–90 in *Der Turmbau zu Babel. Ursprung und Vielfalt von Sprache und Schrift*. Vol. 3A: *Schrift*, ed. W. Seipel. Vienna: Kunsthistorisches Museum.

Zibelius, K.

1972 *Afrikanische Orts- und Völkernamen in hieroglyphsichen und hieratischen Texten*. Beihefte zum Tübinger Atlas des Vorderen Orients B1. Wiesbaden: Reichert.

PLATE I

Pl. I.1. *Wadi el-Ḥôl Sections B (left face of spur) and C (right face of spur) in center left and the Pinnacle of Gebel Roma ͑ in upper right.*

Pl. I.2. *Wadi el-Ḥôl Section C on the western face of the spur.*

PLATE II

Pl. II. *Section C in the Wadi el-Ḥôl; boxes indicate the location of Early Alphabetic Inscription No. 1 (Horizontal Inscription) to the left and No. 2 (Vertical Inscription) to the right.*

PLATE III

Pl. III. *Wadi el-Ḥôl Early Alphabetic Inscription No. 1 (Horizontal Inscription).*

PLATE IV

Pl. IV. *Wadi el-Ḥôl Early Alphabetic Inscription No. 1 (Horizontal Inscription).*

PLATE V

Pl. V.1. *The head sign; sign 1.1.*

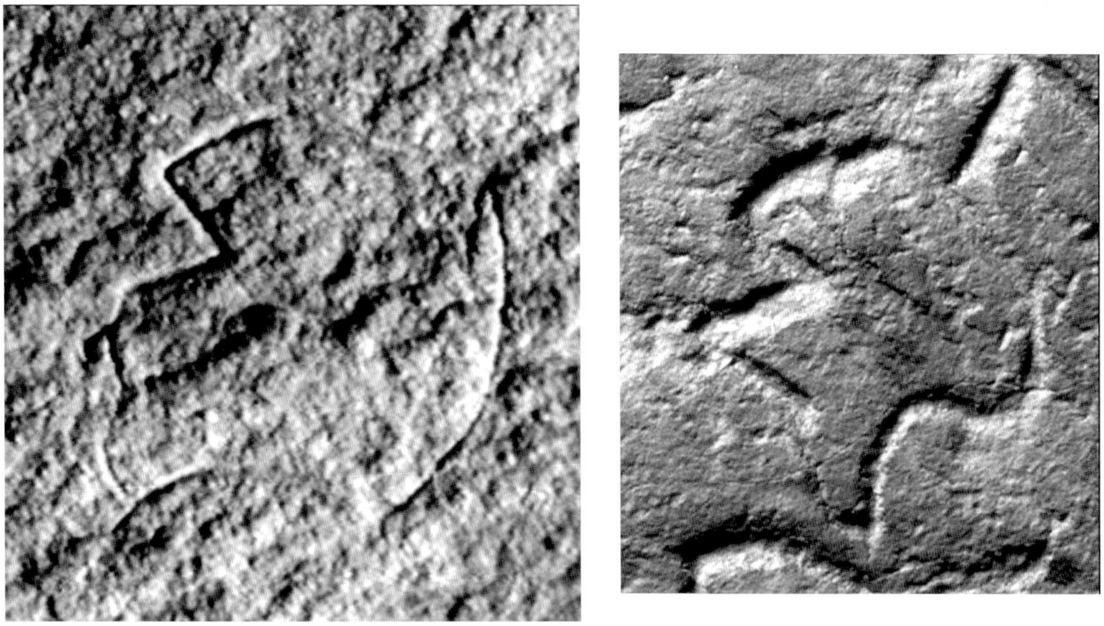

Pl. V.2. *Head signs; signs 1.16 and 2.4.*

PLATE VI

Pl. VI.1. *The courtyard-styled house sign; sign 1.2.*

Pl. VI.2. *The seated man sign; sign 1.7.*

Pl. VI.3. *The seated man sign; sign 1.11.*

Pl. VI.4. *The possible sun sign; sign 1.13.*

Pl. VI.5. *The "twisted flax" sign; sign 1.15.*

PLATE VII

Pl. VII. *Wadi el-Ḥôl Early Alphabetic Inscription No. 2 (Vertical Inscription).*

PLATE VIII

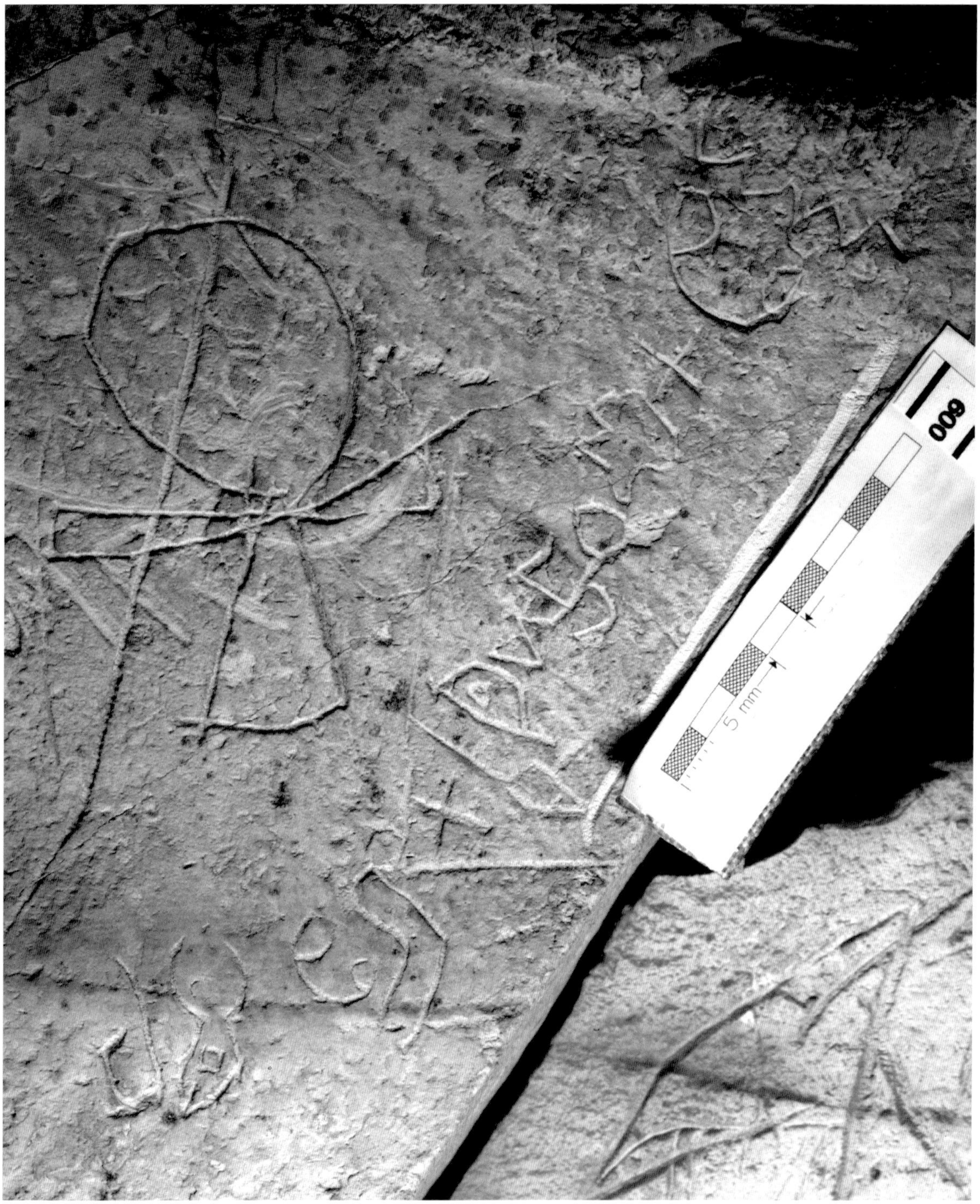

Pl. VIII. *Wadi el-Ḥôl Early Alphabetic Inscription No. 2 (Vertical Inscription).*

PLATE IX

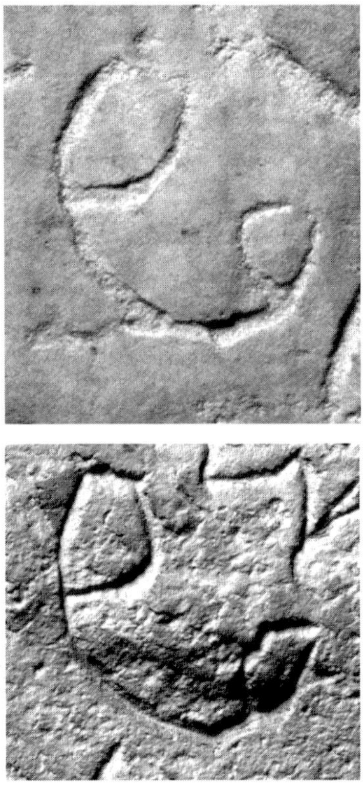

Pl. IX.1. *The "hobble" signs; signs 2.2 and 2.10.*

Pl. IX.2. *The seated man sign; sign 2.5.*

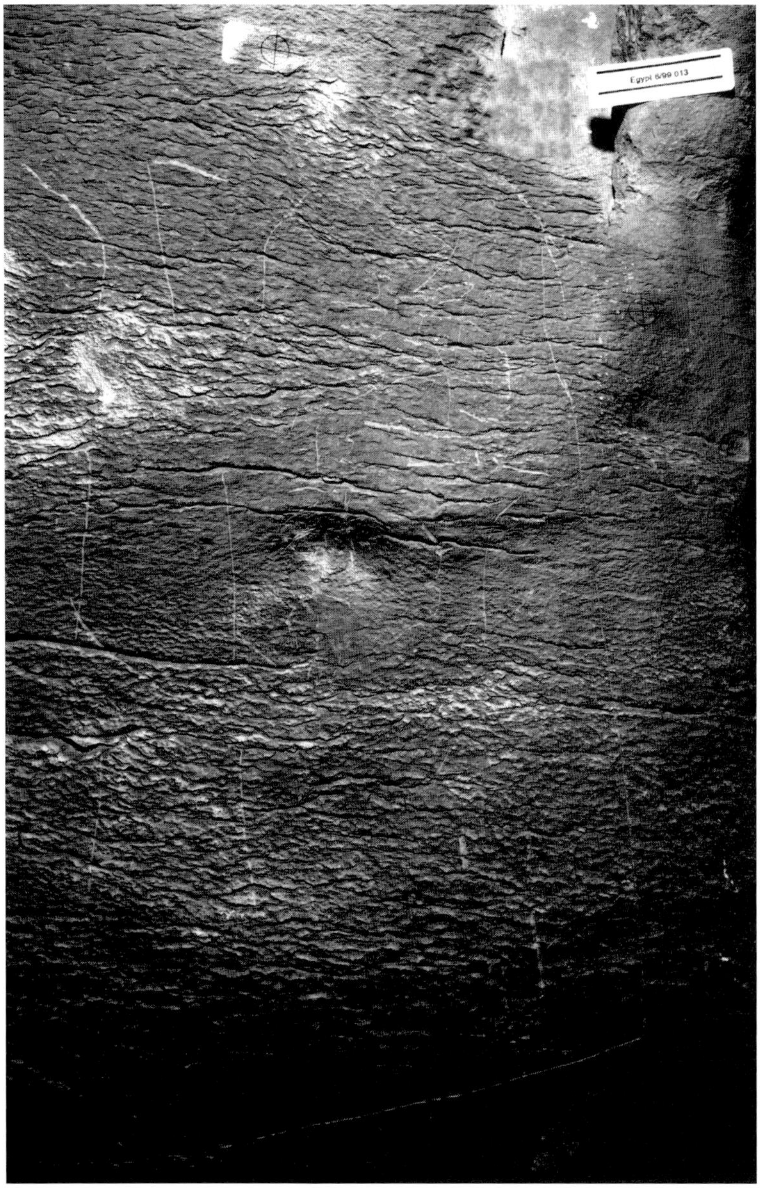

Pl. IX.3. *Detail of the first three lines of the hieratic inscription mentioning the "General of the Asiatics, Bebi."*

PLATE X

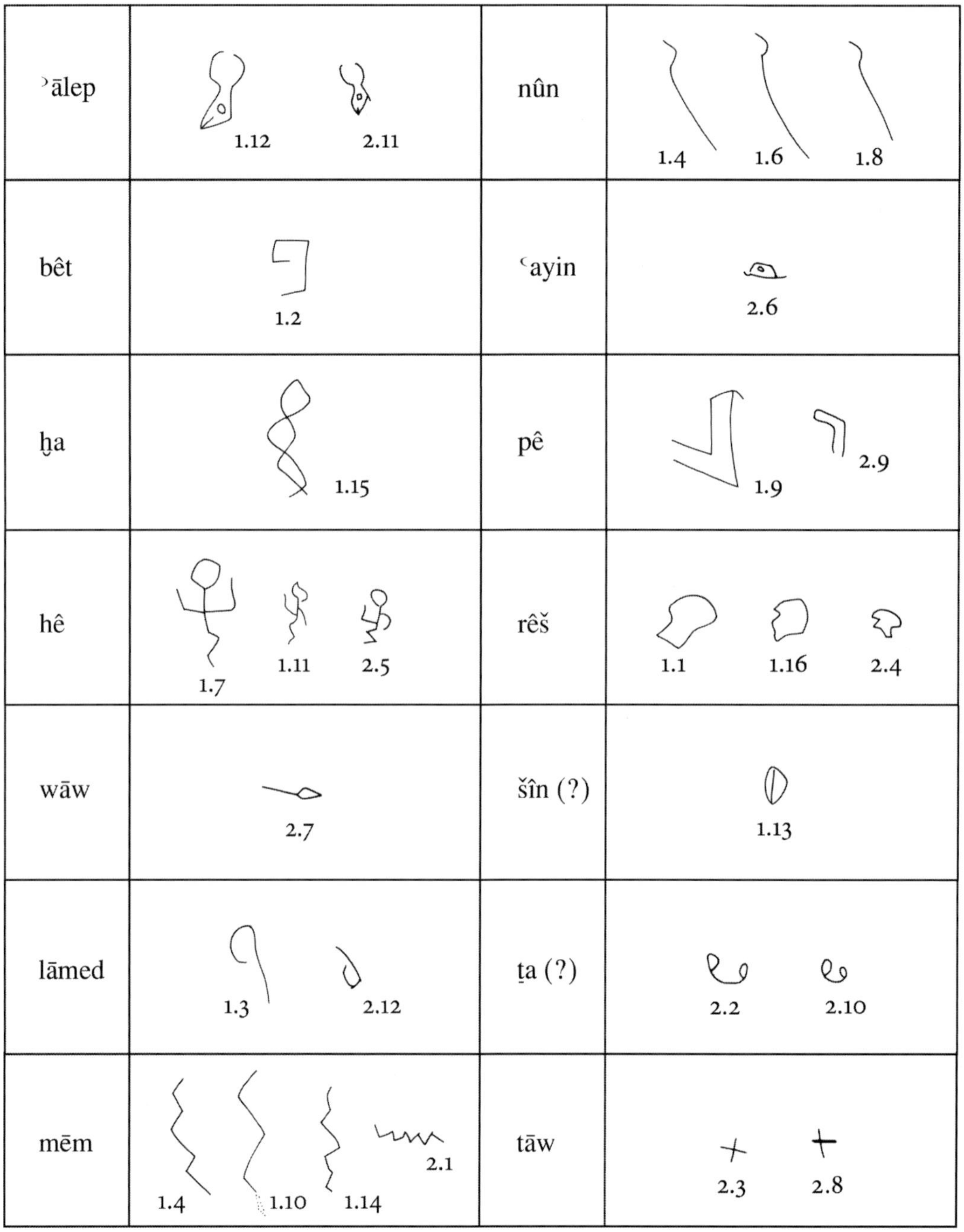
ʾālep
1.12
2.11
nûn
1.4
1.6
1.8
bêt
1.2
ʿayin
2.6
ḫa
1.15
pê
1.9
2.9
hê
1.7
1.11
2.5
rêš
1.1
1.16
2.4
wāw
2.7
šîn (?)
1.13
lāmed
1.3
2.12
ṯa (?)
2.2
2.10
mēm
1.4
1.10
1.14
2.1
tāw
2.3
2.8

Pl. X. *Paleographic chart of the two Wadi el-Ḥôl Early Alphabetic Inscriptions (signs reproduced by scale).*